SAMS
Teach
Yourself

SAP

George Anderson
Danielle Larocca

in **24**
Hours

SECOND EDITION

SAMS 800 East 96th Street, Indianapolis, Indiana 46240 USA

Sams Teach Yourself SAP in 24 Hours, Second Edition

International Standard Book Number: 0-672-32822-4

Library of Congress Catalog Card Number: 2005930224

Printed in the United States of America

First Printing: November 2005

08   07   06   4   3   2

Trademarks

Warning and Disclaimer

Bulk Sales

Sams Publishing offers excellent discounts on this book when ordered in quantity for bulk purchases or special sales. For more information, please contact

U.S. Corporate and Government Sales
1-800-382-3419
corpsales@pearsontechgroup.com

For sales outside of the U.S., please contact

International Sales
international@pearsoned.com

Publisher
Paul Boger

Acquisitions Editor
Loretta Yates

Development Editor
Songlin Qiu

Managing Editor
Charlotte Clapp

Senior Project Editor
Matthew Purcell

Copy Editor
Kezia Endsley

Indexer
Chris Barrick

Proofreader
Jessica McCarty

Technical Editor
AJ Whalen

Publishing Coordinator
Cindy Teeters

Designer
Gary Adair

Page Layout
Kelly Maish

Contents at a Glance

Table of Contents

Part III: SAP Products and Components

Part IV: SAP Technical Guide

Sams Teach Yourself SAP in 24 Hours, Second Edition

About the Author

George W. Anderson currently resides in Houston, Texas, and is a senior SAP Consultant and Project Manager specializing in deploying, implementing, and optimizing SAP solutions. An eight-year veteran of numerous successful implementations, upgrades, technology refreshes, and other SAP engagements, he is a certified SAP Technical Consultant and PMI Project Management Professional. George is the author of *SAP Planning: Best Practices in Implementation* and *mySAP Toolbag for Performance Tuning and Stress Testing*, along with a host of articles and other publications. A former U.S. Marine, husband to the most wonderful woman on Earth, and father of three awesome kids, George's overriding passion revolves around his relationship with our Father in Heaven and our Savior Jesus Christ. You can reach him at George.Anderson@hp.com.

Danielle Larocca currently resides in Weddington, North Carolina. Danielle has earned a bachelor of science degree in psychology and holds certificates and certifications for many areas of SAP, including Human Resources, ABAP programming, and Basis Technologies. She is an ABAP programmer as well as an expert on SAP query-based reporting and the Human Capital Management module. Danielle has documented and instructed multiple computer languages and applications, including ABAP, Visual Basic, Electronic Data Interchange (EDI), as well as Oracle, PeopleSoft, and SAP. Danielle is a featured speaker at many SAP conferences throughout the U.S. Additionally, Danielle is an avid technical reader, perpetual student, and an executive independent SAP consultant. She is currently working for the sixth largest employer in the world, Compass Group, as the Vice President of HR Information Systems.

Dedication

George: To my church family and friends, I dedicate this book to you—
perhaps now you'll finally understand some of what I actually do for a living!

Danielle: To my best friend, Jimmy (and to our best friend, Casey).

Acknowledgments

From George: I'd simply like to recognize the love of our Lord and Savior whom makes everything possible, without whom we are nothing or mean nothing—thank you for giving me life, giving that life purpose, and blessing me beyond what any man deserves. To my family at home, thank you for your love without terms. To my colleagues and management team at work, and my clients across North America, thank you for the opportunity to share time together, learn from one another, and play a part in each others' lives. To the many men and women at SAP, thank you for your dedication toward developing not only practical but truly worthwhile solutions. And finally, to Danielle Larocca and AJ Whalen, thank you for the time you invested in this second edition—you both went above and beyond, and I recognize that fact and appreciate you. Because of your extraordinary efforts, this book will continue to serve its readers well for many years.

From Danielle: Special thanks to the man who saves my life, every day, James Signorile. Thanks for the support of my family Daniel, Carol, Patricia, and Cathy Larocca, Albee Hill, and Nicole Kaupp. Thanks for the support of my extended family Mary and Janeen Signorile and the Tricarico, Workman, Mifsud, and Beato families and the latest addition, Abbey Frances Willis. Warm thanks and appreciation to a wonderful boss, Robert Kovacs, and a wonderful list of colleagues and friends including Raj Pragasam, Kelly Brunsman, Michael Lariosa, Brad Pearce, Sarah Van Aken, Chris Ashcroft, David Lynn, AJ Whalen, Joyce Urguhart, Stevie D, Tom Robb, Phil Wells, Kelly Edington, Kevin Thorpe, Joe Rogers, Bonnie Penzias. Thanks also to the gang at UCG, Rob Watkins, Jon Harris, the Compass Group, HRIS and Business Systems departments, and the rest of the gang that I have the pleasure of working with every day at Compass Group, The Americas.

We Want to Hear from You!

As the reader of this book, *you* are our most important critic and commentator. We value your opinion and want to know what we're doing right, what we could do better, what areas you'd like to see us publish in, and any other words of wisdom you're willing to pass our way.

As publisher for Sams Publishing, I welcome your comments. You can email or write me directly to let me know what you did or didn't like about this book—as well as what we can do to make our books better.

Please note that I cannot help you with technical problems related to the topic of this book. We do have a User Services group, however, where I will forward specific technical questions related to the book.

When you write, please be sure to include this book's title and author as well as your name, email address, and phone number. I will carefully review your comments and share them with the author and editors who worked on the book.

Email: feedback@samspublishing.com

Mail: Paul Boger
           Publisher
           Sams Publishing
           800 East 96th Street
           Indianapolis, IN 46240 USA

For more information about this book or another Sams Publishing title, visit our website at www.samspublishing.com. Type the ISBN (excluding hyphens) or the title of a book in the Search field to find the page you're looking for.

Introduction

Welcome to the newly updated *Sams Teach Yourself SAP in 24 Hours,* your teach-yourself guide to learning one of the most sophisticated and far-reaching set of enterprise solutions available on the market today. And congratulations—you've been paying attention. Over the last few years, we have seen software packages become popular overnight, fading back into obscurity just as quickly. Through every storm that the dot-com bubble, tragedy of September 11, period of global recession, and unparalleled growth of the Internet era mustered, though, it's been impossible not to notice how one company and its products consistently stayed the course. That company is SAP, and its most popular products and technologies are mainstays throughout much of corporate America and indeed the world— R/3, NetWeaver, mySAP ERP, Business Warehouse, Advanced Planner and Optimizer, Customer Relationship Management, Enterprise Portal, and much more. In fact, upwards of 30 products or technical components make up SAP's stable of software solutions today. It is hard to believe that merely a few short years ago, there were only two.

SAP is nothing if not revolutionary. Since 2001, we have witnessed something remarkable, almost unbelievable. The market leader in its industry looked inward and evaluated its core competencies, looked outward at its competitors and paid attention, and then made the necessary adjustments to maintain its market leadership. It didn't shrink back and "right-size" around one or two things it did well, or waffle back and forth between leadership visionaries and their predictions of the future. Instead, faster than a ship its size has any business doing, SAP modified course headings without ever straying *too far* off course. SAP navigated the whole best-of-breed debacle, charted a wide path around the "sell services, not products" trend, embraced Java instead of circumventing it in favor of its own legacy development language, and all the while sped full steam ahead toward a vision of always-on, always-accessible, and eminently adaptable enterprise computing.

Yet, on a number of fronts, SAP remains a model of evolution as well as revolution, explaining at once why this company claims leadership in nearly every market in which it competes. SAP is not content to leave well enough alone. It's not content to hang its hat on market share and product award laurels that, immediately following product announcement, only begin to age at Internet speed. SAP's product design philosophy, its attention to underlying architecture models, and most of all its customer focus, has created the third largest software company in the world. SAP is not afraid to embrace new technologies and computing models, or to embrace new ways of getting work done. NetWeaver proves this: SAP has taken the specialization and integration it has done so well, and added adaptability and agility to the mix. Boldly claiming that the future belongs to Web Services and the rapid adaptation of business processes that such technology enables, SAP has given the world a platform that is not only immediately useful, but ready for the long haul. And its boldness will serve SAP well, especially in light of the fact that SAP is equally concerned with maintaining support for legacy technologies.

Today, SAP AG is the market leader in enterprise application software based on client/server and more recently Service Oriented Architecture (SOA) or more precisely Enterprise Services Architecture (ESA) technology—the latter of which is SAP's take on SOA. As the number one vendor of standard business-application software in the world, SAP AG's products are used by thousands of companies across more than a hundred countries, from multi-national global entities to small/medium business concerns determined to succeed in a global marketplace. And with solutions spanning industry verticals, SAP is also the undisputed leader in providing comprehensive solutions for companies of all sizes and within all industry sectors.

Picking up this book represents a confident step in the right direction. You are going with the market leader, the model of endurance, the preeminent technology frontrunner and enterprise solution enabler. As a result, after about 24 hours of reading, you will possess a solid foundation upon which to build greater capabilities or even a career in SAP. Your knowledge foundation will be broad, certainly, and in need of much bolstering in one direction or the other. But the beauty of the whole thing is that you'll be *aware* of these directions—career options and choices that will enable you to grow and manage your own career in a direction of your choosing. You'll *know* where you want to go. That alone is enough to get you on the road toward making something happen.

And in the meantime, your 24-hour investment will likely serve you well in your current employment position, too. Armed with insight, skills, understanding, and a broad sense of the "big picture" facing nearly every company in business today, you'll no longer look at computing solutions and the people who use and manage them in the same way again. That will make you a valuable asset to your employer, and perhaps the envy of your co-workers.

What's New in This Edition

Sams Teach Yourself SAP in 24 Hours is divided into 24 chapters that can each be completed in about an hour. This book covers everything you need to become well acquainted with the core SAP products and components that are often collectively referred to simply as SAP. The book is organized to provide visibility into key facets of SAP terminology, usage, configuration, deployment, administration, and more. As such, it is necessarily general at times rather than exceedingly detailed, although a certain amount of depth in much of the subject matter is purposely provided where deemed critical to further your understanding. In this structure may be found the book's true value—the content herein is broad enough to paint a picture most anyone can understand, yet deep enough to provide more than an introduction to the subject matter. Certainly, more detailed books abound; use this book as a stepping stone to those various other texts dedicated to SAP architecture, implementation, programming, configuration, administration, performance tuning, and so on.

Who Should Read This Book

Sams Teach Yourself SAP in 24 Hours begins with the basics and terminology surrounding SAP, SAP NetWeaver, and ESA, and from there begins the process of carefully building upon your new knowledge to piece together the complex world of SAP. The pace of the book is designed to provide a solid foundation such that you understand the more advanced topics covered later in the book. In this way, the novice may quickly realize what it means to plan for, deploy, and use SAP, in the process unleashing the power that comes with understanding how all the pieces of the puzzle come together to solve business problems. With this understanding also comes an appreciation of the role that colleagues and partners play with their regard to SAP—perspectives of SAP end users, system administrators, business planners, will ultimately make more sense as you work your way through the book.

Organization of This Book

Thus, from the basics surrounding SAP, to implementation planning and system navigation, to creating your own SAP reports and using the many different SAP components that make up NetWeaver and mySAP business suite today, this book is ideal for people at all levels of education, experience, and familiarity with SAP. Combined with its real-world examples, along with figures, tables, graphics, and actual SAP user-interface screenshots, *Sams Teach Yourself SAP in 24 Hours* serves as an excellent launch pad for using and managing SAP in the real world of business and IT.

To test and reinforce your knowledge, each hour concludes with a Q&A, and Quiz section. These sections provide you an opportunity to put your newfound knowledge and understanding both to the test and into practice. And with the answers to the quiz questions found at the back of the book, it is an easy matter to verify your knowledge and hone in on particularly troublesome topics.

Finally, most hours include an Exercises section as well. Specifically, for those hours that are user-focused or that lend themselves to real-world application, a set of open-ended exercises are designed to get you familiar or comfortable with a particular area. There's no wrong answer when it comes to these exercises (indeed, there are no answers provided); instead, the knowledge you gain as you work through the exercises helps you build upon the foundation provided that hour.

I hope you enjoy the updated *Sams Teach Yourself SAP in 24 Hours,* and learning the new world of SAP. Good luck and regards!

Conventions Used in This Book

Text that you type appears as **bold monospace** and text that appears on your screen is presented in monospace type.

```
It will look like this to mimic the way text looks on your screen.
```

In addition to this, the following icons are used to introduce other pertinent information used in this book.

A By the Way presents interesting pieces of information related to the surrounding discussion.

A Did you Know? offers advice or teaches an easier way to do something.

A Watch Out! advises you about potential problems and helps you steer clear of disaster.

PART I

SAP Introduction

Introduction to SAP NetWeaver and ECC

This first hour provides you an overview of SAP, from its humble beginnings up to our present state of affairs. SAP's structure and philosophy from an architecture perspective, combined with necessary background information on SAP, set the stage for further hours. Welcome aboard!

Highlights of this hour include

- ▶ An overview of SAP
- ▶ An introduction to SAP's architecture
- ▶ Investigating programming and development
- ▶ Discussing the logical unit of work (LUW) concept
- ▶ Reviewing basic inner workings of SAP

Overview of SAP

SAP AG (pronounced ess-aye-pea aye-gee) is based in Walldorf, Germany and is the world's largest enterprise software company. SAP's foundation is built upon the concepts of specialization and integration. That is, each component or product within the SAP family of products and services meets a particular need, like providing web-based access to other SAP systems, addressing product lifecycle planning requirements (SAP PLM), supporting internal company procurement (SAP Enterprise Buyer), interconnecting different systems to ease integration headaches (SAP Exchange Infrastructure), and so on. Many of these components are explained in subsequent hours; suffice it to say here that there are many components, many products, and therefore many potential SAP solutions.

Each product can typically be broken down further into modules—portions of functionality that are more discrete in nature, geared toward addressing a particular piece of the overall component pie. For instance, SAP R/3 and its successor, SAP ERP Central Component (ECC), are comprised of modules like Financials, Sales & Distribution, Materials Management, Warehouse Management, and so on. Individually, each of these modules effectively serves to manage a business area or functional area for which a particular company department often is responsible.

Looking at it from another perspective, individual SAP modules combine to form an SAP component, application, or product. Within a particular module or component, a company's business processes are configured. SAP is well known for reflecting industry's best practices for the different business processes that it supports. By adopting proven best practices, companies grow more efficient serving their customers, constituents, and other stakeholders. Within ECC, for example, you can configure something as complex as an "order to cash" business process, or something as simple as a "credit check" transaction. Many business processes only require a few different modules within the component; others touch many more, however, underscoring the importance of the integration SAP provides.

However, to gain even better business visibility into trends and to maximize revenue and profit, it is becoming increasingly common to extend business processes like "order to cash" so that they inevitably touch multiple components. These so-called *cross-application business processes* might start by accessing ECC or perhaps SAP's Enterprise Portal, and then transfer control to another component such as SAP's Customer Relationship Management (CRM) product to determine customer-buying trends. CRM's business logic might essentially direct or influence the business process in a particular way, seeking to ultimately increase order size or gross margin. Next, SAP's Advanced Planner and Optimizer (APO) system might be accessed to revise a supply chain planning process for a set of potential orders, looking to optimize profitability as the system seeks to balance the needs of many different customers with the organization's access to materials, people, and other resources. Finally, SAP's Business Warehouse (BW) might be queried to pull historical data relevant to the financial terms at hand (so as to offer the best financial terms and discount strategy for this particular customer, for example, given his payment history). After these details are analyzed, control can be turned back over to ECC or Enterprise Portal to track warehousing, drive the pick-list process, manage shipping data and the A/R process, and at some point place the final closing touches on the cross-application business process.

Through all this, take note of the common thread—SAP's products are used to satisfy the needs of enterprises, big and small, enabling an enterprise to tend to the *business* of running a business. After all, every enterprise needs to manage its inventories, generate and track sales, deliver services, maximize revenue, optimize its supply chains, and so on. SAP and its enterprise application competitors—Oracle and to a lesser extent Microsoft—enable this capability on a grand scale, integrating many otherwise discrete functions under a single umbrella. This way, the company (by way of the system's user community) gains greater visibility into how it is conducting business and how it might do so more economically, rapidly, and profitably.

Evolution of SAP AG

Before you go any further, a quick history lesson is in order. SAP AG was founded in 1972 in Mannheim, Germany by a group of ex-IBM engineers with a great idea that fell on deaf ears internally. The five original engineers who developed the concepts ultimately embraced by SAP originally named their company Systemanalyse und Programmentwicklung. Their goal was to develop a software package that integrated a company's myriad business functions in a manner that reflected best practices. Their idea grew into what soon became Systems, Applications, and Products in Data Processing (SAP).

From day one, SAP was designed to be a global software product engineered on a multilingual and multinational platform. Additionally, the engineers from IBM wanted to break away from the monolithic architecture model that defined mainframes and their applications of the day—they wanted to open the doors to a variety of hardware, operating system, and database platforms, thereby giving SAP's customers flexibility and choice. These revolutionary and innovative design features are what made SAP Germany's top software vendor only a few short years after its core product hit the marketplace.

SAP AG Today

Today, SAP AG reigns as the undisputed market leader in Enterprise Applications software. SAP is listed on the New York Stock Exchange (NYSE) under the symbol SAP. SAP AG offers comprehensive industry solutions atop their flagship R/3 and ECC products (so as to afford access to industry-specific best practices and processes), among these SAP Aerospace & Defense, SAP Automotive, SAP Banking, SAP Chemicals, SAP Consumer Products, SAP Engineering & Construction, SAP Healthcare, SAP High Tech, SAP Insurance, SAP Media, SAP Oil & Gas, SAP Pharmaceuticals, SAP Public Sector, SAP Retail, SAP Service Provider, SAP Telecommunications, SAP Utilities, and others— nearly 30 industries are addressed by these *solution sets* (see Figure 1.1).

SAP AG operates around the globe, with offices in more than 50 countries. With more than 32,000 employees and a base of partners exceeding 1,500, SAP AG has such manpower and reach that it literally touches much of the business world we know—with more than 12 million users spread over 91,000 installations.

FIGURE 1.1
SAP provides
industry-specific
solution sets for
nearly 30 indus-
tries.

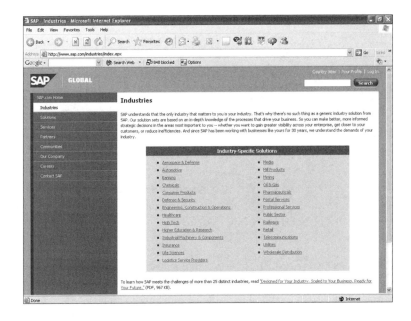

SAP System Architecture and WebAS

Many of SAP's latest products over the last few years, including ECC, are built upon
a relatively new and very powerful platform called Web Application Server, or
WebAS. WebAS offers an "open" front-end in that it speaks the most popular computer communication languages—HTML, XML, Web Services, and traditional "SAP."
WebAS offers the programmers who help customize it a choice, too—SAP's very own
and very powerful ABAP/4 language or the industry standard Java. Finally, WebAS
continues to provide an "open" back-end. That is, many database versions and
releases are supported in which to house all the data and configuration information
that help create a solution rather than a bunch of data and a pile of equipment.

Given the flexibility and power inherent to WebAS, a company deploying it can
navigate a number of different roads. You might deploy an SAP system initially very
similar to how you do business today, and then evolve your own business model
over time, happy about the fact that you don't need to retool your SAP platform to
make this happen. This applies to the use of Web Services, for example. Or better
yet, you might jump in and immediately begin supporting your customers and partners who demand you communicate with them over XML or Web Services, while still
supporting HTML and the traditional SAP user interface when it comes to your company's internal users.

ECC's architecture (one component within the larger mySAP ERP bundle) is different
from its predecessor's (detailed in Hour 11, "SAP ECC and R/3"), but also alike in

many ways as well. For example, both allow for the distribution of a user-based or report-based workload to multiple PCs (front-end clients called "presentation servers" by SAP). These presentation clients are linked together through a network. The SAP system was historically designed so that the presentation layer, application logic, and data management were logically separate as well as potentially physically separate from one another. In this way, a flexible system can be architected, one where additional headroom can be easily added when required. See Figure 1.2 for a classic example.

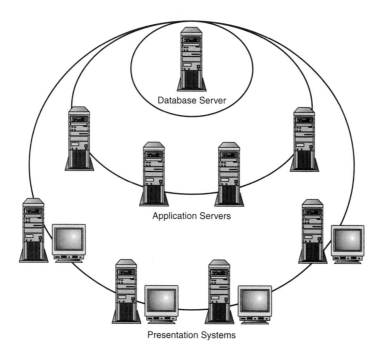

FIGURE 1.2
The SAP classic system architecture requires a database server, one or more application servers, and one or more (typically hundreds or thousands of) front-end presentation servers.

Client/Server Environment

The concept of client/server is still very popular despite the growing popularity of other environments and architectures. SAP R/3 was built around the concept of client/server; ECC, on the other hand, is built around SAP NetWeaver and the concept of Enterprise Services Architecture. Client/server is essentially one of a few different standards used to build computer systems. Illustrated in Figure 1.3, a *client/server environment* is one in which the *client machine* (an individual PC, workstation, mobile computing device, or even another computer system) requests information (via a connection) from the supplying machine, known as the *server*. The communication and interchange of data between the requesting and supplying machine is known as the *client/server relationship*.

FIGURE 1.3
In simplest form, a standard client/server environment connects workstations, printers, and other client devices to a server.

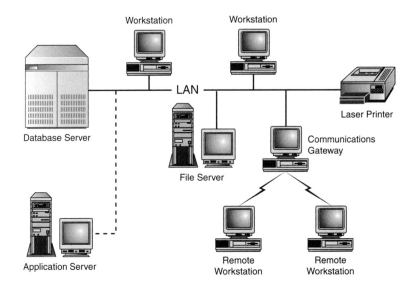

Three-Tiered Architecture

SAP AG's approach to using client/server was brilliant, if not common sense. By constructing a computing solution that could be divided into three discrete layers or tiers, the engineers at SAP solved a couple of sticky issues. Among these issues were scalability (or lack of it, actually), the need to easily upgrade business application logic, and the desire for technical flexibility. To this last point, the engineers at SAP wanted to abstract the database layer so that many different databases could be supported without having to go back and recode existing programs.

The result was SAP's *three-tiered architecture*, which essentially subdivides a higher-level architecture into three layers based on function:

▶ The user interface layer

▶ The business logic layer ("application" layer)

▶ The database layer

The configuration shown in Figure 1.4 is a good example of how the three-tiered architecture applies to SAP in the world of legacy applications as well as in the world of Web Services and ESA.

In this example, a central computer houses the database, known as the *database server*. In terms of a distributed SAP system, it is enough to understand that a database is the place where the data is stored. For the purposes here, assume that only a single database server is set up in a client/server system. I will get into more detail on this in the upcoming Hour 3, "Database Basics."

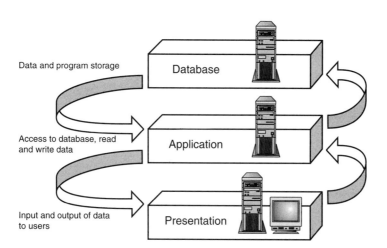

Data and program storage — Database

Access to database, read and write data — Application

Input and output of data to users — Presentation

FIGURE 1.4
The three-tiered architecture is one of the most popular designs for SAP installations.

The *application server* is responsible for the administrative functions of the system. This includes background processing, printing (addressing spool requests), and process request management. Unlike the database server, multiple application servers can exist in an SAP three-tiered design. In the same way, many computers fulfill the role of presentation server (see Table 1.1). These computers, or front-end *clients* as they are more commonly called, display the software and screens that you will use when working with SAP. The specific piece of software that is often installed on these front-end clients is referred to as the SAP *graphical user interface (GUI)*, or SAP GUI.

Graphical user interface: The first practical user interfaces between people and computers were text-and-keyboard oriented. The command-line interface of the MS-DOS operating system (the screen with the C:\ command prompt, which you can still get to from your Windows operating system by executing the cmd command) is an example of a typical text-based computer interface. In contrast, a *graphical user interface* consists of graphic images called *icons* that include buttons, pull-down menus, dialog boxes, and scrollbars, which are typically manipulated with a mouse. Such graphical user interfaces were developed with one purpose in mind—to make computers *user friendly*, a rather tired but still very appropriate term today.

TABLE 1.1 SAP System Architecture

Server	Server Name	Server Description
🖥	Presentation server	Displays the user's communication window with SAP; also known as the SAP GUI.
🖥	Application server	Manages SAP administrative functions, processes, and request management.
🖥	Database server	Provides for the organized storage of all data, in the form of database tables, rows, and other structures.

The Precursor to ESA

Outside of SAP's three-tiered architecture, you might come across two others as well, two-tiered and four-tiered architectures. In the first, the application and database layers are combined onto one server. From an installation perspective, they're still separate (you install first one and then the other on your server). But by installing each of these tiers on the same server, you can quickly and cheaply create a simple-to-administer system. The downside is scalability—when the server runs out of horsepower, it has to be upgraded or replaced entirely. It is primarily for this reason, in fact, that three-tiered architectures became so popular.

Four-tiered architectures came into being when SAP and other enterprise software vendors recognized the value that the Internet or company-internal intranets can provide. By adding an "accessibility tier" or "services tier" in between the application and presentation tiers, a four-tiered system enabled simple browser-based access, solving two other dilemmas—how to reduce the expense associated with installing, patching, and upgrading the SAP GUI user interface across perhaps hundreds or thousands of desktops, and how to integrate web or application services into the overall architecture.

ESA and mySAP ERP

SAP NetWeaver is the ultimate in four-tiered architectures, integrating Web Services and Internet support within the core WebAS platform. And because support is still maintained for the traditional SAP GUI as well as web browsers and other user interfaces, a company intending on moving to NetWeaver does not have to radically change the way it does business. It can do so methodically, in keeping with one of NetWeaver's core benefits to longtime SAP customers and users—legacy support.

Yet SAP NetWeaver is only one piece of the puzzle. SAP AG offers quite a bit more under the guise of mySAP ERP—a suite of applications that has been specifically designed or updated to align with ESA, briefly discussed next.

Enterprise Services Architecture

Hour 10, "SAP NetWeaver," covers Enterprise Services Architecture (ESA) and how it is leveraged in the deployment of SAP NetWeaver. Suffice it to say here, though, that ESA is the new model around which SAP is building its solutions. ESA provides the roadmap or blueprint for designing an adaptable enterprise computing solution. ESA is not exclusive by nature, therefore. In fact, by embracing an Enterprise Services Architecture, R/3 and other legacy SAP solutions can be plugged in as *application services in much the same way that new SAP NetWeaver components are.* The preference might be to move to an ERP system that is architected from the ground up to fit into ESA, like SAP's ERP Central Component. But at the end of the day, if an application can share data via XML, it can be used and accessed like a service. SAP NetWeaver merely provides the vehicle for integrating these application services; it provides the platform. And in doing so, NetWeaver makes it possible for you to adopt an Enterprise Services Architecture.

mySAP ERP

Within the bundle of solutions that SAP AG calls mySAP ERP, you find not only NetWeaver but also SAP ECC. That is, ECC is but only one component (the central component!) of the mySAP ERP bundle. This comprehensive bundle of solutions also contains Business Intelligence (SAP BI), Enterprise Portal (SAP EP), SAP's Exchange Infrastructure (SAP XI), Mobile Infrastructure (SAP MI), and more. And beyond NetWeaver, mySAP ERP also includes SAP's Strategic Enterprise Management application (SAP SEM, a "bolt-on" to SAP BW), SAP's Supplier Relationship Management solution (SRM, which essentially consists of SAP Enterprise Buyer Professional), Employee Self Service (ESS) and Manager Self Service (MSS), and a number of other components designed to simplify web integration or enable collaborative project management and oversight.

SAP ECC

At the core of mySAP ERP is ECC. SAP's ERP Central Component replaces SAP R/3 as the company's core online transaction processing (OLTP) system. Like R/3, ECC addresses a business organization's needs to manage inventories and sales, track orders, plan and execute warehouse movements, and much more. Such activities often constitute the core business activities that must be accomplished day in and day out. Although a number of these functions were mentioned in passing, it's important to point out that many of these functions are now augmented through the deployment of one of four solutions that ship with mySAP ERP.

- ▶ mySAP ERP Financials
- ▶ mySAP ERP Human Capital Management
- ▶ mySAP ERP Operations
- ▶ mySAP ERP Corporate Services

These solutions include all the individual components necessary to fulfill their intended needs, making them easy ways to procure, plan for, and implement such a system. It's also important to note that any of these solutions can be easily tailored for a company's specific business needs by developing and deploying one or more of the *other* components that ship with mySAP ERP (described previously).

When all is said and done, though, the real work of a computing system is not accomplished by business processes, but rather by the individual SAP transactions that make up each business process. The role of SAP transactions is discussed next.

SAP Transactions

At a high level, we talk of computing architectures and business models. But nothing useful can be realized until you understand that the backbone of SAP is at the transaction level. An SAP transaction is any logical process in the R/3, CRM, BW, or other SAP system. A simpler way to define this is to say that a transaction is a self-contained unit, a set of steps with a beginning and an end, resulting in some kind of output and often an update to the underlying SAP database. Creating a new customer, generating a list of existing customers, processing an order, and executing a program are all examples of SAP transactions. SAP transactions therefore do the *work* of the application; everything else simply supports how this work gets done.

An SAP **logical unit of work (LUW)** contains all the steps of a transaction, concluding with the update to the SAP database, if necessary.

Suppose that you are adding a new employee in the SAP ECC Human Resources module. To complete this employee new-hire process, you need to go through several screens to describe and add that new employee to the system. Adding the employee's name and address on one screen and then proceeding to the next screen is considered a *dialog step* within the process. Adding the new employee's salary and paycheck information on another screen is an additional dialog step. At the end of an employee hiring, after you have gone through all the necessary screens (or dialogs) in the process, the data is committed to the SAP database, thus completing your LUW.

Dialog, Dispatch, and Dataflow

Dialog, dispatch, and *dataflow* refer to the information entered on a screen (dialog), the transfer of that screen data to the database (dispatch), and the update to the database and movement to the next process (dataflow). The data typed into a screen by the user is performed through the Presentation Layer via the SAP GUI. Finally, in order to update the database, this data must be manipulated and managed by the dispatcher.

The concepts of logical units of work (LUW), dialog, dispatch, and dataflow can get quite complicated and technical and are usually concerns of your technical team.

A **dispatcher** enables SAP to communicate with the presentation server by managing the information exchange between the SAP GUI and the individual processes within SAP that execute work.

In simpler terms, the dispatcher serves as the go-to guy. Its role is to get things done. You learned about a logical unit of work, the steps performed to complete a task. It is the responsibility of the dispatcher to assure that complete processing of these steps occurs. The dispatcher evenly distributes the work it receives and organizes the communication activities so that, in the end, the database is updated and the transaction is complete (see Figure 1.5).

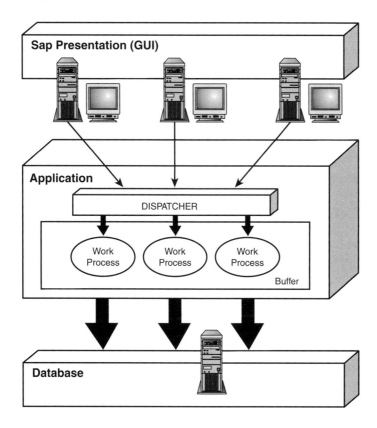

FIGURE 1.5
The SAP Dispatcher is responsible for controlling which processes run on which servers and managing the work to completion.

Summary

This hour provided you with an introduction to the world of SAP. You have gained an understanding of SAP's legacy and more current architectures, and its history. You are now more familiar with many SAP catch phrases and terms, too, such as Enterprise Services Architecture, NetWeaver, ECC, client/server, three-tiered architectures, logical unit of work (LUW), dialog step, and others. You are now in an ideal position to jump with both feet into the SAP world as you progress into Hour 2, "SAP Basics," where you begin to truly explore SAP.

Q&A

Q *Are you required to use a three-tiered architecture for your SAP implementation?*

A Although a popular standard, the three-tiered architecture design is only one architecture used in deploying SAP.

Q *Is there a limit to the number of presentation servers that you can deploy for SAP?*

A Depending on the size of your SAP implementation, you might have hundreds, even thousands, of presentation servers (front-end systems or clients). Although there is not a limit, naturally each presentation server must be licensed for SAP software.

Q *Can you use your SAP system to support multiple languages within a single client?*

A Yes; when you log in to SAP, you specify the logon language. You can log in with any language available in SAP (most of these are added separately as part of the initial software installation).

Workshop

The workshop is designed to help you anticipate possible questions, review what you've learned, and begin thinking ahead to putting your knowledge into practice. The answers to the quiz that follows can be found in Appendix A, "Quiz Answers."

Quiz

1. What does SAP stand for?

2. Name a few of the industries for which SAP offers comprehensive bolt-on solutions.

3. What are the three distinct servers that comprise SAP?

4. What is the successor to SAP R/3?

5. What is the main benefit of SAP's integration?

6. What differentiates a cross-application business process from a standard business process?

7. Describe Enterprise Services Architecture (ESA).

8. A logical unit of work (LUW) is not complete until what action is accomplished?

HOUR 2

SAP Basics

With the introduction to SAP NetWeaver in Hour 1, you are now ready to dive into the world of SAP. If SAP is already installed at your site, and you have access to an SAP User ID, you can follow along as you progress through this hour. If your SAP access is not yet available, you can still follow along in the book; when your access is granted, you will be more prepared to jump right in. Let's get started.

The highlights of this hour include

- ▶ Logging in and off the system
- ▶ Session management and multitasking
- ▶ SAP GUI basics

Session Basics

Each time you connect to SAP via the SAP GUI user interface you begin a user session. An **SAP session** simply means you have started the SAP GUI (the SAP graphical user interface) and established a connection with a particular SAP system—you're connected, so to speak. You can have multiple sessions open with multiple SAP components—such as SAP ECC, R/3, CRM, and so on—or you can open one or more sessions with a single system. The number of the current session is displayed in the status bar, which you will see in a few minutes.

One of the benefits of this multiple session option is that you can multitask. Assume that you are processing a new customer order and your boss asks you to generate a report. There is no need to stop processing the order. You can leave that session (screen) open on your computer and begin a new session. With this new session, you can request and generate your boss's report. By default, you can open up to six sessions at the same time (as I explain later in the section "Session Management"), although the default can be increased by a System Administrator knowledgeable in maintaining SAP from a technical perspective. With six sessions, think about how much more work you can do! Multitasking is indeed alive and well in the world of SAP.

Access the System

Regardless of the particular SAP product, SAP solutions are designed as "end user" or client systems. That is, most of these systems are geared toward satisfying business-oriented requests. What this means is that you have the freedom to operate the system from any computer that has SAP GUI (SAP's user interface, also called *presentation software* by the folks at SAP AG) or Internet Explorer (in most cases). This user interface connects to the SAP *central instance* (the SAP "executables"), which in turn talks to the back-end database holding all the programs, data, and so on. The key in this is that you are not required to be at your particular desk working from a special desktop or client machine to complete your daily tasks. Instead, if you happen to be visiting your warehouse and realize that you forgot to perform a task back at your office, you can perform it from this site (assuming the computer is connected to SAP via the company network or intranet). SAP recognizes who you are and what activities you are allowed to perform through your SAP user ID.

All SAP users are assigned a user name (although it is not uncommon to see infrequent factory, distribution site, and warehouse workers sharing a single SAP user ID). In most cases, it is your own name or initials, similar to the PC logon name you're accustomed to using. When you connect to SAP using your initial password, you are forced to change it immediately upon logging in, thus securing your user ID even from System Administrators and others tasked with maintaining security.

The Client Concept

Your organization will likely have multiple clients. Clients in the world of SAP are the self-contained business entities or units within your various SAP systems. A client retains its own separate master records and own set of tables. The best way to think of this is in the form of a company—within a large multinational organization, for example, you might have five or six companies. Each client within SAP represents a different company. Most of the time, you might log in to a particular client or company and do your work; others might log in to a different client or company on the same SAP system, though. In the end, the results can be easily rolled up so that the multinational organization as a whole can easily report on its cross-company financials, for example.

In the same way, an SAP system also tends to maintain different clients strictly for convenience, or to segregate critical data from perhaps less critical data. Here is a general example. When you are first installing SAP and configuring the system, you will likely have a set of systems that you can log in to. Most SAP customer sites maintain a Development system, QA or Test system, and a Production system.

Within each of these systems you can choose the specific client you want to log in to. For instance, within the Development system you might maintain a "business sandbox" or "crash and burn" client along with your workhorse development client and later a copy of this workhorse client, called a "Golden Master" by many. These very distinct client environments within each system enable you to segregate your critical data (important golden development or production client data, for instance) from your test and what-if configuration data.

You might have *many* clients configured within a particular system. For example, the technical team might implement a new client in your development environment for special developer training purposes, to be used to teach developers how to use the system without actually making any changes to the important development data. This same client configuration is often established in your other systems, too—from production down to the QA and test systems, and so on.

Regardless of the number of clients, each one is assigned a unique three-digit number, which you are required to know and type at login time. This makes it easy to distinguish between clients. A developer might log in to client 100 to do training, client 200 to review and approve new business logic, and client 500 to conduct actual development activities for the company. In the same way, an end-user might log in to client 300 in the production system to do his day-to-day work, and occasionally client 900 in the QA or Test system to check on the status on new functionality being developed for production.

Within the SAP world, the term *client* is used to describe something distinctly different from what the Information Technology (IT) world in general uses it for. In IT, a client represents an individual PC or workstation. For the purposes here, though, I will use client in the manner used by SAP—to describe a logical and separate business entity within an SAP system.

Watch Out!

Initial SAP Logon

The initial screen that you see when first connecting to SAP is the SAP R/3 Logon screen. See Figure 2.1 for an example, keeping in mind that the Logon screen associated with different SAP products or components might look a bit different.

On this screen, you need to provide the client number, your user name, and the initial password that was assigned to you. Enter the information provided to you on this screen, and then select the green check mark (or press the Enter key on your keyboard) to continue.

FIGURE 2.1
The first screen
you see when
starting the
logon process is
the SAP Logon
screen.

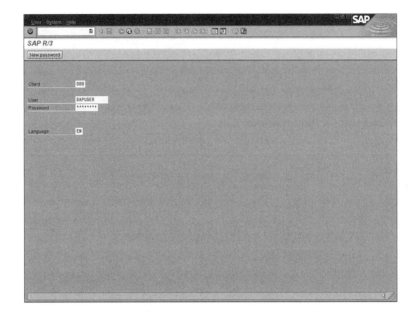

By the
Way

> It is not necessary for you to enter your logon language on this initial logon screen
> (see Figure 2.1). Your system will likely be configured to default to a standard
> language for your organization, such as "EN" for English. If your organization
> requires global (multilingual) logon capabilities, and those particular languages
> have been set up for your system, you can specify a two-digit language code in
> the language box.

Changing Your Password

On first signing in to SAP, you are prompted to change your password. Keep in mind
the following five rules to create your password (with the caveat that some of these
rules can be changed by your System Administrator):

Rule 1   A password must consist of at least three characters (most companies
         go with between five and eight characters at minimum, however).

Rule 2   The first character cannot be ! or ? or another special character.

Rule 3   The first three characters must be unique.

Rule 4   The first three characters should not be contained in the user name.

Rule 5   The password is generally limited to excluding SAP* or pass, along
         with anything that the System Administrator assigns as "no-no"
         passwords in database table USR40. Most sites do not allow their
         company name to be used as a password, for instance.

In addition to the standard rules for governing passwords, your company will almost certainly define a set of rules that pertains to its own operations. A particular minimum length, and requiring the use of special characters or numbers within the body of the password, serves to create stronger passwords and a more secure environment for SAP.

On the Change Password screen, as shown in Figure 2.2, enter your new password on both lines and select the green check mark (or press Enter) to continue.

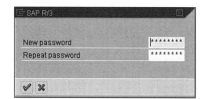

FIGURE 2.2
Upon first logging in to SAP, you are required to change your password. In the same way, if your System Administrator ever resets your password, you are also required to change it the next time you log in. This applies to each client for which you have a user ID.

Logging Off of SAP

To terminate your SAP session or connection, you can select the System, Logoff option from the main menu or select the Windows "X" icon in the top-right corner of your SAP GUI window. You can also execute /nex from the SAP GUI command field. SAP will prompt you with a window confirming the shutdown of your connection to SAP.

The SAP Logon Pad

Until a few years ago, it was common to log in to SAP by double-clicking an SAP icon that the System Administrator set up on each user's desktop. Although simple in approach, it was a bit limiting—especially for companies that deployed multiple SAP systems. Each user's desktop could crowd up quickly with SAP GUI icons. And additional icons set up on each user's desktop to log in to Disaster Recovery systems and so on added to this complexity.

Thus, SAP developed the SAP Logon Pad, a simple utility with a straightforward yet powerful interface designed to help you manage your SAP systems and accounts. As seen in Figure 2.3, the SAP Logon Pad enables you to organize the various systems you need to use.

FIGURE 2.3
The SAP Logon Pad is useful for organizing and simplifying access to multiple SAP systems.

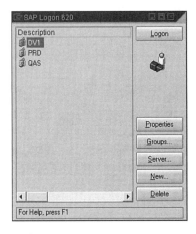

Configuring the SAP Logon Pad

To configure the SAP Logon Pad, you can either manually enter all the systems (using the buttons to add individual servers or groups of systems), or you can copy the saplogon.ini file from another person's personal computer to your own and then customize its contents. The saplogon.ini file usually resides in the C:\windows directory. For existing systems, right-click the current SAP system's description, and then select Properties. Edit the description to reflect something meaningful (I often include the user ID for a particular system in the description, for example, to help me remember it). Most importantly, enter the SAP application server you connect to (either the computer's hostname or its TCP/IP address) and its System ID or SID—a three-character identifier assigned by the System Administrator. You'll also need to include the system number (a two-digit number) and click the R/3 button (which actually comprises all systems except SAP's old mainframe-based R/2 system). See Figure 2.4 for an example. Click the Save button when you're finished.

Low-Speed Connections

One of the most useful features of the SAP Logon Pad is its capability to support low-speed connections. For instance, if your work site is physically far away from the SAP system, or you use a slow connection method (like modem dial-up, or a slow wide-area network link), you can instruct SAP to skip sending you all the pretty graphics and other such constructs that can really slow down an already bogged-down network connection. By giving yourself this extra network bandwidth, you'll be in a position to get your SAP work done that much faster. Click the Advanced button from within the SAP Logon Pad's Properties dialog box, and a new Advanced Options box like the one in Figure 2.5 is displayed. Simply click the Low-Speed Connection check box and save the new setting by selecting OK.

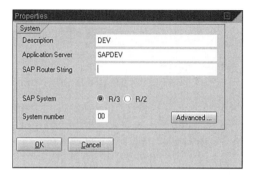

FIGURE 2.4
For each system you intend to log in to, specify at minimum a Description, SAP application server, System ID or System Number, and SAP System type.

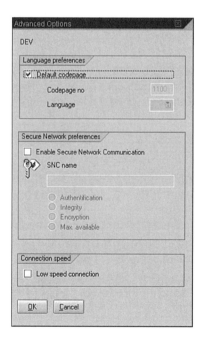

FIGURE 2.5
For SAP GUI users at remote sites or using slow modems or networks to connect to SAP, the Low Speed Connection option can really help speed up system response times.

Session Management

Mentioned at the beginning of this hour, you can create up to six sessions by default. Each session you create is as if you logged in to the system again.

Consequently, the system can be given more work to do (you could launch five long-running reports, for example, while keeping one session available for online "real-time" transactions). Such a workload can obviously affect to some degree how fast the system responds to your real-time requests. That is, your desktop PC and even its network connection back to SAP might perform slower than expected. For these reasons, plus the fact that the back-end SAP system can conceivably suffer a performance penalty as well, your company will normally set limits to the number of sessions that you and your colleagues can create. Alternatively, it might encourage the SAP user community to limit itself to only one or two sessions.

Creating a New Session

In SAP, you can create a session at any time and from nearly any screen in the system. You do not lose any data in the sessions that are already open with each new session you create, either. Create a new session by following the menu path System, Create Session. You will now have two sessions open on your computer. If you want to determine which session you are currently in, check the status bar on the bottom-right side of your screen (see Figure 2.6).

FIGURE 2.6
The SAP GUI window displays the current session number in the bottom-right side of the screen, in parentheses.

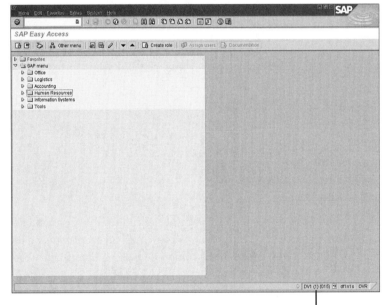

Current session number

Creating a New Session Using the Command Field

Rather than following the menu path, you can also create a new session by typing **/0** (0 for open) in the command field on the top-left side of your SAP GUI window and pressing Enter. You will be prompted with a window like the one shown in Figure 2.7—similar to the same window seen when you enter transaction **SM04**, although with the added benefit of the Generate button.

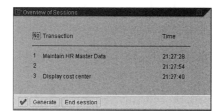

FIGURE 2.7
The Overview of Sessions window displays the number of open sessions and enables you to create a new session or end any existing sessions.

From this box, you can create a new session by selecting the Generate button or terminate an existing session by selecting the End Session button. This box also provides an overview of all the sessions that you currently have open, making it easy to determine what you are doing in each session, for example.

When you generate a session in this way, the system displays the initial SAP R/3 or SAP Easy Access system screen in the new session. But you can change this by changing what you type into the command field, explained next.

Creating a New Session and Starting a New Task at the Same Time

Instead of creating a new session and then executing a desired transaction or task, you can combine these two steps into one. Again, you use the command field. By entering transaction codes in the command field, preceded with the /o, you can quickly call a task or proceed to a specific screen. A **transaction code** is a unique sequence of between three and eight alphanumeric characters that identify a transaction in the SAP system.

To execute or *call* a transaction, enter the transaction code in the command field on the top-left side of your SAP GUI window and press Enter. Give it a try using the transaction code SE38. Type **/oSE38** in the command field and press Enter. You should not only open a new session, but arrive at the ABAP Editor Initial screen as well.

> Transaction codes are not case sensitive, which means that you can enter them in lower- or uppercase. For information on finding and using transaction codes, see Hour 5, "Navigation in SAP."

By the Way

> Depending on your system's security authorization, you might not be able to enter certain transaction codes or navigate to certain screens. Work with your System Administrator to understand your personal user ID authorizations and limitations.
>
> Also, it is important to note that, when using transaction codes from any screen except the initial screen, you need to add an **/N** prefix before the transaction code or an **/O** to create a new session and start a new transaction.

Ending a Session

After you are done using a session, it is a good idea to end it. Each session uses system resources that can affect how fast the SAP system responds to your requests, and that of your colleagues. Before you end a session, it is important to note that you must save any data that you want to keep. When you end a session, the system will *not* prompt you to save your data if you are in the middle of a transaction, for instance.

Ending a session is similar to creating a session. You follow the menu path System, End Session (or enter **/O** as previously discussed). From the Overview of Sessions box, you can selectively close a session by selecting it and then selecting the End Session button. Give it a try. Assuming you've followed along and opened a number of SAP GUI sessions, select number 2 by single-clicking on it, and then select the End Session button. It might not initially appear that anything has happened, but the session was indeed closed. To verify this, return to the Overview of Sessions box by typing the transaction code **/O** in the command field. Transactions 1 and 3 should still be listed, but number 2 is no longer open. Follow the same steps to end session 3, leaving only session 1 open.

Overview of Users

Have you ever been curious to see what your co-workers are running in the system, or what your boss is working on? SAP has a snooping screen in which you can see a list of every user currently logged on to the SAP system. The Users Overview screen available via transaction SM04 lists the client number they are logged in to, the number of sessions that they currently have open, and the transaction code that they are currently running (their first session only, though).

By the Way

> Depending on your SAP system's configuration, your SAP System Administrator might have blocked your access to execute transaction /nSM04.

To access this transaction, type **/nSM04** in your command field and press Enter. The screen should appear similar to the one shown in Figure 2.8. The User ID, time entered, and user's terminal (desktop "host" ID) may be displayed in this way.

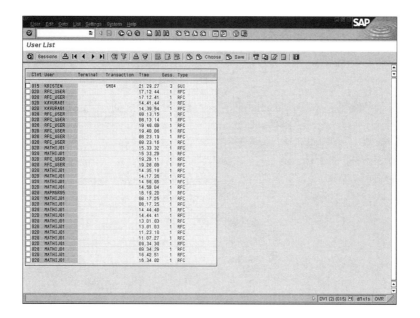

FIGURE 2.8
Use /nSM04 to review the transactions your colleagues are executing, and end these sessions if authorized and necessary.

As mentioned earlier, the Users Overview screen only displays the transaction code of the first session that a user has logged in to. What if the user has multiple sessions open, though? To look at a list of all the transactions a user is currently processing, double-click on any user's name. An Overview of Sessions box will appear, listing all the current transaction codes that the user is processing, along with the powerful option to end the user's session.

> Be careful when snooping with this transaction, and never select the End Session button for another user's session unless directed to do so by competent authority; he might lose data. Besides, it's a very simple matter to determine how a user's session was ended.

**Watch Out!**

SAP GUI Basics

The SAP GUI window is the user interface to most SAP systems available today. At the very top of the window is the *title bar,* which gives the screen (or transaction) description for the window that is displayed. The standard elements of an SAP GUI window are shown in Figure 2.9, and are explained in the following sections.

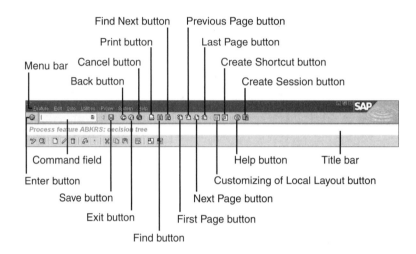

FIGURE 2.9
Your SAP GUI
window might
appear slightly
different
depending on
which transac-
tion you are
currently pro-
cessing, and
which particular
version or tech-
nical release of
SAP you are
executing.

Find Next button   Previous Page button
Print button   Last Page button
Menu bar   Cancel button   Create Shortcut button
Back button   Create Session button

Command field   Help button   Title bar
Enter button   Customizing of Local Layout button
Save button   Next Page button
Exit button   First Page button
Find button

The Menu Bar

The *menu bar* contains all the menu options available. The menu bar changes from screen to screen to match the function module that you are currently processing. The last two items on the menu bar, System and Help, remain constant on all SAP's screens and contain the same submenu options.

The Standard Toolbar

The *standard toolbar* is easy to identify because of all the buttons. It varies slightly, but generally contains the same basic components on every screen. The main navigational, printing, page viewing, and help functions are all made available here. It contains the following elements:

▶ **Enter button**—This button has the same function as the Enter key on your keyboard and is used to check your entry in a field or your work in a transaction when you have finished entering data on a screen. This button should not be confused with the Save button.

▶ **Command field**—The command field is located to the right of the Enter button and is used to enter transaction codes to call a task without having to choose menu options for navigation.

▶ **Save button**—The Save button saves your work and performs the same function as selecting Save from the Edit menu.

▶ **Back button**—The Back button is quite similar to the back button used in most web browsers, and it does just as its name implies. It will take you back to the previous screen. If you use this button to return to the previous screen, your data will not be saved unless you save it first using the Save button on the toolbar.

▶ **Exit button**—The Exit button is used to leave the current application. The system returns you to the previous application or to the main menu screen.

▶ **Cancel button**—The Cancel button is used to exit the current task without saving and performs the same function as selecting Cancel from the Edit menu.

▶ **Print button**—The Print button is used to print data from the screen in which you are currently working. (There are some advanced settings that the user should set up in order for the print setting to work more efficiently. These are covered in Hour 5.)

▶ **Find button**—This button is used to perform a search for data on the screen in which you are currently working.

▶ **Find Next button**—This button is used to perform an extended search for data on the screen in which you are currently working.

▶ **First Page button**—This page navigation key is generally used in reports. It is used to travel to the top of a screen (or page) if the information on the screen is too long to fit on a single screen.

▶ **Previous Page (Page Up) button**—This page navigation key is generally used in reports. It is used to travel up one screen (or page) if the information on the screen is too long to fit on a single screen. This button is equivalent to using the Page Up key on your keyboard.

▶ **Next Page (Page Down) button**—This page navigation key is generally used in reports. It is used to travel down one screen when the information on the screen is too long to fit on a single screen. This button is equivalent to using the Page Down key on your keyboard.

▶ **Last Page button**—This page navigation key is generally used in reports. It is used to travel to the end of a screen (or page) when the information on the screen is too long to fit on a single screen.

▶ **Create Session button**—Open a new session by clicking this button. Alternatively, execute /0 in the command field.

▶ **Create Shortcut button**—This is handy for creating a shortcut on a user's desktop for any SAP transaction, report, or other task that is executed frequently.

▶ **Help button**—The Help button is used for context-sensitive help. That is, when you place your cursor on any object on the screen and select the Help button, you receive specific help for that item (you will learn more about the Help button and SAP's Help system in Hour 23, "Support Overview").

▶ **Customizing of Local Layout button**—This customizing button allows a user to customize SAP GUI display options; details are provided in Hour 4, "Customizing Your SAP Display."

The Application Toolbar

The *application toolbar* is located under the standard toolbar. This toolbar is application- and in some cases transaction-specific and varies depending on the screen (or transaction) that you are currently processing in. For example, if you are in the Finance module, Create Rental Agreement screen, your application toolbar will contain buttons that enable you to copy or retrieve master data from SAP. But if you are in the ABAP/4 Workbench Initial Editor screen, your application toolbar will contain buttons for the Dictionary, Repository Browser, and Screen Painter.

Summary

Hour 2 walked you through exploring the SAP graphical user interface, or SAP GUI. In the process, you learned about its basic features and functionality. You also were introduced to the concepts of session management, session navigation, and basic user access. The fundamentals you have learned in this hour will serve you well as you work your way through the remaining hours in this book.

Q&A

Q *Can a user navigate to the same transaction code in more than one session?*

A Using multiple sessions is like logging in to the system again and again; you can have all your sessions running the same transaction at the same time if you want.

Q *If the Production and Development clients reside on different servers, can they both be viewed on the Users Overview screen (snooping screen)?*

A Only the clients installed on the server that you are logged in to are visible in the Users Overview (snooping screen). SM04, like most SAP transactions, can only "see" the local SAP instance (including users logged in to multiple application servers); other SAP instances are not visible.

Q *If your security access prevents you from navigating to a particular screen using the menu paths, can you jump there using a transaction code?*

A All system security configurations are different, but essentially all users who are not permitted to enter a particular SAP screen cannot access it via a menu path or a transaction code either.

Workshop

The workshop is designed to help you anticipate possible questions, review what you've learned, and begin thinking ahead to putting your knowledge into practice. The answers to the quiz that follows can be found in Appendix A, "Quiz Answers."

Quiz

1. What is the default maximum number of sessions that you can have open at one time in SAP?

2. What is the transaction code to execute the Users Overview screen?

3. If you are on any screen in the SAP system except the main screen, what two-character code must you enter in the command field before typing in a transaction code?

4. What two items on the menu bar are consistent across all SAP screens?

5. What is one of the most important benefits of using multiple sessions in SAP?

6. Which three items are required in order for you to log in to the SAP system?

7. What is the menu path to create a new session in SAP (without using the command field)?

Exercises

1. Create a new session and navigate to the Users Overview screen (snooping screen), and then view all your open sessions.

2. Using the SAP Logon Pad, set up a new connection to one of your SAP systems. Log in to the system and execute a few transactions. Then log out, change the connection speed option in the SAP Logon Pad, log back in to your system, and note the difference in the speed and performance of your SAP GUI session.

3. Execute the transaction code /nFS10 to navigate to the GL Account: Initial Screen Balances display, and then select Help to obtain help for a particular field within your open session.

HOUR 3

Database Basics

All enterprise applications like SAP are essentially made up of programs along with the data that are both used by and created by those programs. The data are organized in a meaningful way within a database, making it easy for the programs to access and find the data necessary to do something useful like run a financial report or create a sales order. In the case of an SAP component or product like ECC, the programs and data reside *together* in the same database. Each component generally has its own database (although exceptions exist)—a production system landscape composed of SAP ECC, SAP Business Warehouse (BW), and SAP Customer Relationship Management (CRM) consists of three production databases. Given its fundamental station in the life of an SAP system, it is important to therefore understand the overall role of the database. This hour, I explore the different features and structures in a database, including the various industry-standard database vendors/brands supported by SAP.

Highlights of this hour comprise

▶ Exploring the concepts and structures of an RDBMS

▶ Discovering which databases are supported by SAP

▶ Learning the difference between a primary and foreign key

▶ Discovering why indexes speed up data retrieval

Database Structure

A **database** is essentially an electronic filing system that houses a collection of information organized in such a way that allows a computer program to quickly find desired pieces of data.

In the simplest form, a database is composed of tables, columns (called *fields*), and rows (called *records* or *data*). A classic example of a database is a telephone book, which is organized alphabetically so as to make it possible to quickly find a desired piece of data. The telephone book can be considered a table, a storage container for information (see Figure 3.1). Within this table is typically found three columns (or fields)—name, address, and telephone number. Within each of these fields exists rows (or records), the simplest form of data in the database.

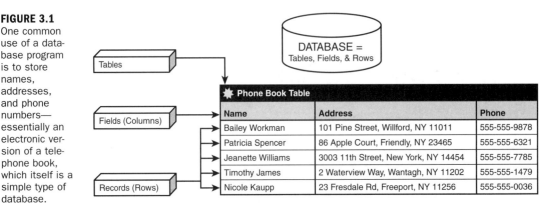

The basic structure of a database is quite similar to a Microsoft Excel spreadsheet wherein columns (fields) store row after row of records (data). The biggest difference between a database and a spreadsheet is simply that databases can contain multiple tables that are connected to one another through relationships. Thus, a database can be thought of as a much more complex, and ultimately much more useful, spreadsheet.

The database plays a key role in each SAP system, as it houses all the data that are used by that particular SAP component or product. Many brands of databases exist, making it easy for an IT shop to select a database vendor with which they are probably already familiar. Currently, SAP can use a variety of different brand name database releases ranging from very expensive and imminently flexible to very inexpensive and yet quite capable. A list of supported databases appears in Table 3.1.

TABLE 3.1   SAP-Supported Databases

Partner	Website
Microsoft SQL Server	www.microsoft.com
MySQL MaxDB	www.mysql.com
IBM DB2 (various versions)	www.ibm.com
Oracle	www.oracle.com

It is important to note that not *all* database vendors and versions are supported by SAP. SAP tends to stick with the market leaders, over the years adding and removing support for certain vendors. In this way they not only limit the amount of database-specific customization they must perform, but they provide IT shops with flexibility and choices, keys to success both for SAP and the IT organizations tasked with deploying and supporting SAP solutions.

Relational Database Management System (RDBMS)

The SAP database contains literally thousands of tables that store information. Some products like ECC and R/3 have more than 30,000 tables in fact, whereas other products like CRM might have fewer than 10,000. Regardless of the number, these tables are tied to each other through established relationships. This connection of multiple tables through relationships creates what is known as a **Relational Database Management System (RDBMS)**.

An important benefit in the design of an RDBMS is that it eliminates redundancy. To understand this better, look at the concept of an RDBMS using the phonebook example. In this example, the phonebook represents a table that stores the names, addresses, and phone numbers for everyone in your city. Say that you obtain a different phone book for your same city, one that includes email and website addresses along with the other data. Now you have two separate tables that store much of the same information, although the second source includes data not available in the first.

Say that you wanted to create a report listing all the Names and Phone numbers from the first table, and include the email addresses in this report by pulling data from the second book. This data is stored in two different tables, and hence problematic. If you updated the first phonebook table with all the information from the second directory, the same information would be stored in two different tables.

Besides being redundant and therefore a waste of resources, this is more cumbersome from a maintenance perspective too. Say that someone's physical home address changes, as they often do: You would then be required to change this data in both tables. Using an RDBMS database design, these problems are no longer a concern, because the tables and therefore their discrete data are associated with one another through relationships specified within the database. In the example, both the tables contain a column (or field) containing the person's name. In an RDBMS, these two tables could therefore be linked by the name field, or any other field they have in common (see Figure 3.2).

Primary Key

Database tables in an RDBMS are required to contain a unique field that individually distinguishes one particular record from all others in the database. This unique field is called a **primary key** and is composed of one or more fields that make every record in a database unique.

FIGURE 3.2
The phonebook
example using
an RDBMS to
link tables.

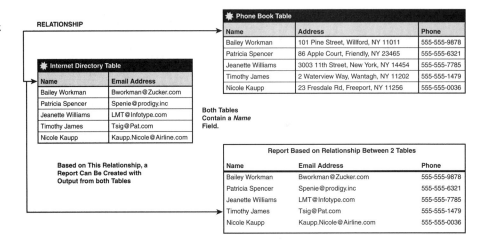

I'll use the SAP R/3 Human Resources functional area as an example of a primary key. The Human Resources module stores all your company's employee data. Some of your employees will have the same department number, some will have the same job title, and some will even have the same salary. Thus, none of these are good primary key candidates. In order to uniquely distinguish each employee of a U.S.-based company, a primary key could be used based on the employee's Social Security number, though. Because a person's Social Security number is truly unique, it would be a good candidate for a primary key in your employee's table. Figure 3.3 gives a sound example of two different tables and their unique primary keys.

FIGURE 3.3
Primary keys in
an Employee
table and a
Department
table.

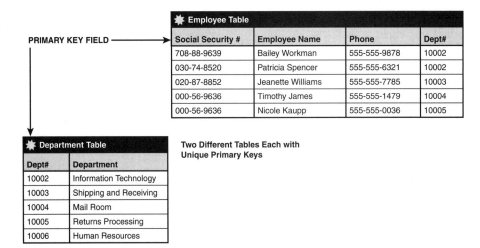

Foreign Key

You use the primary key field in one table to link it to another. The common link field in the other table is usually not the primary key in the other table: It is called a **foreign key**.

Let's use the Human Resources employee example again. You have an employee table that stores the basic employee data with a primary key defined as the Social Security number, and you have a Department Table that stores all the department numbers and departments for employees with a department number as the primary key (see Figure 3.3). In these two tables, you have the same field, Department Number. In the Employees table, the department number is the foreign key linking it to the department table (see Figure 3.4).

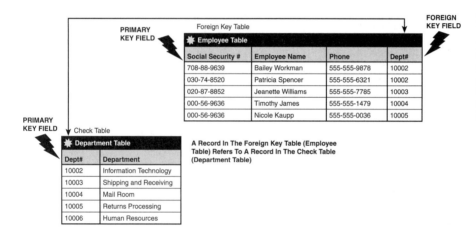

FIGURE 3.4
The department numbers in the Employee Table are checked against the Check table using a foreign key relationship.

The foreign key is used to establish *consistency* between tables. An example of consistency would be that you do not want an employee entered into the system with a department number that is not currently in the database table in which department numbers are stored. The use of a foreign key relationship is to check that the number entered exists in the department table, as shown in Figure 3.4, and reject any records that do not. This way all the data is consistent in your tables.

Check Table Violation

Your SAP database will not accept data in any fields that contain a foreign key to a Check table in which the data entered does not exist in the Check table (see Figure 3.5).

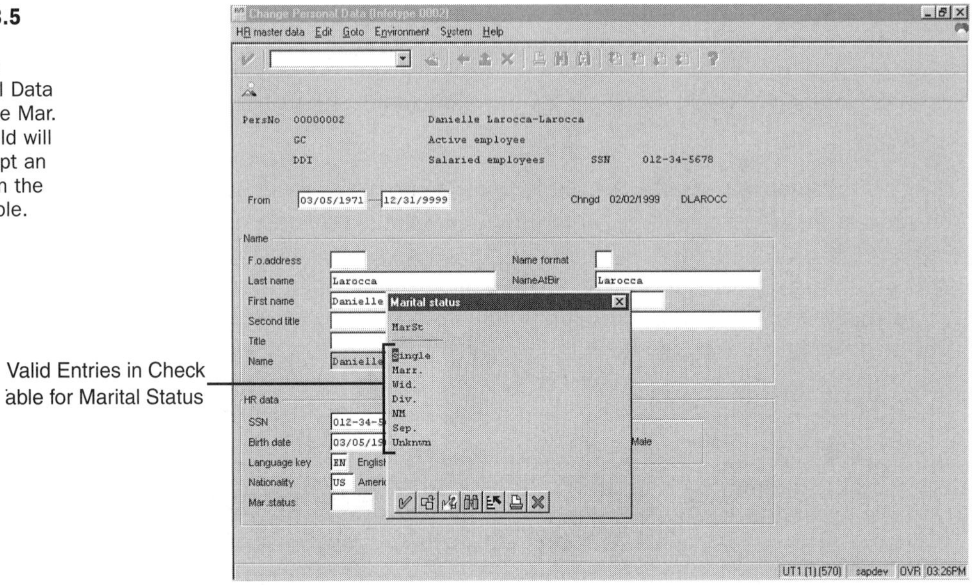

FIGURE 3.5
On the Employee Personnel Data screen the Mar. status field will only accept an entry from the Check table.

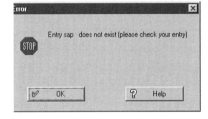

Valid Entries in Check table for Marital Status

In this example, you need to enter a Marital Status for the employee. The possible values in the Check table are listed in the small window. If you enter a value that is not listed in the Check table as a valid entry, you will receive a check violation error like the one shown in Figure 3.6.

FIGURE 3.6
A Check violation message appears when you enter data into a field that is not in the Check table for that field.

An error message will appear when you enter a value (in this case in SAP) that is not a valid entry in the Check table.

Database Concepts

The SAP system contains many types of constructs and structures within the R/3 (or other SAP component) Data Dictionary (DDIC). The majority of these constructs tend to get very technical. I will however provide an overview of many of these constructs and related concepts later in Hour 17, "ABAP Data Dictionary and

Repository." The topics discussed next give you an idea of how different elements of the database are usually designed with the end result of increased performance and system scalability in mind.

Database Indexes

Database indexes are used to speed up the retrieval of data from tables (see Figure 3.7). An index might best be described as a copy of a database table reduced to only the key fields. The data in this reduced copy are sorted according to some predefined criteria, enabling rapid access to the data. Not all fields from the copied table exist in the index, and the index contains a pointer to the associated record of the actual table.

FIGURE 3.7
SAP database indexes are used to speed up the retrieval of data from tables in the database.

Index

	Index	
Dept #	Pointer
10002	Record 101
10003	Record 273
10004	Record 33
10005	Record 5
10006	Record 576
10007	Record 11
10008	Record 460
10009	Record 33
1010	Record 411

Table

	Employee Table				
Record #	Social Security	Employee Name	Phone	Dept #
Record 1	708-88-9639	Bailey Workman	555-555-9878	10002
Record 2	030-74-8520	Patricia Spencer	555-555-6321	10002
Record 3	020-87-8852	Jeanette Williams	555-555-7785	10003
Record 4	000-56-9636	Timothy James	555-555-1479	10004
Record 5	000-56-9636	Nicole Kaupp	555-555-0036	10005

The Index is Accessed and the Pointer is Used
To Locate The Actual Record in the Table

In Hour 17, I go into more detail about databases and tables when we take a closer look at the SAP Data Dictionary.

Transparent Tables

SAP uses another concept called transparent tables, which are SAP database tables that only contain data at runtime. A transparent table is automatically created in the database when a table is activated in the ABAP/4 Data Dictionary. This transparent table contains the same name as your database table in the ABAP/4 Dictionary. Each of its fields also contains the same names as their database counterparts although the sequence of the fields might change. The varying field sequence makes it possible to insert new fields into the table without having to convert it, all of which allows for more rapid access to data during runtime.

The concept of transparent tables can get quite technical and is more of a concern to your ABAP/4 programmers. The concept is only discussed here to provide you basic familiarity with the term.

By the Way

Database Structures

Database structures is another technical term that you really do not need to concern yourself with too much, but is important nonetheless. Simply remember that database structures are a group of internal fields that logically belong together. Structures are activated and defined in the ABAP/4 Data Dictionary and only contain data temporarily—during the execution of a program. Structures are differentiated from database tables based on the following three criteria:

▶ A structure does not contain or reflect an associated ABAP/4 Data Dictionary table.

▶ A structure does not contain a primary key.

▶ A structure does not have any technical properties like class, size, category, or buffering specifications.

Summary

The SAP suite of applications are based on an RDBMS, or Relational Database Management System. The database serves as the core repository for all programs and data, the latter of which consists of database tables and indexes. This hour you learned about the structure of a database and what it contains. The concepts covered in this hour are the key to understanding the behind-the-scenes functioning of your SAP system, especially as you build upon this foundation in the next few hours.

Q&A

Q *Will the business logic configured in the SAP system function the same regardless of the database used, for example, Oracle, DB2, SQL Server, and so on?*

A The SAP business logic configured in the system functions the same regardless of the brand or release of the database storing and managing the data. Of course, the particular brand or release of database must be supported in the first place by the SAP software installation process.

Q *Will the SAP system permit you to create a new record that has the same primary key as another record?*

A No. The SAP system prevents you from being able to create new records with a primary key that already exists.

Workshop

The workshop is designed to help you anticipate possible questions, review what you've learned, and begin thinking ahead to putting your knowledge into practice. The answers to the quiz that follows can be found in Appendix A, "Quiz Answers."

Quiz

1. What is a database?

2. A database is composed of which three components?

3. What kind of database contains multidimensional relationships between its tables?

4. What kind of key in a database table requires unique values in each field?

5. What is the field or fields used to link a primary key field in another table called?

6. What causes a "Check key" or "Check table" violation?

7. What is used in a database to speed up the retrieval of records/data?

Exercises

1. Look in your workplace or home for paper-based database examples like the phonebooks discussed previously.

2. In a Microsoft Excel or other spreadsheet, observe how a database (workbook) complete with fields (columns), records (rows of data), and even tables (different worksheets) can be created. Consider how this structure is applied in a true RDBMS.

3. Go to http://help.sap.com, click on the Search Documentation link, and then search on the phrase "supported databases." Note the variety of database releases supported by SAP AG for different products and components.

4. If you have access to a SAP system, and authority to do so, execute transaction /nDB02. Note how much space is consumed by data, and how much by indexes. Is it close to a 50-50 ratio?

HOUR 4

Customizing Your SAP Display

Regardless of whether you are an SAP user, System Administrator, or manager of a team tasked with supporting or using SAP, there will come a time when you want to customize the SAP user interface to your liking. With the basics under your belt from Hours 1, 2, and 3, you are ready to do so. In this hour, I cover tasks that show you how to manipulate the SAP GUI to your custom specifications.

The highlights of this hour include

▶ Selecting the best version of the SAP GUI

▶ Customizing the SAP front-end to your specifications

▶ Customizing colors and fonts

▶ Changing the way SAP responds to you

Which SAP GUI Is Right?

With the JavaGUI, WebGUI (for Windows-based browser system), and a number of flavors of the SAP GUI at your disposal, a bit of insight is in order so that you can select the best user interface for your purposes. Take into consideration the following points when choosing a user interface:

▶ The functionality required by the end users

▶ The average user's front-end client hardware platform (hardware details, including CPU speed, amount of RAM, and amount of disk space available)

▶ The average user's front-end client Operating System platform (Windows, Unix, Linux, Mac OS)

▶ The network infrastructure servicing the users (don't forget about remote users—do they access SAP over a slow WAN link or even slower dial-up?)

▶ Installation ramifications (are there resources available to deploy the SAP GUI, and then patch and maintain it?)

In the next few pages, the benefits and drawbacks of each SAP GUI flavor are outlined.

JavaGUI—SAP GUI for Java

For users of Unix, Linux, and Mac OS, the JavaGUI might well be the only choice for connecting to and working with SAP. The JavaGUI supports Windows 32-bit systems as well, and for users still hanging on to OS/2 machines (and not forced for other reasons to upgrade beyond SAP GUI 6.20), you're in luck as well. Support for Mac OS was less than desirable until SAP GUI 6.10. This and later versions work well, though—they install smoothly and offer the basic and advanced functionality seen in the SAP GUI for Windows.

Installation of the SAP GUI for Java requires a Java Runtime Environment (JRE). After it's installed, the total footprint is small—only 8MB is required for the Java Virtual Machine (VM) and only another 9MB is required for the JavaGUI itself. And the product works well. It's as fast as the SAP GUI for Windows, and offers most of the functionality.

If the best description of your desktop environment is "variable," you will do well to consider the JavaGUI. It supports more than 20 languages, and it operates in an identical manner on all supported platforms, despite its platform independence. It supports all R/3 transactions, boasts an ultra-thin network protocol (it is very efficient), and you can natively view all MS Office documents. To obtain the latest version, or pull down older versions, see ftp://ftp.sap.com/pub/sapgui/java/. The .JAR files range from 20MB to 40MB—quite reasonable compared to the SAP GUI for Windows, and just another reason to seriously consider the SAP GUI for Java.

WebGUI—SAP GUI for HTML

SAP introduced the user interface for HTML at the end of 1996, when R/3 3.1G was released along with another then-new product, Internet Transaction Server. Much has changed in the subsequent years, obviously, but the WebGUI is still an excellent interface to SAP. Originally, the WebGUI supported a number of browsers but supported perhaps only 90%–95% of SAP's user transactions out of the box. Today, the SAP GUI for HTML emulates the full features of the traditional SAP GUI with no real difference, except for the fact that a web browser is used. The two most popular browsers are still supported—Microsoft Internet Explorer (IE) and Netscape Navigator.

In the last few years, the SAP GUI for HTML has been much improved. Recent features and enhancements include:

- ▶ Improved flicker-free rendering performance of HTML pages
- ▶ Smaller network bandwidth required
- ▶ Support for the vast majority of SAP transactions
- ▶ New Enterprise Portal–compliant design (SAP Streamline, discussed later)

▶ Elimination of hanging SAP sessions (when the users close WebGUI on their desktops or laptops, it terminates the back-end SAP session)

▶ Support for moveable pop-up windows

▶ Accessibility features that enable blind users to access SAP systems

Because the hardware footprint is minimal (no disk space is necessary per se, assuming IE or Netscape is installed by default), the SAP GUI for HTML makes a lot of sense for many SAP users. Drawbacks exist though. The WebGUI does not support the same level of Microsoft Office integration as the SAP GUI for Windows, nor does it support the variety of business graphics or desktop access mechanisms supported by the WinGUI. Finally, until recently, the WebGUI moved 3–5 times the amount of network traffic than its Windows and Java counterparts, making it the chunkiest (least efficient) member of the SAP GUI family from a network perspective.

WinGUI—SAP GUI for Windows

Because it is the most mature user interface offered by SAP, it comes as no surprise that a number of SAP GUI for Windows "flavors" are available. For years, the only option was the plain gray screen displayed in Figure 4.1, now called the Classic SAP GUI. In typical German fashion, it was very functional. However, it was not known for its good looks. All that changed after Hasso Plattner, one of the founding engineers of SAP AG, toured a customer facility and was given such feedback personally. The result was EnjoySAP—a much more attractive and greatly updated interface, as seen in Figure 4.2.

To easily obtain the latest SAP GUI for Windows, see ftp://ftp.sap.com/pub/sapgui/win/. From here, select the version (for example, 640), and then select what you want to download. Typically, the latest compilation is available along with add-ons, patches, and scripting tools. Be prepared to download more than 500MB.

Enjoy

EnjoySAP, also known as Enjoy, is the most popular SAP GUI flavor today. A bit fatter than its predecessor in terms of desktop CPU and network bandwidth consumption, Enjoy initially suffered from performance issues primarily because it required more data to be moved per transaction than the classic SAP GUI. Old network infrastructures struggled with this requirement until SAP provided the option through the SAP Logon Pad to reduce or "throttle" the bandwidth back to a more bare-bones level. It does this by *not* sending bitmaps and other such "extras" that, although pleasant on a screen, require time to download and display. This low-speed connection throttling option is discussed in more detail in Hour 2, "SAP Basics."

FIGURE 4.1
The classic
SAP GUI.

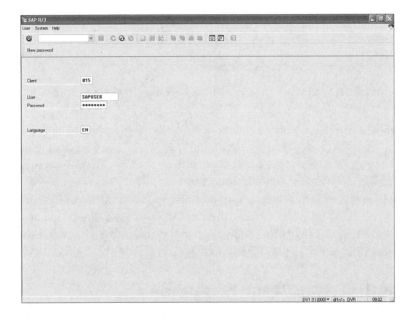

FIGURE 4.2
The EnjoySAP or
simply "Enjoy"
SAP GUI.

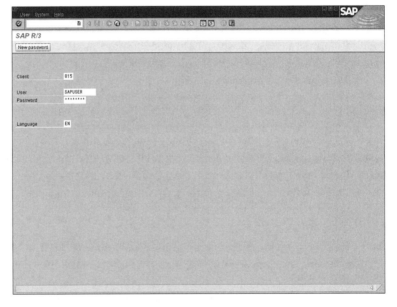

Enjoy is heavier, at least initially, for another reason too. Before EnjoySAP, functions such as scrolling, navigating, scrolling, and searching used to require another network "roundtrip" between the desktop and SAP. With Enjoy, this roundtrip is eliminated with the downside that a bit more traffic is generated up front. However, because subsequent navigation often requires no extra network traffic (there is more information on each SAP screen, often in tabbed format), Enjoy can be both fast and efficient in the long run. Enjoy is available for the JavaGUI as well as the SAP GUI for Windows.

Deploying the SAP GUI for Windows does not require special administrative rights; any user can install the product. With SAP GUI for Windows support for common software management and distribution utilities (like Microsoft SMS), you can easily deploy it across a widely dispersed enterprise. Finally, you no longer need to uninstall previous SAP GUI versions as long as you are running 4.6D or later, a great time-saver for those IT shops that grew accustomed to running the once-mandatory SAPsweep utility prior to each GUI upgrade.

High Contrast and Streamline

A "High Contrast" theme was introduced to make the SAP GUI easier to read. It was intended for visually impaired users. I like using this mode when creating screenshot-based documentation, though—the high-contrast mode makes for easy to read documents, both printed and on the screen.

When SAP GUI 6.30 was released, yet another new theme, called "Streamline," was introduced. Streamline helped create a uniform look and feel between the different GUIs, especially useful when multiple systems and user interfaces were involved. Its green-blue color mocks the default color scheme found in some versions of the WebGUI.

Tradeshow

The latest edition to the standard SAP GUI stable of interfaces is called "Tradeshow." Released in 2003, Tradeshow is easily readable because its strong SAP GUI controls contrast with a bright background.

It's easy to tell at a glance if you're running in Streamline or Tradeshow mode. Just look at the background color of a button. Light blue (almost gray) buttons indicate Streamline, whereas Tradeshow uses a light yellow color.

The Customizing of Local Layout Button

On the top-right side of every SAP GUI window, you can see a multicolored button (next to the yellow Question Mark Help button). Called the Customizing of Local Layout button, and informally referred to as the Customizing or Settings button, it gives you access to the following menu options (see Figure 4.3):

▶ Options

▶ New Visual Design

▶ Set Color to System

▶ Clipboard

▶ Generate Graphic

▶ Create Shortcut

▶ Activate GuiXT

▶ Script Recording and Playback

▶ Script Development Tools

▶ SAP GUI Help

FIGURE 4.3
The Customizing of Local Layout button lets you change the appearance and functionality of your SAP screens, and provides access to many features, simple tools, and utilities.

There are a number of other menu options that are self-explanatory, like a spell checker, a character set selector, the ubiquitous About option, and so on. The About option is especially useful because it not only displays the version and patch level of the SAP GUI, but it also identifies the version of each loaded DLL, provides system information details, and provides a button useful for saving this detail into a text file for safekeeping (see Figure 4.4).

FIGURE 4.4
Many valuable options and system insight are available from the SAP Version Information screen.

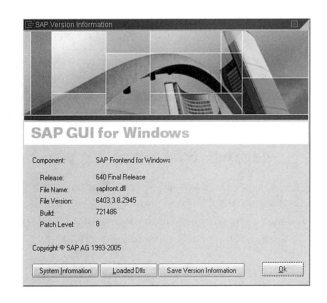

From the Customizing menu, select Options. An Options window appears similar to the one shown in Figure 4.5.

From this Options window, through the use of different tabs, you can

▶ Define when dialog boxes pop up (with success, warning, and/or error messages) and whether such an action incurs a beep

▶ Change cursor width and enable a block cursor (for Overwrite mode)

▶ Specify your default working directory for local data (that is, data that you save from the SAP GUI via %pc or other means, discussed in later hours)

▶ Set Trace options

▶ Set Scripting options

The Options Tab

From the Options tab, you can change how the system notifies you of certain events and how quickly SAP Help is invoked. These used to be termed "general screen settings" in the days before EnjoySAP. It is important to note the default settings for this tab in case you are unhappy with any changes that you make, so that you can easily restore the defaults.

Quick Info

The Quick Info option controls how quickly the Help information (simple description) launches whenever you place the pointer or cursor over an item in the button bar. For example, if you hover over the Customizing button for a period of time, you'll note that a description displays with the button's full name and its shortcut (in this case, Alt+F12). The Slow setting is indeed pretty slow; I recommend the Quick option. Users who tend to execute the same transactions daily (know-it-alls!) should go with None.

There is also an option to enable On Keyboard Focus Change. With this option enabled, if you tab between buttons, for example, the help information is displayed as each button is highlighted. I also find this setting useful, especially when I'm in new SAP territory. For users who tend to repeat many of the same functions over and over, this setting will grow tiresome.

Messages

These options enable you to configure how the SAP system presents you with information. The default setting is that any messages from the system appear in the status bar in the bottom-left side of your screen. By default, all messages pertaining to system output, warning messages, and error messages appear in the status bar. You can set these messages to appear in a pop-up box as well by selecting the appropriate box. I tend to keep none of these checked. Users new to a particular module, or with a critical need to ensure they don't miss an error message, should enable the dialog box at Error Message.

System

This option refers to the location from where SAP retrieves its help files, along with a default time-out. It is best to leave this setting as it is; any changes need to be tested and made by the System Administrator.

The Cursor Tab

The Cursor tab enables you to make custom setting changes to the position and appearance of your cursor. The default setting is usually best, as shown in Figure 4.6. In some cases, though, you might want to make modifications. You can change how the cursor is displayed in lists, for example, so that the cursor marks an entire column or simply one character. And the default cursor position or cursor width can be changed as well, discussed next.

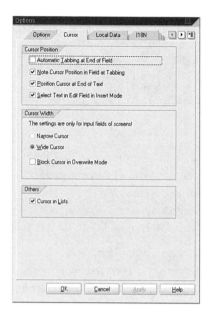

FIGURE 4.6
Your SAP cursor placement can have a big impact when you are doing a lot of data entry in your SAP system.

Cursor Position

With the Automatic Tabbing at End of Field option, you can determine whether the system automatically moves the cursor to the next input field when the cursor reaches the end of the current input field.

> For data entry, Automatic Tabbing (AutoTAB) is useful when you must enter data in many fields and you don't want to press the Tab key to move from field to field.

Did you Know?

In the SAP system, you can determine where you want the cursor to appear when you click in the blank area of an input field. The place where your cursor appears in an entry field is called the cursor position. You can change this setting so that your cursor automatically tabs to the end of a field (when you use the Tab key on your keyboard to navigate between fields). You can also set the cursor to appear exactly where you place it in the field, whether there are blank spaces or not.

You can also set your cursor to note the cursor position in the field at Tab, or position the cursor to the end of the text. These options are designed to make your SAP environment more user friendly and enable you to set the screen and placement of the cursor to your liking.

> If you primarily work in tasks that require a great deal of data entry, it is helpful to place the cursor at the end of any text when you click anywhere behind the text. This is the SAP default setting. This way, when the input field is empty, the cursor appears at the beginning, enabling you to freely enter data without worrying about extra spaces in front of the cursor.

Cursor Width

Cursor width is just as it sounds: Use it to fatten up or thin down your cursor. And use the check box option in this section to enable Block Cursor in Overwrite mode, which enables you to block out all the text when replacing data in a field. This is handy for users who often must overwrite existing field data, as it saves time compared to pressing the Delete or Backspace key to clear a field.

If you want to change your SAP system from Overwrite mode to Insert mode, select the Insert key on your keyboard. You then see the abbreviation in the bottom-right corner of your SAP window change from OVR to INS (see Figure 4.7). With each new session you create, the system defaults back to Overwrite mode.

FIGURE 4.7
The Insert and Overwrite modes determine how text entry functions in SAP.

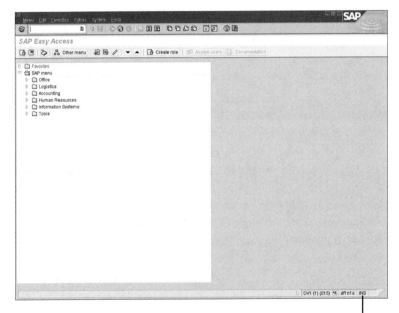

OVR indicates Overwrite mode. INS indicates Insert mode.

The Local Data Tab

As illustrated in Figure 4.8, the Local Data tab lets you configure history and local cache settings, enable front-end security, and specify the default directory for any local data you choose to save in the course of conducting work with the SAP GUI. I find the defaults to be quite useful, although at times I change the local data directory to suit the needs of various SAP customer systems or sites.

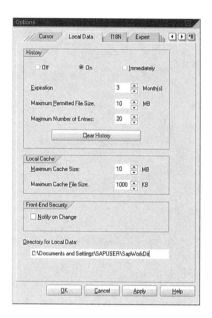

FIGURE 4.8
The Local Data tab is useful in configuring history and local cache settings as well as the default directory for saving local data.

The Trace Tab

The Trace tab has options that enable you to create a file to trace activity in the system. The settings under the Trace tab are managed by your System Administrator in an effort to monitor and diagnose system concerns. Traces can be set to keep a record of errors and warning messages a user receives. In addition, traces are used to monitor where a user has been by keeping a file of each transaction code for each screen visited by the user.

Because such granularity in terms of what is traced is made available, the Trace tool is very powerful. As shown in Figure 4.9, a great number of SAP GUI controls, actions, and conditions can be traced. Use the Select All and Deselect All buttons to work through the list faster, keeping in mind that the more items that are traced, the greater the load placed on the front-end client machine.

FIGURE 4.9
The Trace tab is ideal for diagnosing system problems experienced by a user; its use has a performance effect on the speed of the system, however.

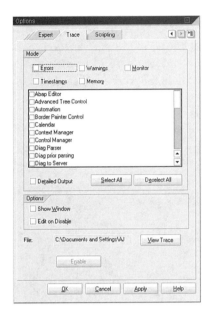

The Scripting Tab

SAP GUI scripting is a powerful tool. Besides providing the interface for powerful load-testing tools to simulate real-world workloads, it also gives average users the capability to automate their daily work. Note that a minimum version of SAP GUI 6.20 is required. SAP GUI scripting is supported on R/3 4.6C and newer systems, though, making it eminently useful.

Scripts are recorded, saved, and played back later. You can drop a script onto a SAP GUI screen and your script will start running. Scripting is only accessible through the SAP GUI for Windows and SAP GUI for Java interfaces, though. Further, if your screen changes (because of the introduction of a new SAP Support package, for example), your script might very well "break" and therefore need to be re-recorded. Although scripts can be shared between users, if a particular user is not allowed to execute a transaction, any script given him by his colleagues does not work for him.

Use the Scripting tab to first verify that scripting support is indeed available (as seen in Figure 4.10), and then enable it and select one of the two Notify options.

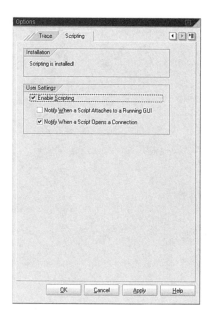

FIGURE 4.10
The Scripting tab lets you verify scripting is installed and enabled for your SAP GUI.

New Visual Design Selection

Beyond the Options selection, the Customizing button offers users great flexibility in configuring SAP GUI settings through the New Visual Design selection. This is accomplished through two tabs

▶ The General tab

▶ The Color Settings tab

The General Tab

Within the General tab, a number of high-level options are available, as displayed in Figure 4.11. You can select the active theme or mode used by the SAP GUI, for instance. Selections include Enjoy, High Contrast, Streamline, Tradeshow, and System Dependent. You can easily change the font size from here as well (making additional changes to fonts are covered later in this hour). You can also enable or disable audio from the General tab.

FIGURE 4.11
The General tab
lets you make
high-level
changes to the
theme employed
by the SAP GUI
as well as to
font size and
audio status.

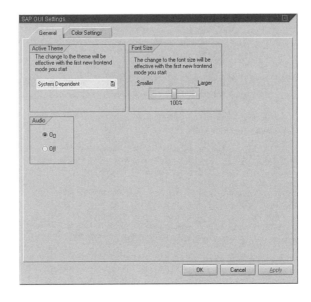

The Color Settings Tab

Like the General tab, the Color Settings tab also lets you change the theme. The idea
here, though, is that the display within this particular window is changed real-time,
enabling you to see the impact that different selections and color settings has relative to each theme. Given its maturity, it comes as no surprise that the Enjoy option
has the greatest number of color settings available. Use it to quickly walk through
different options, and then customize your display.

Clipboard Selection

Although rather simplistic, the Clipboard selection from the Customizing button's
drop-down menu gives you basic power to cut and paste items. This includes

Select	(Ctrl+Y)
Cut	(Ctrl+X)
Copy	(Ctrl+C)
Paste	(Ctrl+V)

Font Selection

There are a number of places where you can make font configuration changes. This
particular selection, from the Customizing button, is the most powerful. Select Font,

and from this window, you can change the appearance and size of the fonts used in your SAP GUI.

> I use this option most often when my screen resolution varies from desktop to desktop, or monitor to monitor.

To change the font, perform the following steps:

1. Under the Font section, select one of the possible entries.

2. Under the Font Style, choose regular, italic, bold, or bold italic.

3. Under the Size section, choose the font size.

As you make changes, a sample of text in the font and size that you have chosen appears in the Preview box display. I suggest you document your default settings so that you can easily return to them. Finally, to get a true sense of the impact your font changes have on your screen, select OK.

> In order for the "font" option to be available in a default GUI configuration, you have to activate the IME config and the multibyte functionalities. Do this by using the tab I18N. Doing so makes the "font" option available as a menu choice.

Status Field's System Information Icon

At the bottom of the SAP GUI, you can click the small white arrow (see Figure 4.12) to display or hide a set of status fields. These fields include the following:

▶ System

▶ Client

▶ User

▶ Program

▶ Transaction

▶ Response time

These fields are mutually exclusive, in that only one can be displayed at a time. I normally enable the response time tracker, although I often instead use the transaction option when documenting a system's configuration or performance (so as to automatically capture the current transaction's T-code in the screenshot).

The status field next to the System Information icon displays the server to which you are connected. Finally, the status field to the rightmost of the screen indicates your data entry mode—Insert (INS) or Overwrite (OVR).

FIGURE 4.12
Clicking the small white arrow alternatively displays and hides a set of useful fields, including the System Information icon.

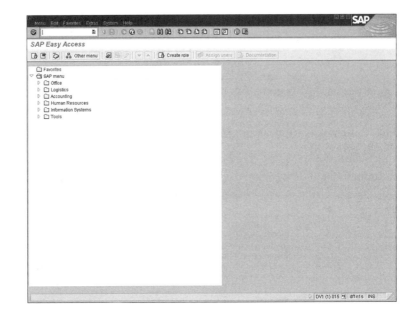

Summary

In this hour, you learned about the three primary flavors of the SAP GUI and how they are alike as well as different. You also learned how to customize your SAP front-end environment to best suit your needs, likes, or personality. From changing your system colors and fonts to customizing your SAP screens and enabling various options, the SAP GUI offers amazing flexibility. As you become more accustomed to working in your SAP system, you will find certain settings and other configuration changes to your liking.

Q&A

Q *When you make changes through the Customizing button, do they apply only for the current session?*

A Changes made through the Customizing button apply to any SAP system that you log in to via the front-end machine you customized, independent of the server or SAP "client" you are processing in.

Q *Is there any benefit to having warning and error messages set to appear in dialog boxes as opposed to appearing only in the status bar?*

A The behavior of system messages is usually a matter of preference. There is some argument about this; many feel that error messages only should appear as dialog boxes, with all other messages appearing only in the status bar, for example. Certainly new users might benefit from the additional dialog boxes, whereas long time users benefit less.

Workshop

The workshop is designed to help you anticipate possible questions, review what you've learned, and begin thinking ahead to putting your knowledge into practice. The answers to the quiz that follows can be found in Appendix A, "Quiz Answers."

Quiz

1. What is the name of the colorful icon to the right of the Help icon on the top-right side of your SAP GUI window?

2. What should you always do before changing a setting via one of the Customizing button options?

3. How do you change the SAP system setting from Overwrite mode to Insert mode?

4. Which SAP GUI flavor supports Linux, Unix, and Mac OS?

5. Where do you change the setting if you want your SAP GUI error messages to display in a pop-up window (dialog box)?

Exercises

1. Change the theme of your SAP GUI between Enjoy, High Contrast, Streamline, and Tradeshow.

2. From the main SAP screen, enter your name into the command field and select the Enter key. An error message will appear in the status bar. Change your settings in the General tab of the Interface menu so that your error message appears as a dialog box.

3. Modify your Quick Info setting in the Interface menu to gain fast access to the help information (description) of fields.

Navigation in SAP

This hour provides an overview of navigation within the SAP system. It goes into detail relative to how to navigate SAP using both menu paths and transaction codes (T-codes). It also gives you some helpful hints on how to determine the transaction code for a screen that you reached using a menu path, along with similar matters of convenience.

Highlights of this hour include

▶ Menu path navigation

▶ Transaction code navigation

▶ Using the SAP history list

Performing Tasks Using Menu Paths

Using the menus in the SAP menu bar, you can navigate to the application and the task you want to begin, or you can choose the function to start the task. With menus, you can easily drill down into business-specific application transactions and other functions without having to memorize T-codes.

Navigation Using the Mouse

To select a menu, single-click on the menu to display the various options listed underneath that menu. Menu entries that contain an additional list of objects (submenus) include an arrow (see Figure 5.1).

Navigation Using the Keyboard

Menus can be selected with the mouse or by using the keyboard. To select menu paths using your keyboard, press F10 (to activate the menu bar), and then use the navigational arrow keys on your keyboard to select and display the menu. You choose a function by highlighting it with the arrow keys and then pressing Enter.

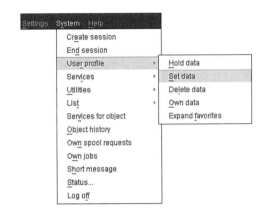

FIGURE 5.1
Menus and sub-
menus can be
selected using
your mouse.

Performing Tasks Using Transaction Codes

As you learned earlier, you can jump directly to any screen in the SAP system by entering an SAP transaction code into the command field on the standard toolbar. A transaction code is an alphanumeric code, essentially a shortcut, that takes you directly to the screen for the task you want to perform. For example, to display an existing sales order in R/3, you can enter **VA03** in the command field and then press Enter. Similarly, to update a vendor's credit limit you can enter **FD32**. Such T-codes save a considerable amount of time otherwise spent navigating the menu system.

SAP provides a T-code for nearly every transaction. The alphanumeric codes themselves vary in length, but do not exceed 20 characters. Most are generally fewer than six or seven characters, in fact. And SAP provides you with the capability to create your own transaction codes to augment those that already exist. Such custom T-codes start with the character Y or Z. Use custom T-codes to execute custom versions of transactions or reports.

By the Way

From any SAP screen except the main screen, you need to enter /n (or /N) before the transaction code in the command field to execute a new transaction (for example, /nVA03). To open a new SAP GUI session and execute a new task, instead of /n, use a /o plus the transaction code (for example, /oVA03).

Finding the Right Transaction Code

To find a transaction code for a certain task, begin by using the Standard SAP menu or SAP Easy Access menu. You can often display this menu from the main SAP screen by entering /n in the command field and pressing Enter. A screen will appear similar to the one shown in Figure 5.2.

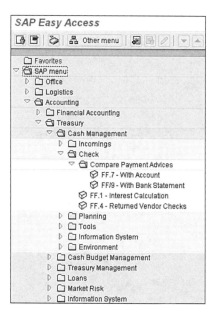

FIGURE 5.2
You can use the SAP Easy Access menu to search for transaction codes.

> Depending on the SAP modules that you are using, the client that you are logged into, and your system configuration, your SAP Easy Access or other standard menu might be different.

By the Way

On the screen, you see a list of the SAP application areas, with arrows (or plus signs, in the case of older SAP releases) to the left of every item that has sublists attached underneath it. On the menu bar, select Edit, Technical Name, Technical Name On. This turns on the feature allowing all transaction codes to be displayed next to the tasks. To display one of the application area sublists, double-click on it. The sublist appears containing tasks, more sublists, or both. You can identify a task by the fact that no arrow (or plus or minus sign) appears to the left of it, and a transaction code is listed instead.

Continue to drill down until you see the task you want. You can start the function now by double-clicking on it. Otherwise, you can use this transaction code to start this task from any screen in the SAP system. When you use a transaction code to start a task, the SAP system closes, or ends, your current task and then displays the initial screen of the new task.

As you can see, this seems like a lot of work to find a particular transaction code. Fortunately, a number of shortcut methods exist. For example, after you have entered a particular task's screen, there's a simple method of determining its relevant T-code, as Iexplained in the following section.

Finding the Transaction Code for the Current Task

From nearly every screen in SAP, the system allows you to easily determine its relevant transaction code. From the SAP screen, select the menu path System, Status. This displays the System Status screen that provides a great amount of detail and technical information regarding the screen you are on (see Figure 5.3).

FIGURE 5.3
The System Status window provides useful information, including the transaction code for the screen that you are currently on.

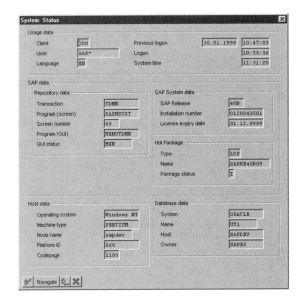

In addition to all the detailed and technical information, the System Status screen gives you the transaction code for the screen. Look in the field under the SAP Data heading called Transaction. This gives you the multicharacter transaction code for the current screen. In the example shown in Figure 5.4, for example, the transaction code is TDMN. You can use this method from nearly any screen in the system.

By the Way

> In some instances, an SAP action or event consists of a series of screens. Some of the screens within that action might contain the same transaction code as the first screen in the action, in essence telling you that you cannot start this particular transaction midway; it must be started from the beginning.

Using the History List to Find Transaction Codes

A list of all the transaction codes processed since you logged on is called a *history list*. To access the history list, use your mouse to select the down arrow to the right of the command field (see Figure 5.4).

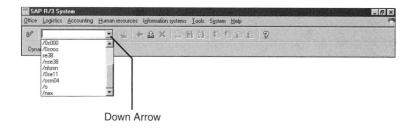

Down Arrow

FIGURE 5.4
The history list is quite useful for navigating back and forth between different transactions that you have executed or accessed within your current session.

From the history list, select the transaction code you want to execute by highlighting it and pressing the Enter key on your keyboard or clicking the green check mark on the toolbar. The initial screen of the task associated with that transaction code will appear.

Scrolling Techniques

When you view information in reports or view the SAP online help, occasionally some of the information will not fit in your window. To see the additional information, you can use the scrollbars. Your window has a vertical and a horizontal scrollbar.

You use the vertical scrollbar to move, or scroll, up and down through the information in the window. You use the horizontal scrollbar to scroll left and right through the information in the window, as follows:

To Scroll	Do This
Up or down one line	Click on the up or down scroll arrow on the vertical scrollbar.
Left or right one character	Click on the left or right scroll arrow on the horizontal scrollbar.
Up or down one screen page	Click above or below the slider box on the vertical scrollbar.
Left or right the width of the screen page	Click to the right or left of the slider box on the horizontal scrollbar.
To a certain position in the information up or down	Drag the slider box on the vertical scrollbar to the approximate location of the desired infor mation; then release the mouse button.
To a certain position in the information left or right	Drag the slider box on the horizontal scrollbar to the approximate location of the desired infor- mation; then release the mouse button.

You can also use the scroll (page up and down) buttons in the standard toolbar to view information in windows, as follows:

Destination	Toolbar Button	Function Key Shortcut
First Screen Page		F21 Ctrl+PageUp
Last Screen Page		F24 Ctrl+PageDown
Previous Screen Page		F22 PageUp
Next Screen Page		F23 PageDown

Using the Clipboard

You can transfer the contents of SAP fields (and in some cases, the entire contents of an SAP screen) onto your Windows Clipboard and then paste the data into other SAP fields, or into other applications like Word and Excel.

Moving Data

To select a field or the text you want to move, perform the following steps:

1. Click and drag the pointer over the text you want to select. The selected text then appears highlighted.

2. To move the information in an input field onto the Windows Clipboard, use the keyboard combination Ctrl+X. The selected text no longer appears and is now stored in your Windows Clipboard.

3. To paste this information into another SAP screen or into a different application, go to the destination and use the keyboard combination Ctrl+V to paste the data.

The Cut (or move) command is generally used on input fields.

Copying Data

To select a field or the text you want to copy, perform the following steps:

1. Click and drag the pointer over the text you want to select. The selected text then appears highlighted.

2. To move the information in an input field onto the Windows Clipboard, use the keyboard combination Ctrl+C. The selected text still appears and is also stored in your Windows Clipboard.

3. To paste this information into another SAP screen or into a different application, go to the destination and use the keyboard combination Ctrl+V to paste the data.

The transferred data remains in the Clipboard until you use Cut or Copy again to move or copy new text onto the Clipboard.

If you are viewing your Help via a browser like Microsoft Internet Explorer, you can give this functionality a try using the following steps:

1. Begin with the menu path Help, and then select the Library option from the menu bar. Your SAP help application launches and brings you to the library main screen.

2. Select the ABC Glossary button on the top right of the screen. This brings you to the SAP Glossary main screen and a definition appears in the right of the screen. Depending on your version number, the definition that is displayed on your screen might appear different from the one shown in Figure 5.5.

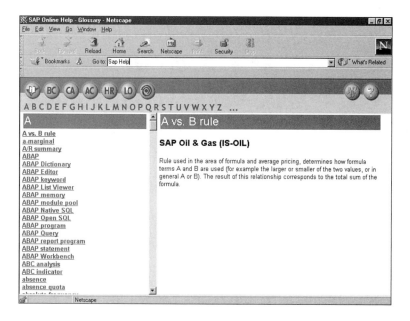

FIGURE 5.5
If you are viewing your SAP Help application via a standard browser, your SAP Glossary main screen will appear like a web page.

3. Next, select the text of this definition and copy it to the Clipboard. Select the text by using your mouse to highlight it.

4. After all the text is selected, use the keyboard combination Ctrl+C to copy it to the Clipboard.

5. You are going to paste this definition into the Windows Notepad. From your Windows Start menu, select Start, Run. Type the word **notepad** and press Enter (see Figure 5.6). The Windows Notepad launches.

FIGURE 5.6
All Windows
applications can
be executed
using Start,
Run.

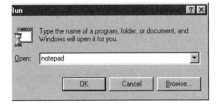

6. Place your cursor at the top of the blank Notepad and use the keyboard combination Ctrl+V to paste the data. Your selected text now appears in the Notepad application.

The formatting might appear a little strange, but this sometimes occurs when you copy and paste information across applications.

Copying Unselectable Data

You are not able to select certain data displayed on SAP screens using your mouse and the method previously described. To give you an example, return to your main SAP window and use the transaction code /nSE11 to travel to the SAP Data Dictionary Initial screen. Place your cursor in the Object Name field and select the F1 key to launch the field-specific help, as shown in Figure 5.7. (If you do not have access to transaction code /nSE11, place your cursor in any SAP field and select the F1 button on your keyboard.) A window will appear giving detailed definitions and technical information for the field that you selected.

By the Way

I will go into more detail about using the SAP Help system in Hour 23, "Support Overview."

Try to use the mouse to select the text displayed on this screen. You will see that you are unable to select the data. In cases like these, you will need to add one more keyboard combination. Use your mouse to tap once anywhere on the screen. Next use Ctrl+Y to change your mouse to a crosshair cursor. Use this cursor to select the desired text and follow the same steps as before: Ctrl+C to copy the text and Ctrl+V to paste the text.

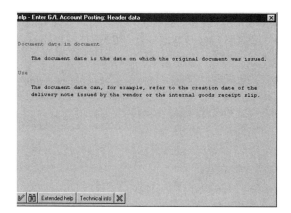

FIGURE 5.7
Field-specific Help can be accessed for any SAP field by selecting the F1 button on your keyboard.

Creating Screen Prints from SAP

There might be times when you want to obtain a print or "screenshot" of an SAP screen. Although the Print function is available on most SAP screens, there might be an occasion when you want to print a copy of a status message (that appears on the bottom-left side of the window) that would not appear using the standard SAP Print function.

To take a screen print of an SAP screen, perform the following steps:

1. Select the Print screen button on the upper-right side of your keyboard. This stores a snapshot of your current screen in the Windows Clipboard.

2. Next, launch the Windows Paint (formerly Paintbrush) application to paste the file for output. Follow the Windows menu path Start, Programs, Accessories, Paint to launch Windows Paint (or execute pbrush.exe from Start, Run).

3. On the Edit menu of the Paint application, select the Paste option (if you are prompted to enlarge the bitmap, choose OK).

Your screen print will now appear in the Windows Paint application. From here, you can print or save it to a bitmap file on your computer for later reference. The same kind of process can be applied to Microsoft Word if you simply need to save a screen print, rather than potentially manipulating the image in Paint.

On the Interface menu, there is an option called Generate Graphic. The screen capture facility allows you to pick up table data from any screen in the SAP system and display it using SAP Business Graphics.

To save screen output (like that found in a list) to a file on your desktop or the network, enter %pc on the command line, and then press Enter. A print window pops up, defaulting to saving the screen's contents in an unconverted or XLS file format. Choose the format most appropriate (for example, XLS or RTF for Excel or Word-based output, respectively), press Enter, browse to the desired directory path, type the name of the output file you want to create, and then press Save to save the list data to the filename you specified.

Printing in SAP

Printing enables you to make hard copies of lists, tables, and reports from SAP. The SAP Print button is available on most SAP screens (see Figure 5.8).

Print button

FIGURE 5.8
The Print button allows you to create a hard copy of your SAP output.

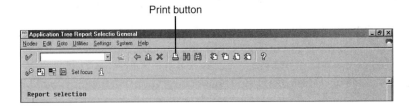

Let's take a look at the printing features in SAP. If you are not connected to a printer, you can still follow along.

In order to print from SAP, your workstation needs to be connected to a printer, via a network or directly plugged into your PC.

The SAP Print Screen List

Start with the SAP transaction code /nSM04, which you might recall is the SAP Overview of Users screen that you learned about earlier. If you do not have access to this screen, you can use any SAP screen where the Print button is available. Select the Print button on the standard toolbar. You will be prompted with the SAP Print List Output screen similar to the one shown in Figure 5.9. Select the Print button, and the data that you wanted to print is sent to the output device specified in your settings.

If you are not presented with this screen or if you receive a warning message saying your system is not connected to a printer, contact your system administrator for assistance in connecting to a printer. Alternatively, you might be presented with the

Print Screen List window, which is used to enter the output device (printer) you intend to print to—select or type the name of your printer, make any other updates to the number of copies or pages (see Figure 5.10), and select the green check box to continue.

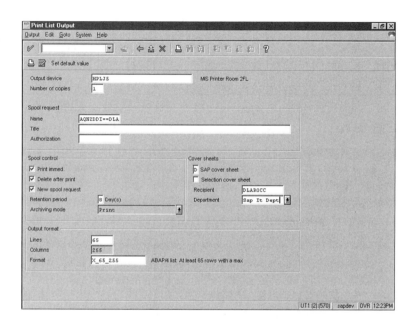

FIGURE 5.9
The Print List Output screen allows you to customize your printer settings.

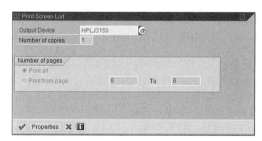

FIGURE 5.10
The Print Screen List window enables you to specify your printer, number of copies, and specific pages to print.

Output Device

This field contains the name of the output device. This could be a printer, a fax machine, or some other hardware device connected to the SAP system. In the example provided in Figure 5.10, it contains my printer name—HPLJ3150. To see a list of available output devices connected to your SAP system, select the down arrow to the right of this field.

Number of Copies

The Number of Copies field is where you specify the number of copies of the document you want to print.

> Sometimes in SAP, your reports might be lengthy. It is always a good idea to determine how many pages your output is going to be before printing one or multiple copies. Use your scrolling options on the toolbar, covered earlier in this chapter in "Scrolling Techniques," to navigate through your output to determine its length before printing.

Spool Request

The Name field contains the name of the spool request. As you will learn, everything in SAP is assigned a name or an identifier within the SAP system. This name designates the item, in this case, a print request to the system. For example, if you go to your printer and you do not find your output, you can search in the SAP system by this Spool Request Name and find out what happened to your output.

The Spool Request Name can consist of letters, numerals, special characters, and blanks. The standard name proposed by the system for a spool request comprises the eight-character report name, the separator '_', and the first threecharacters of your user name. You can, however, add a description of your own in the Spool Request Title field, although it is usually a good idea to accept the name proposed by the system.

The Title field contains a description of the spool request. It might consist of any combination of letters, digits, special characters, and blanks. This field can help you to identify your spool request.

The Authorization field contains the authorization for the spool request. Say that a Human Resources Manager created a report of all employee salaries and sent it to the printer. As this item sits in the SAP spool waiting to be printed, only users with the correct authorization are allowed to display the contents of the spool request.

Spool Control

The Print Immed. option determines whether the spool request (that is the report output) should be sent to the output device immediately. This setting is usually marked at runtime if you are printing a small report. This designation will bypass the standard spool routing and get sent directly to the designated printer.

The Delete After Print option determines whether to delete the spool request immediately after it has been sent to the output device or only after the spool retention period has expired. The default setting for this option is blank, indicating that the spool requests are saved for the duration of the spool retention period set in the retention period box. This is helpful in the previous scenario I detailed. If the spool request was immediately deleted, you would not be able to go back and search for the item, in case the output had been misplaced.

Most users mark this box in an effort to conserve space by not saving a spool request for every item printed. The box is cleared only when the user feels it is necessary to retain the request for very important spool requests.

The New Spool Request option determines whether to append the current spool request to an existing request with similar attributes or whether to generate a new spool request. If left blank, this option allows users to add their spool request to an existing request.

To append the current spool request to an existing spool request, the values contained in the Name, Output Device, Number of Copies, and Format fields must be the same, and the existing spool request should not yet have been completed. This setting applies particularly when a spool request is released for output. If no suitable spool request is found, a new one is generated.

The Retention Period field determines how many days a spool request is to remain in the spool system before it is deleted.

Archiving Mode allows the user the option to send the file to Print, Archive, or Archive and Print. The default setting is for Print (so that the data is output on paper). Sending output to an archive is a function managed by your system administrator.

Cover Sheets

The SAP Cover Sheet field determines whether to include a cover sheet with your output that is sent to the printer. Information such as recipient name, department name, format used, and so on can all be included on your SAP Cover Sheet. The permitted values for this field are

> ' ' (left blank): No cover sheet
>
> 'X' : Output cover sheet
>
> 'D' : Cover sheet output depends on the setting of the output device (printer) being used

The Recipient field contains the spool request recipient's name that appears on the cover sheet of hard copy printouts. The default value for the name of the recipient is the current user name.

The Department field contains the name of the department originating the spool request. On hard copy printouts, the name is displayed on the cover sheet.

Output Format

The Lines field determines the number of lines per list page. If this field contains a zero or is blank, the number of pages is unlimited, which is not permitted during printing. The length of the list is then determined by its content alone. When printing, the maximum number of lines per page depends on the formatting you choose. If you want to change the number of lines, you must use different formatting. It is a good idea to accept the default setting for this field.

The Columns field contains the current line width of the list; the maximum line width of a list is 255 characters. When printing, the maximum line width depends on the format. If you want to change the line width, you must also choose a different format. It is a good idea to accept the default setting for this field.

The Format field contains the spool request format for output. Selecting the down arrow to the right of this field brings you a list of available formats for your selected device. This setting defines the page format: that is, the maximum number of lines and columns that print per page. It is a good idea to test the different formats listed to find one that is most acceptable for the output you are printing.

Setting Default Values for the Printer

Each time you select the Print button in the SAP system, you will be prompted with the SAP Print Screen List. You can set a default value for each field in this screen so that you need not re-enter your settings each time you print. After you have entered all the settings to your specifications, select the User-Specific Print Parameters button from the application toolbar. This brings up a Print List Output window useful in selecting user-specific and other print options.

> Don't forget when you select the Print button from the standard toolbar, you will always be prompted with the Print List screen. You must select the Print button from this screen in order to send the output to your printer.

Summary

In this hour, you have learned about the different methods of navigation within SAP. You should now be more familiar with the concept of navigation using transaction codes and how to find a transaction code for any screen within the SAP system. You should also be comfortable with the scrolling concept in reports and screens, as well as how to use the Windows Clipboard to store data as you move between screens and applications. Finally, a very important topic that I covered in this hour is the concept of retrieving print screens from the SAP system and of setting your preferences for printing using the SAP Print List screen.

Q&A

Q *If you make your own screens, can you make your own transaction codes?*

A Yes, when you create your own screens using the Screen Painter, you also create your own transaction codes for your screens.

Q *Can you set up your SAP desktop to be connected to more than one printer at a time?*

A Yes, you can configure your SAP system to be connected to multiple output devices including printers and fax machines. Each time you select the Print button, you must specify the output device.

Q *If you are working in multiple SAP clients, does your history reflect navigation in both clients?*

A Yes, your history list saves all transaction codes used on your system, at any given point, regardless of the specific client you have logged into.

Workshop

The workshop is designed to help you anticipate possible questions, review what you've learned, and begin thinking ahead to putting your knowledge into practice. The answers to the quiz that follows can be found in Appendix A, "Quiz Answers."

Quiz

1. What is the transaction code for the main SAP screen?

2. Which Windows application can you launch to paste and save SAP screen prints in?

3. Which check box on the SAP Print List screen do you select if you do not want your spool request saved in the SAP system for the duration of the retention period?

4. To select SAP menu paths using your keyboard instead of your mouse, you first need to select which function key?

5. How do you find the transaction code from nearly any screen displayed in SAP?

6. How do you access the history list?

7. What is the Retention Period used for on the Print Screen List window?

Exercises

1. Find the transaction code for the main SAP screen.

2. Place your cursor in the command field and then select the F1 key on your keyboard to select the field-specific help. Copy this help and paste it into your Windows Notepad application.

3. Print the Overview of Users screen to your local printer.

HOUR 6

Screen Basics

This hour helps you begin to understand the fundamental elements of the SAP screens. This overview will familiarize you with the screens and discuss how you will interact with them.

Highlights of this hour include

- ▶ Entering data in SAP screens
- ▶ Using the SAP Possible Entries Help function
- ▶ Saving your data
- ▶ SAP screen objects

Understanding and Using Fields

The SAP system houses a large database of information. This database is composed of tables that store data (master data, transactional data, programs, and more). The tables are composed of columns (called fields) and rows (called records or data). SAP screens display these database fields on their screens. From R/3, use the command field to navigate to transaction code /nFF7A. This transaction code will take you to the Cash Management and Forecast screen in the Financial Accounting module (see Figure 6.1). For help navigating in SAP, refer to Hour 5, "Navigation in SAP."

Input Fields

This screen displays a series of fields that are linked to database tables in the system. Most screens in the SAP system contain fields in which you enter data. These types of fields are called *input fields*. An example of an input field is shown in Figure 6.2.

Input fields vary in size: The length of a field determines how many characters you can enter in the field. In the example shown in Figure 6.2, the Display As Of date input field is 10 characters. The length of the rectangular box indicates the length of the longest valid data entry for that field.

The **active** field is the field that currently contains the cursor and is waiting for input.

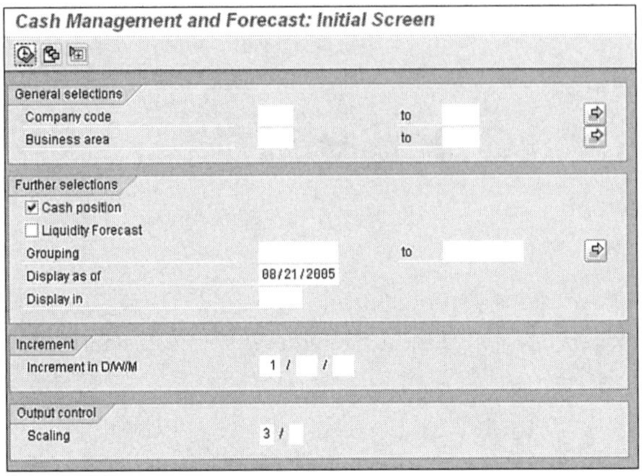

FIGURE 6.1
The Cash Management and Forecast screen gives a good example of an arrange-ment of fields presented on an SAP screen.

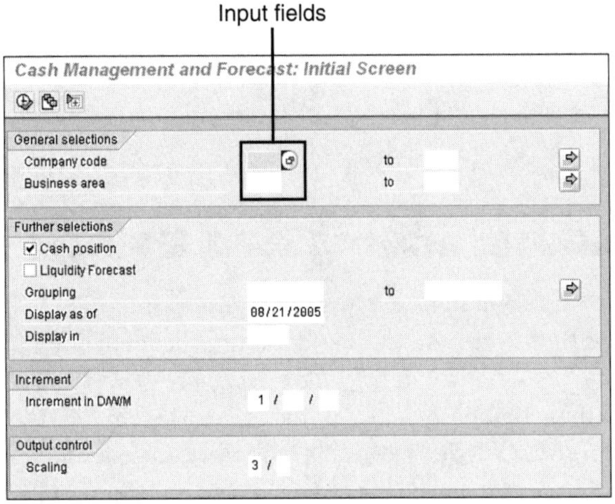

Cash Management and Forecast: Initial Screen

FIGURE 6.2
SAP input fields accept the entry of the data and are tied to fields in your SAP Data Dictionary.

Input fields

Cash Management and Forecast: Initial Screen

When you place the cursor anywhere in an empty input field, the cursor appears at the beginning of the field, making data entry simple. Remember that the field can only hold data that fits into its rectangular box. After entry, the cursor remains in the input field until you press the Tab key to move it to the next field, press the Enter key to check your entry, or click on another input field.

Did you Know?

> The initial placement of the cursor in a field is determined by your system set-tings, and can be modified. See the section "The Cursor Tab" in Hour 4, "Customizing Your SAP Display," for more information.

Replace and Insert Modes

Your computer keyboard has a button called Insert on its top-right side above the Delete button. This Insert key toggles your computer setting between two writing modes. The Insert mode enables you to insert data into an existing field without typing over it. The Overwrite mode enables you to type over existing data in a field. The Overwrite mode is the SAP default.

You can tell which setting your SAP system is using by looking at the bottom right of your screen. In the box to the left of the system clock, you will see the abbreviation OVR for Overwrite mode or INS for Insert mode. This setting is usually user-specific, as indicated by the following:

▶ Most users familiar with the Microsoft family of products, such as Microsoft Word and Excel, are used to the Insert mode.

▶ Users familiar with WordPerfect and similar products prefer the Overwrite mode.

Either way, the system will adjust to your suiting; however, keep in mind that with each new session you create, the default Overwrite mode setting will be active unless you change it.

Possible Entries for an Input Field

As I explained at the beginning of this hour, each input field is linked to a database table. If you are unsure of a valid entry (that is, the exact name of a field that already exists in the table), you can use the Possible Entries button to select a valid entry from the list (see Figure 6.3).

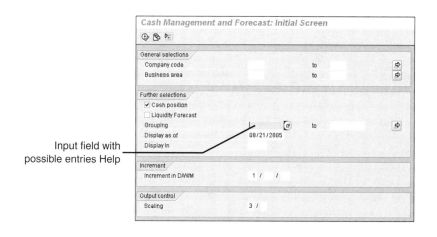

Input field with possible entries Help

FIGURE 6.3
Many fields in the SAP system contain Possible Entries Help where you can select an appropriate value from a list instead of typing it.

Any field containing a down arrow (like the one indicated in Figure 6.3) on the far-right side has a Possible Entry function. Give one a try. Use the Transaction code /nFK10 to travel to the Vendor: Initial Screen Balances Display screen. This screen contains three input fields. Use your Tab key to navigate between the three fields. You will see that as you travel from one field to another, the Possible Entries down arrow appears only when the field is active. You will also see that the Possible Entries down arrow is not present on the Fiscal Year field. Use your Tab key to return to the Company Code field. Use your mouse to select the Possible Entries arrow, as displayed in Figure 6.4 (the Possible Entries Help button down arrow disappears when the Possible Entries window opens).

By the Way

Not all input fields have lists of possible entries. You cannot determine whether such a list is available for an input field until you place the cursor in the input field. Also, some fields that contain Possible Entries Help do not have a down arrow even when the field is active. You can select the F4 button on the top of your keyboard to retrieve the Possible Entries Help in any SAP field where it is available.

FIGURE 6.4
The Possible Entries window displays available company codes.

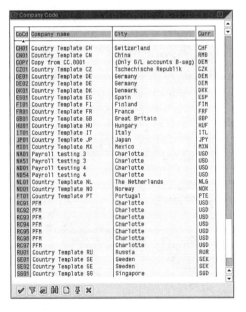

In this example, after selecting the Possible Entries down arrow for the Company Code field, you are presented with a list of possible entries that are acceptable and valid for that field.

Keep in mind, depending on your system's configuration, your possible entries list might appear slightly different from the one displayed in Figure 6.4.

By the Way

To select an item from a Possible Entries list, you can double-click it or use your mouse to highlight it once, and then choose the green check mark Enter key. The list will disappear and the value selected will then be present in your Company Code field.

See what happens when you enter a value that is not an item listed in the Possible Entries Help. Return your cursor to the Company Code field, type your initials, and press the Enter key. A warning or error message appears in the Status bar area. This error or warning message prevents you from progressing to additional screens until the issue is corrected.

Editing the Data in an Input Field

Now that you have an invalid entry in your Company Code field, you need to return to that field to correct the input. Place your cursor in the Company Code box and then select the Possible Entries Help down arrow for the Company Code field. Select any item from the list of possible entries and press the green check mark. Now your invalid entry is replaced by a valid one. Press the Enter key, and SAP checks your entry to confirm that it is acceptable and removes your warning message from the status bar.

Sometimes the SAP system saves the last value entered in an input field into memory. Even when you replace it with a new value, it retains the old one. To clear the SAP memory for an input box, select the exclamation point key (!) and press Enter; this clears the memory for that input field.

Did you Know?

Required Input Fields

On SAP screens, some fields require you to fill them with data before proceeding. These are called *required fields* and in the early days of SAP contained a question mark (?). Today, these required fields contain a square with a check mark inside it, as shown in Figure 6.5. The following are examples of required fields:

▶ A purchase order number field on a Create Purchase Order screen in the Financials module

▶ An employee personnel number on a Change Basic Pay screen in the Human Resources module

▶ A date of accepted delivery field in an Inventory Management Control screen in the Logistics module

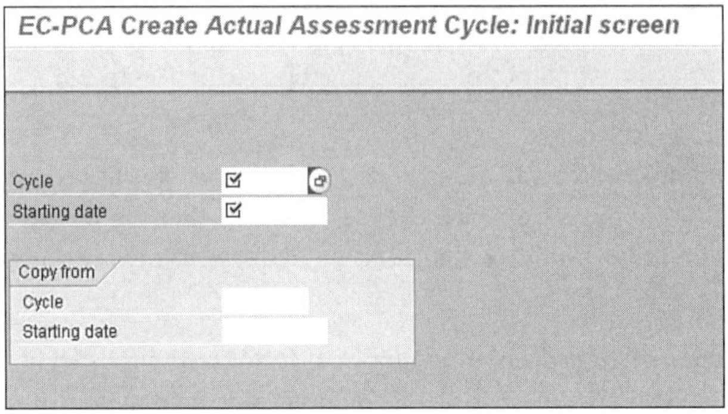

FIGURE 6.5
Required fields
require data
before enabling
you to save or
proceed past
the screen.

Generally, if a screen does not contain a square with a check mark, you can navigate to the next screen without entering data in any fields. However, some screens that contain required fields are not marked in this way. This situation can occur when you enter data in an optional field that has required fields associated with it, for example.

If you have not completed all the required fields on a screen and then try to proceed to another screen, the SAP System displays an error message in the status bar. At the same time, it returns the cursor to the first required field that needs data entered so that you can make the necessary change.

Field Entry Validation

After entering data into input fields on the screen, use the Enter key or the green check mark on your SAP toolbar to check the validity of your entries. If your entries are valid, the system will advance to the next screen in the task. If the system checks your entries and finds any errors—for example, entries in the wrong format—it displays a message in the status bar and positions the cursor in the field that you need to correct.

Canceling All the Data Entered on a Screen

To cancel all the data you just entered on a screen, use the menu path Edit, Cancel or use the red X Cancel button on the toolbar. In most instances, you will be prompted with an SAP window confirming that data will be lost if you proceed to exit the current screen. See Figure 6.6.

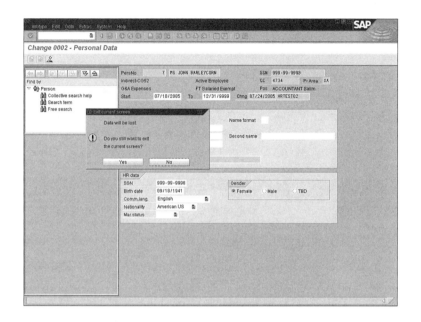

FIGURE 6.6
The Exit current screen box confirms that data will be lost if you choose to exit the current screen.

Saving Your Data on the Screen

The SAP Save button appears on the standard toolbar and looks like an open folder. When you are working in a task that consists of several screens, the system temporarily stores the data that you enter on each screen. After you complete all the necessary screens in your task, you need to save your data by selecting the Save button. The Save button processes your data and sends your changes to the database.

> If you are doing a task for the first time and you do not know which screen is the last screen, the system prompts you to save when you reach the last screen.

By the Way

Printing Data Displayed Onscreen

Use the Print button on the standard toolbar for sending the information on your screen to the printer. Advanced printing options are covered in Hour 5.

Replicating Data

No one likes entering data. SAP has a way to simplify the process. Say that you need to enter a handful of new employees into the SAP R/3 or ECC Human Resources or Human Capital Management (HCM) modules, respectively. All the employees have the same hire date. Using the Hold Data or Set Data SAP functions, you can set the hire date to automatically default to the date you set for each of the employees that you need to enter, without having to rekey it each time.

Hold Data

To use the Hold Data function on any SAP screen (except the login screen), enter the data that you want to hold in an input field. While your cursor is still in the input field, navigate to the menu path System, User Profile, Hold Data, as shown in Figure 6.7.

FIGURE 6.7
Hold Data is a
useful tool for
entering data
in SAP.

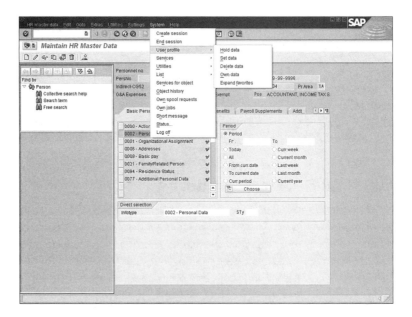

The data will be set in memory for that field for each new record you create until you turn the Hold Data setting off. The Hold Data feature also has another advantage: The input field defaults to the data that you have set to hold, yet it also allows you to override the data. If you want to hold data and not give the user the capability to change the default, you would use the Set Data setting.

Set Data

The Set Data feature works in the same fashion as the Hold Data setting, but it does not enable the user to override the default in the input field. The advantage to using the Set Data setting is that it gives you the capability to automatically skip fields with held data, so you do not need to tab from field to field during data entry.

To use the Set Data function on any SAP screen (except the login screen), enter the data in an input field that you want to set. While your cursor is still in the input field, go to the menu path System, User Profile, Set Data, as shown in Figure 6.8.

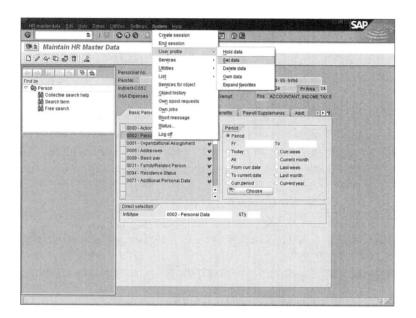

FIGURE 6.8
Using the Set Data option restricts users from changing the set value in the field.

Deleting Data That Is Held or Set on a Screen

You can hold data for as many different screens as you like. The data you enter and hold on a screen is held for that screen until you delete it or until you log off the SAP system. If you want to remove the setting without having to log off the system, place the cursor in the input field that you want to delete and follow the menu path System, User Profile, Delete Data. The data will be deleted, and the next time you access the screen the data will not be displayed.

> You can also simplify the input of repeated data using parameters and variants. Parameters are a more advanced topic that is not within the scope of this book. For more information on parameters, search your SAP Help for more information. Variants are discussed in Hour 19, "Reporting Basics."

By the Way

Display Fields

Another type of SAP field is a display field. This type of field is not used to enter, but only to display data. Display fields are always shaded with a gray background to indicate that the field cannot be changed.

Display fields are often used for values that were set according to some configuration in the system or by previous steps in a process. What this translates to is that fields are often assigned values based on configuration that occurs behind the scenes. For example, if you add a new employee to your Human Resources Module, on their New Hire screen, there will be a display field listing the employee's status as active. This value is assigned by the system and cannot be changed by the user.

By the same token, when system administrators run processes for maintaining the system, their screens often include date fields storing the current date, which are display only. The system does not enable you to change the value in these fields because in most cases the values are used by the SAP system for accurate processing. Using the Human Resources example, if you hired a new employee and were able to change his status from active to terminated, the new employee would not be recognized in SAP as an active employee. Therefore, he would not be paid or receive benefits as an active employee.

By the Way

> Some fields come predelivered from SAP as display only, but you can also customize your system to change additional fields to display only so users cannot make changes to the data.

Screen Objects

This section covers the different types of items that you see on the SAP screens. Regardless of the SAP component's module that you are processing in, the same types of screen objects will generally appear on the different SAP screens.

SAP promotes itself as very logically designed and organized; a user can easily navigate through its system. The style of the SAP system is much different than many popular applications available on the market today, including the Microsoft Windows and the Microsoft Office family of products. Often absent in SAP are the friendly pictures, detailed formatted text, or elaborate design. Most screens in SAP are designed in tabbed formats or tree structures through which the user navigates by drilling "down."

SAP Trees

You will soon become accustomed to using SAP trees in navigating through the SAP system (see Figure 6.9). SAP's logically devised environment centers on a basic tree structure. The SAP trees appear similar to the Windows structure that you see in Windows Explorer. The tree structure is formulated so that you can drill down in the tree to reach deeper levels within a concept. To use an SAP tree for navigation, you need to select the arrow sign to expand or compress the tree to view more or fewer selections, respectively. Older versions of SAP use plus or minus signs to expand or compress the tree.

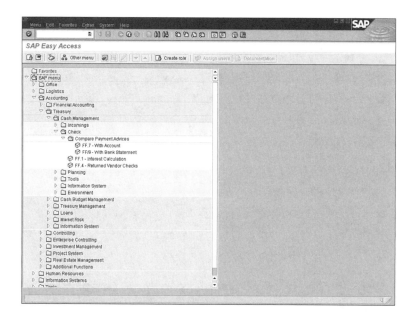

FIGURE 6.9
The SAP ECC and similar SAP systems are based on an elementary tree structure.

Check Boxes

When you are working in SAP, entering information sometimes involves selecting options. These options can be in the form of check boxes like the ones shown in Figure 6.10. A check mark placed in the check box indicates that the box is selected, and an empty box indicates that the box is not selected.

Check boxes are used when a person has the opportunity to select more than one option. On a single screen, a person can select multiple check boxes.

Radio Buttons

When you are permitted only *one* option among a selection of many, you will see a group of radio buttons provided instead of check boxes. A group of radio buttons accepts only one selection for the group. That is, you cannot mark more than one radio button in a group.

A mark placed in the circle indicates that the radio button is selected, and an empty circle indicates that the radio button is not selected (see Figure 6.11). An example of a radio button is the designation of an employee in the Human Resources module as male or female.

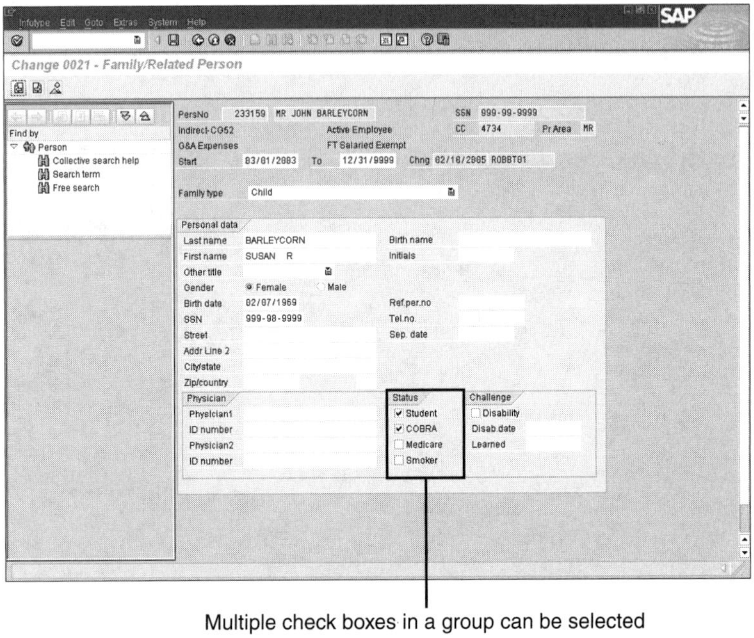

FIGURE 6.10
Check boxes
are used to
respond with a
yes or no to a
selection.

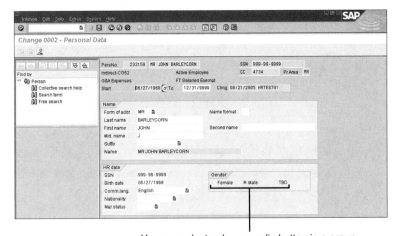

Multiple check boxes in a group can be selected

FIGURE 6.11
Radio buttons
are always
shown in a
group of at
least two or
more; choices
are mutually
exclusive.

You can select only one radio button in a group

Dialog Boxes

A dialog box is a fancy word for a window that pops up to give you information.
These are also sometimes called Information windows. Two situations in which a
dialog box appears on your screen are described as follows:

▶ The system needs more information from you before it can proceed.

▶ The system needs to give you feedback, such as messages or specific information about your current task.

For example, you might receive a dialog box on your screen when you are logging off SAP. If you select the SAP icon in the top-left side of your screen and then select the Close button, you are prompted with a dialog box confirming that you indeed want to log off the system.

Table Controls

A final object you will see on most SAP screens is Table Controls, as shown in Figure 6.12. Table controls display data in a tabular format similar to a Microsoft Excel spreadsheet. Table controls are popular for displaying or entering single structured lines of data. The term *table control* is covered in more detail in Hour 18, "Designing Screens and Menus." Just as you can use a check box object for selection for some data, you can use a table control object to display data in a tabular format.

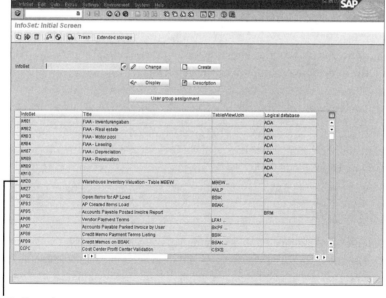

FIGURE 6.12
Table controls are very popular in SAP for presenting data in a simple structured format.

SAP Table Control

Summary

At this juncture, as a user you should feel very comfortable working in the SAP system. Many of the once-obscure objects, functions, and concepts should now be familiar. For instance, you should be well equipped to enter data into the SAP system, and you are quite familiar with the SAP objects that you will encounter on the different screens, including dialog boxes and radio buttons. You also should feel more comfortable with SAP terminology as it applies to screens and controls.

Q&A

Q *How is case used in SAP?*

A This is a popular question when implementing SAP to replace a very old legacy system. As technology continues to evolve away from old uppercase-based systems toward systems that support both upper- and lowercase, this can become problematic. Data that comes delivered with SAP is presented in title case, and all data converted into SAP from your existing systems should first be translated to title case as well for consistency.

Q *Is there a standard setting that companies should be using with regard to the Insert and Overwrite modes of SAP?*

A Generally, this setting is unique to an individual and should be maintained by the individual on his or her own workstation.

Q *Can you set your own required fields?*

A In SAP, you can configure your own required fields. Keep in mind that any fields you configure as required will prevent the users from proceeding if the data is not readily available to them. Be cautious when setting required fields.

Workshop

The workshop is designed to help you anticipate possible questions, review what you've learned, and begin thinking ahead to putting your knowledge into practice. The answers to the quiz that follows can be found in Appendix A, "Quiz Answers."

Quiz

1. How do you check your entries on a screen?

2. Is it the Hold Data or Set Data option that enables you to overwrite the default entry in an input field?

3. What item on an SAP screen that contains an SAP tree do you need to select in order to expand the tree?

4. What is the name of a window that pops up to give you more information or supplies you with feedback on your current task?

5. When looking at a screen, what determines how many characters you can enter in an input field?

6. What do you need to do to display a list of available entries for an input field that is linked to a database table?

7. What type of fields contain a square with a check box?

Exercises

1. Navigate to transaction code /nFB02 and determine which of the fields on the Change Document: Initial Screen contains Possible Entries Help.

2. Find two screens in SAP that contain required fields.

3. Use the Hold Data tool to hold the data in an SAP field.

4. Use the Set Data tool to set data in an SAP field.

PART II

Implementing SAP

Implementing SAP: Resources and Timelines

Implementing SAP is a very large and expensive undertaking spanning six months to perhaps a few years. As such, it usually comes at the culmination of an in-depth "needs analysis" and subsequent SAP vendor- and partner-comparison processes. Equally as important as the SAP product being implemented is the SAP Project Team assembled to deploy and manage your SAP system. This hour underscores some of these SAP implementation details and provides recommendations for successfully implementing SAP into your organization. Highlights of this hour include

▶ Assembling a first-rate Project Team

▶ Addressing SAP training

▶ Identifying members of a successful Steering Committee

Assembling the Project Team

The design, makeup, and skill sets embodied in the SAP Project Team are critical to the success of your implementation. The design and structure of this team must encompass all areas of your company's affected business units as well as executive management support and underlying IT support. Areas of consideration in determining the structure of your team should include the following:

▶ Assessment of the business areas that will be affected by the SAP installation (such as the Finance department, Accounting department, Warehousing group, Plant Maintenance organization, Executive decision makers, and so on).

▶ Assessment of the skills required of each team member, from managerial and leadership to professional and technical skills.

When you determine what areas will be affected and what skill sets will be needed by the various Project Team members, you also need to look for individuals who either possess or can be enlightened to possess the strategic vision required by those tasked with implementing SAP. More specifically, the vision of change and the re-engineering of your current processes is essential to a successful implementation.

Your company's Project Team also needs to be comprised of individuals from all levels of the business who will be impacted by the SAP implementation. Even more importantly, upper-management support is required for efficient decision making and project direction. And throughout the Project Team, members must be focused on results as much as on satisfying a long-term vision. To this end, an ideal Project Team "strawman" structure is illustrated in Figure 7.1.

FIGURE 7.1
An SAP Project Team structure should reflect these fundamental design and role tenets.

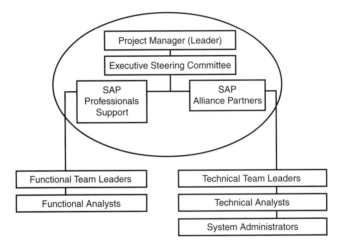

Five key characteristics that your ideally structured Project Team should possess include

▶ Ability to assess how the new system will enable or affect individual and collective business processes company-wide.

▶ Ability to identify the impact on current business processes.

▶ Ability to comprehend the requirements for re-engineering identified business processes hosted by SAP.

▶ Individuals who collectively have the knowledge to design and complete the integration of the SAP structure, hierarchies, and business process configuration across your enterprise.

▶ Individuals who will provide an efficient transfer of knowledge throughout the implementation and post-Go-Live maintenance of your SAP system.

Project Sponsor

At this point, certain senior-level executives are already convinced that implementing SAP is the right thing for the company and its stakeholders. Typically, others must still be convinced that the business units are on the right track, and that the investment in SAP is not only warranted, but in the company's best interests. This is where the Project Sponsor spends his or her time initially, gaining consensus within the impacted business areas, executive circles, and various IT organizations that will ultimately contribute to supporting the project.

The Project Sponsor also plays a key role in initially guiding the Steering Committee, discussed later in this hour. The Project Sponsor builds momentum, gaining buy-in and "talking up" the project throughout the company. When the Project Sponsor works with the various business units to help them understand how important they will be to the project, and how much better the project will address their needs, excitement and buy-in around the project naturally grows in these early days.

Project Management

Another key role is the company *Project Manager* (*PM*), who is responsible for the overall management of your SAP implementation. This individual is responsible for coordinating a cooperative productive environment between all the different team members, so that together the team can achieve success. This position is often named by the Project Sponsor or Steering Committee, and held by a company-internal manager or assigned consultant. Alternatively, a triumvirate of PMs can be assigned, one each from the company, primary SAP consulting or integration partner, and SAP itself.

The PM, like the Project Sponsor, must tailor his or her language and other communications skills to the audience, be it the board room, shop floor, IT group, or any number of functional organizations like Accounts Payable or the Supply Chain team. The PM must also be aware of the politics surrounding the various organizations. This includes determining who the informal decision makers are, as well as the ones granted this authority through formal leadership positions.

Executive Steering Committee

The highest level within your Project Team structure should consist of your high-level managers, executive decision makers, and other stakeholders with a keen interest in seeing the SAP implementation through to completion. It is this committee's ability to steer the project in the right direction with their management experience and decision-making power that makes them the vital foundation of a successful Project Team. The Project Sponsor is often a part of the committee, whereas the Project Manager is typically not part of this "circle," but instead guided to some extent by the committee. Key members include

▶ The Project Sponsor or "Chair," often a senior executive tasked with making SAP a reality.

▶ A high-level representative of each functional area for which SAP will be deployed. For example, this might include representatives from Finance, HR, Manufacturing, Logistics, and Worldwide Sales.

▶ A senior representative of the Company's Chief Information Officer, or the actual CIO.

▶ The Project Sponsor, if not already identified previously.

▶ The company Project Manager (as opposed to other PMs who are often appointed from consulting and integration partners and SAP itself).

▶ The manager or director of Enterprise Computing Systems (or an equivalent title); this person is usually responsible for the systems currently in place, systems that will be retired when SAP is introduced.

▶ A senior-level SAP Solution Architect (SA), or sometimes SAP's appointed Project Manager; the Steering Committee's technical liaison.

Tasks crucial to the Executive Steering Committee include

▶ Identifying and approving the scope of project

▶ Setting priorities

▶ Settling disputes

▶ Committing resources to the project

▶ Monitoring the progress and impact of the implementation

▶ Empowering the team to make decisions

> The importance of upper management's buy-in cannot be underestimated—it has a direct impact on the success of the implementation. The projects that have the most problems are often the ones where upper-management support is unclear or divided.

Project Management Support

The second highest level of support in an ideal Project Team structure includes your Project Management function. The project management team or Project Management Office (PMO) is usually comprised of SAP consulting and support professionals and your SAP alliance partners—the Big 4 and any number of hardware-oriented and boutique SAP consulting and support organizations. It is their job to direct and work in conjunction with the larger team to assure that your SAP implementation is a success.

SAP Consulting and Support Professionals

The support you receive from SAP should ensure that you take better control and ownership of your SAP project. Your SAP support professionals are also crucial in accelerating your teams' learning process through education and instruction by using their SAP knowledge and experience. The SAP Consulting and Support professionals obtained from SAP assist your team with project organization throughout the duration of the project.

SAP Alliance Partners

SAP Alliance partners consist of any SAP-approved partner companies that offer an additional level of support for your SAP system. This includes additional general SAP consulting and integration support as well as support for SAP-partnered third-party products.

Team Leaders

It is the responsibility of your Team Leaders to work with the Project Manager to plan and manage your project's scope, schedule, and resources. They identify the impact on, and the requirements for, business processes to support the organization's re-engineered vision through the deployment of SAP.

The Team Leaders hold the responsibility for leading the design, integration, and testing of SAP across your company's functional business processes. They also serve as leaders and role models for their teams and are an integral part of the knowledge-transfer mechanism between team members—that is, between the consultants and company-staffed teams.

Functional Analysts

Functional Analysts design your SAP solution for your company based on your individual and unique requirements. These are usually nontechnical managers who, on a day-to-day basis, manage some functional area of your business. Examples of Functional Analysts include

- ▶ Financial Accounting Director
- ▶ Human Resources Supervisor
- ▶ Shipping and Receiving Manager

It is their job to foresee the impact that the implementation will have on your employees and your company's business processes. They also need to evaluate the output that is currently generated and determine the functions and processes that will produce the output in the future. A very important function for a Functional Analyst is to determine the teams' training requirements and performance support.

Technical Analysts

As opposed to the Functional Analysts, the Technical Analysts are your skilled Information Technology (IT) professionals. These individuals have the computer skills and savvy and will serve as the technical leaders for your team. It becomes the responsibility of the Technical Analysts to technically deploy and configure your SAP system to successfully support your company's unique processes.

They are also responsible for designing any interfaces or customizations that your SAP system might require. These technically inclined associates also hold the task of designing your conversion plan and the actual migration of data from your old system to the new. As such, the Technical Analysts hold key enabling positions within the larger scope of the implementation.

System Administrators

System Administrators are responsible for the maintenance of your actual hardware/software technology stack and your SAP installation. It is their duty to administer, maintain, and protect your SAP data. This includes preparing and verifying scheduled backups, maintaining spools, installing upgrades, and applying hot packages, legal change packages (LCPs), and so on. System Administrators often begin managing the systems for which they will be responsible months before Go-Live, and then carry on with this responsibility ad infinitum.

Hot packages are fixes that you download or otherwise receive from SAP on a periodic basis. They are designed to correct or enhance your current SAP version. Hot packages include any tweaking done to the SAP system that can be installed as a fix before the next release of the product.

Legal change packages are enhancements that are issued occasionally to accommodate legislative and governmental regulation changes that are required before the next official release of the software.

Training the Project Team

It is the responsibility of the Project Manager to develop a training strategy for all the different levels of the Project Team. SAP has identified three levels of training, as summarized in Table 7.1, illustrated in Figure 7.2, and described in the following sections.

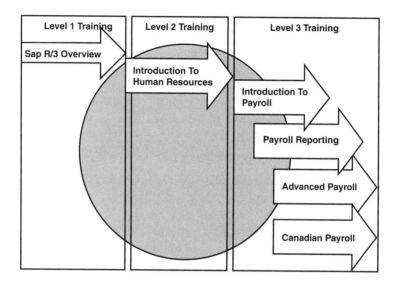

TABLE 7.1 Training-Level Class Descriptions

Level	Prerequisites	Description
1	None	Level 1 courses identify entry-level or high-level overview classes designed to introduce a general theme to the student for the first time (for example, an SAP Overview course).
2	Level 1	Level 2 courses are usually an introduction to a specific subject matter (that is, ABAP Workbench Basics).
3	Level 1 and Level 2	Level 3 courses delve deeper into subject content introduced in Level 2 courses.

The SAP training methodology is based on three principles: Awareness, Readiness, and Proficiency.

Level 1 Training

Level 1 focuses on *customer awareness*. Level 1 courses generally focus on introductory features and functions to familiarize you with the SAP environment and terminology. Level 1 classes include

▶ SAP ECC or BW Overview

▶ SAP Basis/Technology Overview

Level 2 Training

Level 2 training is also known as the *readiness phase*. At this level, you begin to focus on the core business process courses that will empower you with the skills to apply SAP to your company's way of doing business. Level 2 classes include

▶ Introduction to Human Resources

▶ Introduction to Financial Accounting

Level 3 Training

When embarking on the Level 3 training, you generally want to master or become proficient in a particular area. Level 3 classes are more advanced courses that help you to acquire specific expertise in a particular SAP area. Level 3 classes include

▶ Advanced Customizing and Configuration

▶ Joint Venture Accounting: Processing and Configuration

▶ Advanced Payroll

By the Way

> SAP publishes updated training catalogs approximately every six months. You can obtain hard copies of these catalogs from your SAP sales contact or you can download them and other up-to-date training information from SAP's primary website: www.sap.com.

Summary

The careful preparation and groundwork dedicated to your SAP implementation is essential in assuring a smooth transition from your legacy systems to the new SAP environment. One of the most important aspects that will contribute to the success of your SAP implementation is a skilled, appropriately represented, and well-balanced Project Team. The level of expertise and project commitment of the team has a direct relationship on the success of your SAP project.

Q&A

Q *At what point should training begin?*

A After SAP is selected as your vendor of choice, Level 1 training, to familiarize the users with the basic SAP environment, should begin almost immediately.

Q *Should your Project Manager be a company employee or a consultant?*

A If you have an employee with SAP and project management experience for SAP implementations, by all means an employee should hold this role. In most cases, however, a consultant usually fits the skill set better than any employee. It is a good idea to have an employee shadow the project lead so that when it is time for the consultant to move on, there is a proper transfer of knowledge to the employee.

Q *How much do these SAP courses cost?*

A The easy answer is that the price varies depending on the course, the length of the course, and the location. Courses generally cost a couple of thousand dollars each, although some of the Level 1 courses are less than a thousand dollars.

Q *Where can you get more information on different options available for SAP Training and Support?*

A For more information on different options available for SAP education and other training opportunities, visit the website at http://www.sap.com/services/education/index.epx.

Q *How can you find out when new courses become available for SAP training?*

A For more information on new courses available for SAP training, visit the website at www.sap.com.

Workshop

The workshop is designed to help you anticipate possible questions, review what you've learned, and begin thinking ahead to putting your knowledge into practice. The answers to the quiz that follows can be found in Appendix A, "Quiz Answers."

Quiz

1. How many levels of SAP training are available?

2. What level of SAP training does not require any prerequisites?

3. What is the difference between a Functional and a Technical Analyst on your Project Team?

4. What is one of the most important factors contributing to the success of your SAP implementation?

5. What is the highest level of structure in your Project Team hierarchy?

Exercises

1. Investigate the latest SAP training and education offers for your favorite SAP component, product, or technology area via www.sap.com.

2. Obtain a copy of your company's SAP organization chart(s) and identify the client Project Manager, Steering Committee members, overall Project (or executive) Sponsor, and other key decision makers.

HOUR 8

Implementation Tools, Methodologies, and the IMG

Given the complex business processes involved, along with the equally complex information technology requirements, implementing SAP is no easy task. In response, SAP has developed options for rapidly deploying and enhancing SAP. This hour I discuss the evolution of SAP implementation tools and methodologies, including ASAP, ValueSAP, Solution Manager, and the IMG.

Highlights of this hour include

▶ Reviewing your implementation options

▶ Learning about the ASAP roadmap

▶ Reviewing the role of SAP Solution Manager (SolMan)

▶ Viewing the SAP procedure model

▶ Tracking tasks in the IMG

ASAP—AcceleratedSAP

Everyone knows that introducing SAP into your business will be challenging. After all, it's nothing like installing Microsoft Word or some other desktop application. It entails a re-engineering of your current environment, structure, systems, and processes across both business and IT organizations. AcceleratedSAP (ASAP) is a long time tool used to help make this transformation easier by assisting in the implementation of SAP.

Its purpose is to help design your SAP implementation in the most efficient manner possible. Its goal is to effectively optimize time, people, quality, and other resources, using a proven methodology to implementation. ASAP focuses on tools and training, wrapped up in a five-phase process-oriented roadmap for guiding implementation. The roadmap is composed of five well-known consecutive phases:

Phase 1: Project Preparation   Phase 4: Final Preparation

Phase 2: Business Blueprint   Phase 5: Go-Live and Support

Phase 3: Realization

This roadmap is illustrated in Figure 8.1, and the five phases are described in the following sections.

FIGURE 8.1
The ASAP
roadmap.

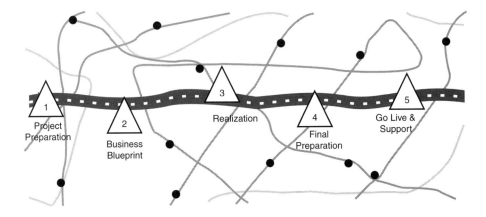

Phase 1: Project Preparation

Phase 1 initiates with a retrieval of information and resources. It is an important time to assemble the necessary components for the implementation. Some important milestones that need to be accomplished for Phase 1 include

- ▶ Obtaining senior-level management/stakeholder support
- ▶ Identifying clear project objectives
- ▶ Architecting an efficient decision-making process
- ▶ Creating an environment suitable for change and re-engineering
- ▶ Building a qualified and capable Project Team

Senior-Level Management Support

One of the most important milestones with Phase 1 of ASAP is the full agreement and cooperation of the important company decision-makers—key stakeholders and others. Their backing and support is crucial for a successful implementation.

Clear Project Objectives

Be concise in defining what your objectives and expectations are for this venture. Vague or unclear notions of what you hope to obtain with SAP will handicap the implementation process. Also make sure that your expectations are reasonable considering your company's resources. It is essential to have clearly defined ideas, goals, and project plans devised before moving forward.

An Efficient Decision-Making Process

One obstacle that often stalls implementations is a poorly constructed decision-making process. Before embarking on this venture, individuals need to be clearly identified. Decide now who is responsible for different decisions along the way. From day one, the implementation decision makers and project leaders from each area must be clearly defined, and they must be aware of the onus placed on them to return good decisions quickly.

Environment Suitable for Change and Re-engineering

Your team must be willing to accept that, along with the new SAP software, things are going to change—the business will change, and the information technology enabling the business will change as well. By implementing SAP, you will essentially redesign your current practices to model more efficient or predefined best business practices as espoused by SAP. Resistance to this change will impede the progress of your implementation.

Building a Qualified Project Team

Probably the most important milestone early on is assembling a Project Team for the implementation. Your Project Team must be a representative sample of the population of your company. If you are implementing the Materials Management and Plant Maintenance modules in ECC, for example, you need to include people from both of these departments, as well as from your Information Technology department, on the team. The team should also represent management as well as non-management or "functional" personnel. Sometimes management is less aware of the day-to-day functions of an organization, including how implementing SAP will tactically influence those functions.

Phase 2: Business Blueprint

SAP has defined a business blueprint phase to help extract pertinent information about your company that is necessary for the implementation. These blueprints are in the form of questionnaires that are designed to probe for information that uncovers how your company does business. As such, they also serve to document the implementation. Each business blueprint document essentially outlines your future business processes and business requirements. The kinds of questions asked are germane to the particular business function, as seen in the following sample questions:

▶ What information do you capture on a purchase order?

▶ What information is required to complete a purchase order?

AcceleratedSAP Question and Answer Database

The Question and Answer Database (QADB) is a simple although aging tool designed to facilitate the creation and maintenance of your business blueprint. This database stores the questions and the answers and serves as the heart of your blueprint. Customers are provided with a Customer Input Template for each application that collects the data. The question and answer format is standard across applications to facilitate easier use by the Project Team.

Issues Database

Another tool used in the blueprinting phase is the Issues Database. This database stores any open concerns and pending issues that relate to the implementation. Centrally storing this information assists in gathering and then managing issues to resolution, so that important matters do not fall through the cracks. You can then track issues in the database, assign them to team members, and update the database accordingly.

Phase 3: Realization

With the completion of the business blueprint in Phase 2, "functional" experts are now ready to begin configuring SAP. The realization phase is broken into two parts:

1. Your SAP consulting team helps you configure your baseline system, called the Baseline Configuration.

2. Your implementation Project Team fine-tunes that system to meet all your business and process requirements as part of the Fine Tuning Configuration.

The initial configuration completed during the Baseline Configuration is based on the information that you provided in your blueprint document. The remaining approximately 20% of your configuration that was not tackled during the Baseline Configuration is completed during the Fine Tuning configuration. Fine Tuning usually deals with the exceptions that are not covered in Baseline Configuration. This final bit of tweaking represents the work necessary to fit your special needs.

Configuration Testing

With the help of your SAP consulting team, you segregate your business processes into cycles of related business flows. The cycles serve as independent units that enable you to test specific parts of the business process. You can also work through configuring the SAP Implementation Guide (IMG), a tool used to assist you in configuring your SAP system in a step-by-step manner (covered in detail later in this hour).

During this configuration and testing process, it becomes necessary to send your Project Team to Level 3 SAP training. This in-depth instruction provides your team members with SAP component–specific expertise that they can map to the business' unique requirements.

Knowledge Transfer

As the configuration phase comes to a close, it becomes necessary for the Project Team to be self-sufficient in their knowledge of the configuration of your SAP system. Knowledge transfer to the configuration team tasked with system maintenance (that is, maintenance of the business processes after Go-Live) needs to be completed at this time.

In addition, the end users tasked with actually using the system for day-to-day business purposes must be trained. Level 1 and Level 2 training should therefore begin in earnest for the people for whom the SAP system is being deployed. This is also a good opportunity to send the implementation Project Team to additional functional Level 2 and Level 3 training in the areas upon which they want to focus post-Go-Live.

Phase 4: Final Preparation

As Phase 3 merges into Phase 4, you should find yourselves not only in the midst of SAP training, but also in the midst of rigorous functional and stress testing. Phase 4 also concentrates on the fine-tuning of your configuration before Go-Live and more importantly, the migration of data from your old system or systems to SAP.

Workload testing (including peak volume, daily load, and other forms of stress testing), and integration or functional testing are conducted to ensure the accuracy of your data and the stability of your SAP system. Because you should have begun testing back in Phase 2, you do not have too far to go until Go-Live. Now is an important time to perform preventative maintenance checks to ensure optimal performance of your SAP system.

At the conclusion of Phase 4, take time to plan and document a Go-Live strategy. Preparing for Go-Live means preparing for your end users' questions as they start actively working on the new SAP system.

Phase 5: Go-Live and Support

The Go-Live milestone itself is easy to achieve; a smooth and uneventful Go-Live is another matter altogether. Preparation is the key, including attention to what-if scenarios related not only to the individual business processes deployed but also to the functioning of the technology underpinning these business processes. And preparation for ongoing support, including maintenance contracts and documented processes and procedures, are essential. Fortunately, a wealth of information and additional resources are available. Turn to Hour 24, "Additional SAP Resources," for more details.

Newer SAP Implementation Tools and Methodologies

Because it has proven itself effective, many SAP implementation partners continue to embrace ASAP or a customized version of it. At the turn of the century, in response to the need to more rapidly and completely deploy R/3 and a host of growing solutions offered by SAP AG, though, ASAP evolved into GlobalSAP and later ValueSAP. ASAP was always limited in that it assumed a very rigid phased approach; the fact that implementation phases often overlapped, or that businesses found themselves in the midst of multiple ASAP phases as a result of a geographically phased rollout, was contrary to ASAP. The new SAP deployment methodologies therefore added Evaluation and Continuous Business Improvement to their core focus on implementation. These changes help overcome some of the previous shortfalls, although not all of them. During this time, the roadmap changed a bit as well, shrinking from five to four phases.

In 2001, SAP AG released an improved delivery vehicle—SAP Solution Manager, or SolMan—when it introduced Web Application Server (WebAS) 6.10. By the end of 2002, Solution Manager had matured considerably, offering not only multiple roadmaps to implementation but also improved content. Some of this content included sample documents, new templates, a repository for canned business processes, and better project-management tools.

SAP Solution Manager has built upon the groundwork created by ASAP. Robust project monitoring and reporting capabilities have been recently augmented with Learning Maps, which are role-specific Internet-enabled training tools featuring online tutoring and virtual classrooms. In this way, the Project Team can more quickly get up to speed. With training and related support of the ASAP and ValueSAP methodologies replaced by SolMan, Project Teams do well to transition from ASAP-based and other methodologies to those facilitated by SAP Solution Manager.

It's important to remember, though, that at the end of the day these approaches all amount to little more than frameworks or methodologies with supporting templates. Even SolMan only *facilitates* an implementation—there's still much real work that needs to be done. But if you are seeking to deploy well-known and mature SAP functionality, and are focused on avoiding too much custom development, SolMan is a wonderful tool in your implementation arsenal.

The SAP Implementation Guide (IMG)

If you return to the realization phase, you will remember that the Implementation Guide (IMG) plays a central role in assisting you with configuring SAP. The IMG is essentially a large tree structure diagram that lists all actions required for implementing SAP, guiding you through each of the steps in all the different SAP areas that require configuration. For each business application, the SAP Implementation Guide (IMG)

▶ Explains all the steps in the implementation process

▶ Communicates the SAP standard (default) settings

▶ Describes system configuration work (tasks or activities)

The guide begins with very basic settings including "what country are you in?" and ultimately drills down into very specific matters like "what number do you want your purchase orders to begin with?" Everything said, it is nearly impossible to complete an SAP implementation without SAP Implementation Guide familiarity. To begin, execute transaction code /nSPRO or follow the menu path Tools, AcceleratedSAP, Customizing, Edit Project. The main screen appears similar to the one shown in Figure 8.2.

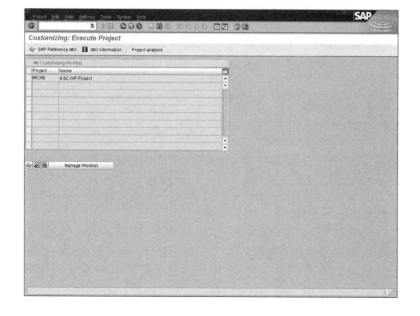

FIGURE 8.2
The Implementation Guide main screen varies depending upon your SAP component, installation, and the amount of configuration that has been completed.

Different Views of the IMG

There are different ways that you can look at your Implementation Guide (IMG) within SAP. Each of these is called a *view*. Depending on the type of information that you want to see and the order in which you want it presented on the screen, you select a different view of the IMG. You can also create your own custom views of the IMG. Note that there are four levels of the SAP Implementation Guide (IMG):

- ▶ The SAP Reference IMG
- ▶ SAP Enterprise IMGs
- ▶ SAP Project IMGs
- ▶ SAP Upgrade Customizing IMGs

The SAP Reference IMG

The SAP reference IMG contains documentation on all the SAP business application components supplied by SAP and serves as a single source for all configuration data (see Figure 8.3).

The SAP Enterprise IMG

The SAP Enterprise IMG is a subset of the SAP Reference IMG, containing documentation only for the components you are implementing. It appears the same as the Reference IMG but lists only the configuration steps necessary for your company's implementation. For example, if you are implementing only logistics within SAP R/3 or ECC, your IMG would not contain any information on configuring payroll from the Human Resources module (see Figure 8.4).

The SAP Project IMGs

SAP Project IMGs are Enterprise IMG subsets and contain only the documentation for the Enterprise IMG components you are implementing (such as a Customizing project). For example, if you are implementing ECC Logistics only, but you have divided it into two projects—one for Sales and Distribution and a second for Materials Management—you can have two different projects set up.

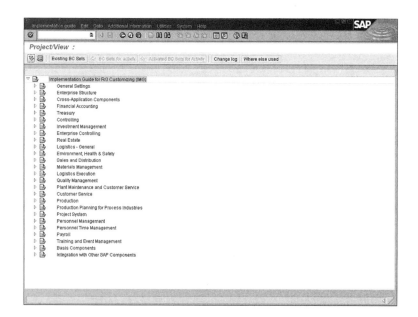

FIGURE 8.3
Using the SAP Reference IMG, you can customize your entire SAP implementation in a single place.

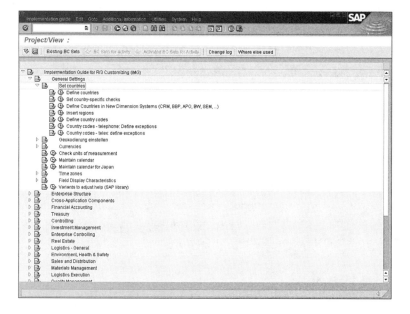

FIGURE 8.4
This display structure in the Enterprise IMG provides for the configuration of your country global parameters.

The SAP Upgrade Customizing IMGs

SAP Upgrade Customizing IMGs are based either on the Enterprise IMG or on a particular Project IMG. They show all the documents linked to a Release Note for a given release upgrade (see Figure 8.5).

FIGURE 8.5
The SAP
Upgrade
Customizing
IMG enables
you to specify
configuration
based on
specific SAP
releases.

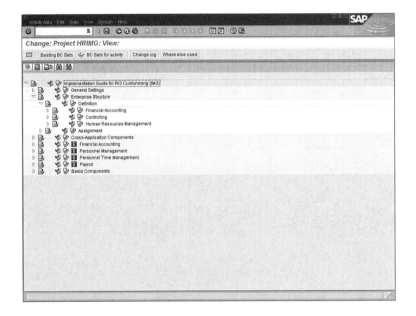

IMG Basics

Using transaction code /nSPRO, your initial view of an IMG structure is always a tree diagram with symbols shown to the left. You can use the plus (+) signs to the left of each item (for older SAP releases) or the triangles (for newer SAP releases) in the tree structure to expand that branch of the tree to view its substructure. You can also expand branches by placing your cursor on a line item and then following the menu path Edit, Expand/Collapse or by placing your cursor on a line item and pressing the F5 key on your keyboard. To expand all possible branches, place your cursor on the highest level and select Edit, All Subnodes.

Looking at the IMG with the subnodes expanded gives you a good idea of the IMG's purpose—to configure basic settings for SAP. Taking a look at each of the line items, it is easy to see how this tool facilitates implementation.

Help in the IMG

The first thing you should learn about the IMG is how to retrieve help for any individual line item. Just by looking at the description of each line item, it is not always clear exactly what the configuration of that item entails. You can access selection-specific help by double-clicking any activity (line item) in the IMG. This brings you detailed help on the configuration activity that you have selected. In some cases, it launches a small window describing the reasons for the activity and what it entails, including describing actual examples of what the activity is used to configure. In other instances, it might launch your SAP Help application, thus enabling you to search for more information. Help is also available after you execute a line item in the IMG. Most activities in the IMG bring you to a screen where you need to add or modify values in a table in order to configure your SAP system.

The field descriptions and selection-specific help might not have provided all the information necessary for you to understand what to do. Placing you cursor in any field and then selecting the F1 key on your keyboard from any IMG activity screen launches field-level selection specific help. The Help file is presented as a small window describing the possible values for entry in that field. Using the Help in the IMG is essential in obtaining additional information on the activities required for configuring your SAP system.

Documentation in the IMG

The Implementation Guide is usually your main source for configuration. That is essentially why it is the ideal location for documenting your configuration. Use the Status Information icon to navigate to the Memo tab of the Status Information screen. From there, record your comments, notes, or configuration information on the appropriate configuration step provided in the IMG. Alternatively, use your cursor to select the documentation symbol, and your screen launches into a screen like the one shown in Figure 8.6.

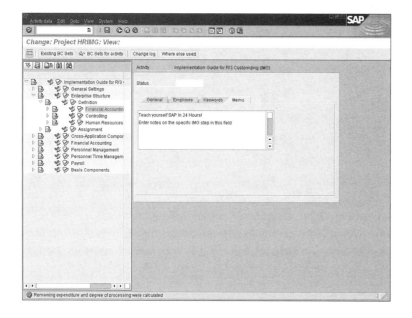

FIGURE 8.6
The IMG's Memo tab in the Status Information screen is an ideal resource for writing configuration notes documenting particular activities.

For each line item in the IMG, you can enter text in this way and, in doing so, document the system as you go along. This is therefore a very helpful tool, not to mention a great reference to use after your implementation is complete or during SAP upgrades and changes. You can type configuration notes into the space provided in the Memo tab and save them with that line item in the IMG. You can then use the Read Note symbol to review any of these notes at a later time.

Status Information

Selecting the Status Information symbol brings you to the General tab, as shown in Figure 8.7. This tab allows you to record the status and progress of your configuration for a particular line item, including planned versus actual start and end dates, and more. Other tabs include the Employee tab, Keywords tab, and the aforementioned Memo tab.

FIGURE 8.7
The Status Information screen records the status of the item, planned versus actual start and stop dates, the percentage complete, and much more.

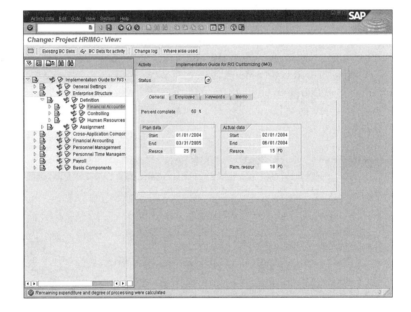

Status

One purpose of the Status Information screen is to maintain a record of your configuration to date, and to track your implementation progress. It is also a good place to see who is working on what. One of the first things that you need to assign on this screen is the Status field. Example Status types include

▶ In Process

▶ In Q/A Testing

▶ Completed

You set up the different status levels, as determined by your company's specifications. This Status designation segregates your configuration tasks into different completion categories.

Percent Complete

The Percent Complete field is used to display a processing status for an activity expressed as a percentage. Example percent completed values include 25%, 50%, 75%, 100%, and so on. At one time, these values were up to the individual to maintain. In newer releases of SAP, though, the percent complete is actually calculated by SAP.

Plan Start and End Dates

The Plan Start Date is where you record the initial projected date on which this particular activity should commence. Select the Possible Entries Help button on this field to display a calendar that enables you to select the date rather than entering it directly. The date is selected using the calendar control by selecting the month, date, and year and then double-clicking or by selecting the green check mark.

The Plan End Date is where you record the projected activity completion date for this particular activity. The SAP calendar is also available on this field.

Plan Work Days

The Plan Work Days field records the planned duration of an activity in days. The planned expenditure can be maintained manually. If neither actual expenditure nor processing status is maintained, the remaining expenditure is calculated.

Actual Start and End Dates

In the real world, things do not always go as planned. The Actual Start Date field records the actual date that an activity was started. Similarly, the Actual End Date records the actual date that an activity was completed. These fields are maintained when the Planned Start Date and the Actual Start Date differ.

Actual Work Days

The Actual Work Days field records the actual duration in days of an activity. This field is usually maintained only when the Planned Start and End Date conflict with the Actual Start and End Date.

Remaining Work Days

The Remaining Work Days field records the remaining expenditure for an activity in days. The remaining expenditure is calculated from the actual expenditure and the processing status, or from the planned expenditure, if these fields are not maintained. You can also set the remaining expenditure manually.

Using the Employee Tab for Resource Assignments

For each particular task in the IMG, you can assign resources (or people) responsible for that task. Use the Employee tab in the Status Information screen to denote these resource assignments. By using the Possible Entries Help button in the resource field, you can select the resources responsible for performing an activity. As the multiple resources boxes depict, you can assign multiple resources to a single task.

Release Notes

Release Notes contain specific relevant information on changes to the SAP system since the last release. They contain functionality and screen changes, as well as menu path and table structure changes. Release Notes are helpful when you are migrating from one SAP version to another. They are also a good tool for retrieving additional information about how something works in the SAP system.

There is an indicator, which you can turn on in your IMG, that displays a marker next to each activity, thereby revealing whether the Release Notes are available for that particular activity; see Figure 8.8 for a sample Release Notes screen.

FIGURE 8.8
Selecting the Release Notes symbol brings you to a screen containing documentation about the line item and how it has been changed since earlier releases.

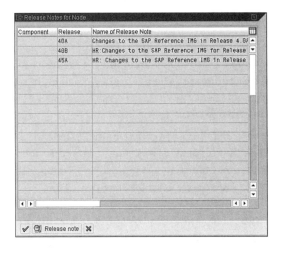

Summary

The decision on the implementation strategy affects the time, cost, and path you follow in your SAP implementation. SAP rapid implementation options are effective and efficient solutions that might not be the best fit for your company. Because no two companies are alike, you should discuss your company's individual needs with your SAP representative and take it from there. When an "empty" shell of SAP is installed, the Implementation Guide is the tool used to assist you in customizing and implementing your SAP system. The Implementation Guide is designed to pinpoint the configuration activities that you are required to perform in order for your SAP implementation to be a success. It also enables you to tweak your SAP system to ideally suit your company's individual needs through custom configuration.

Q&A

Q *Why use an accelerated solution in my implementation?*

A The use of an accelerated solution can incorporate best business practices using a bundled hardware/software solution that includes a dedicated team of experts assembled to get you system up and running, a range of tools, including AcceleratedSAP, to streamline your implementation, and training to bring you and your user community up to speed quickly.

Q *Is there a general method for working with the IMG?*

A The IMG is designed so that steps that need to be completed first are contained at the top so that you work your way "down" through the IMG.

Q *How many different project IMGs should I create?*

A You generally only need to create a single project IMG for each module. In some cases, modules like Human Resources or Human Capital Management dictate that two project IMGs be created.

Workshop

The workshop is designed to help you anticipate possible questions, review what you've learned, and begin thinking ahead to putting your knowledge into practice. The answers to the quiz that follows can be found in Appendix A, "Quiz Answers."

1. What does knowledge transfer in Phase 3 of the ASAP methodology refer to?

2. What are the five consecutive phases of the ASAP roadmap?

3. How many different levels are offered of the SAP training courses?

4. Besides ASAP, list some alternative methodologies or tools for SAP implementation.

5. Which view of the IMG contains only the relevant documentation for the SAP components that your company is implementing?

6. What are three different project views of the IMG?

7. What is the transaction code to launch the IMG?

HOUR 9

Implementation Lessons Learned

Specific reasons for implementing SAP vary as much as the companies that implement it. But a number of general themes are common, including improved business application integration, better operational reporting, close–to–real-time strategic reporting, and support for creating new or extending existing business processes. Throughout all this activity, an implementation team walks away with experiences and other lessons learned. This hour will explore some of these lessons learned.

Highlights include

▶ Discover strategic business-oriented lessons learned

▶ Discover end-user best practices

▶ Learn how technology challenges impact implementations

▶ Uncover implementation process lessons learned

Strategic Business Lessons Learned

Lessons learned of a strategic business type reflect project management and systems integration challenges, along with the number one stumbling block: executive buy-in. These lessons learned are reviewed next.

Sound Project Management

A lack of sound project management invites failure. Although this might be considered a broad "do not do," it's actually common in a number of manifestations. To achieve sound project management, first be sure to understand and document your desired-state solution vision, or where you want to go. Second, follow a proven SAP deployment methodology to take you step by step toward realizing that vision. Third, ensure that the objectives of the implementation are clear, measurable, and actively managed. And fourth, engage project managers with excellent leadership, administration, and resource-management skills.

Managing Timelines by Working Backward

When developing a project plan for an implementation, it is advantageous to work "backward," especially when hard deadlines exist in regard to specific implementation milestones. Hard deadlines often represent milestones on the critical path, which is project-management speak for items that tend to hold up a lot of other milestones. Common milestones like this include

▶ Building and fleshing out the SAP Project Management team

▶ Designing and preparing the SAP Data Center

▶ Getting hardware "on the ground" and readied for use

▶ Deploying the SAP Development environment for each component being deployed, so that developers can get to work

The SAP sizing process and determining when to start technical and incremental "new SAP product" user training can also represent hard deadlines for organizations in the midst of an implementation. Regardless, when you identify tasks on the critical path, you need to understand the dependency between these and other tasks, not just their duration. Once the time needed to complete each task is understood, and intertask dependencies are clear, it is a simple matter to plug in the numbers and arrive at a critical-path-oriented project plan. With this data, you can then look "forward" again, building and identifying slack-time, concurrent activities, and so on, and complete your SAP Implementation Project Plan.

Application Integration

Integrating islands of data and complex business processes spanning many systems represents a key implementation challenge. The fact that many legacy systems might be replaced one day by one SAP component does little to smooth matters initially; integration points still need to be established to facilitate data sharing until the legacy systems are completely retired.

Lack of Buy-In

Although it seems obvious, too many times executive sponsorship wavers throughout an implementation, especially when unanticipated complexities and costs give rise to issues. Long-term buy-in is important to gain up front. And it is just as important to manage and nurture this buy-in throughout the project's deployment life cycle.

Buy-in not only means gaining executive-level approval, but also the approval and a sense of ownership on the part of the end users who will ultimately use the system. This includes functional organizations, organizational leadership, and the end users themselves. Pay particular attention to the super-users or power-users distributed across most organizations. These well-respected and often very senior users tend to have great informal power and influence within their respective organizations. They can therefore help make or break a project, as you read in the following sections.

End User Lessons Learned

End users walk away from an SAP implementation with a great amount of knowledge that needs to be captured quickly lest lost. This is especially important for SAP implementations that are phased over time or across locations, where lessons learned can be easily applied again and again, and therefore reap quick benefits for the company. Important end-user lessons learned include

- ▶ Poorly communicated service level expectations
- ▶ Unwillingness to change current business practices
- ▶ Staying focused on core SAP implementation requirements
- ▶ Understanding the "Adult Learning Model"

Poorly Communicated Service Level Expectations

Too many organizations have failed in the past to coordinate with the IT and business teams the specific service levels they require. If a key online transaction needs to complete 95% of the time in one second or less, ensure this requirement is communicated early in the implementation. Otherwise, time will be wasted in needless testing of discrete business transactions and screens, or even an entire business process.

In the same way, if a certain report needs to be completed within a particular time frame or *execution window*, this requirement needs to be noted as well. Examples include month-end financial reports or reports that fundamentally impact the profitability of the company. Reports required to meet legal, health-oriented, and environmental obligations or regulations can be similarly critical.

Unwilling to Change Current Business Practices

Of all end-user lessons learned, this is perhaps most prevalent. Failing to change business processes represents one of the most common causes of failure for SAP development projects. Sometimes, it is under the guise of maintaining business-as-usual (so that an implementation presumably goes smoothly) that an end user pushes back on the best practices that SAP brings to the table regarding business process design and execution. In other cases, an unwillingness to adopt new processes is the result of not having a strong executive order to implement best practices. Sometimes, it is merely a problem of deploying the wrong people on a project—people without the leadership skills or functional background necessary to make hard decisions. That is, instead of staffing the project with decision makers, the company might have staffed the project with people with nowhere else to go, or people without day-to-day knowledge of a particular business area. You need the A team when deploying SAP; anything less invites problems of potentially great magnitude.

Staying Focused

Early on, the business units must differentiate between "must haves," "should haves," nice to haves," and "blue sky stuff." If the project leadership and end-user community can stay focused on delivering the first two, chances are that the users will indeed *use* the system. Later, more attention can be given in helping the business deliver additional value uncovered by implementing the latter two. Staying focused makes for a quick win, and sets the stage for long-term success as well.

Understanding the Adult Learning Model

It should come as no surprise that most adults learn by doing; SAP training before and after SAP is implemented must therefore reflect this, or risk wasting a great amount of time and money. A focus on delivering end-user training in a hands-on approach is ideal. "Death by PowerPoint" or through the use of printed manuals can certainly provide a good foundation (and in the latter's case, an ongoing foundation for support), but without hands-on experience prior to actual Go-Live, a project team will only set itself up for considerable on-the-job training (OJT) post-Go-Live. For teams that are supporting ever-changing business processes after Go-Live, the same concept holds true.

Technology Lessons Learned

Technology-based lessons learned span the gamut from ignoring the need to test the performance and throughput of various workloads to validating a particular computing component works as expected. Some of the most important or often-overlooked matters in this regard follow.

▶ Maintaining a tight partnership between the IT group and "the business" is critical. If these entities fail to work effectively together, the implementation will fail to realize its potential.

▶ Technical Change Control—the process of managing and testing hardware, firmware, and software upgrades in a non-production environment before making upgrade to production—is just as important as managing functional and other application layer software changes.

▶ Developing and adhering to IT standards saves time and money over the life of the implementation, if not immediately. Be prepared to defend deviations to the standards, of course. More importantly, though, be prepared to spend a bit more budget money more up front to save considerably in the long term.

▶ Just because a vendor indicates that a particular piece of technology works in a particular way does not mean it does so in the world of SAP. SAP technology stacks are complex, and therefore options tend to be more limited than in other types of business/IT projects.

▶ In the same way, it pays to ensure early on that your particular technology stack is indeed supported not only by SAP AG, but also by your server, disk subsystem, OS, and RDBMS vendors. Re-engineering and re-architecting an SAP solution's technology stack is best done at the onset of a project, not mid-way through.

▶ Failing to *load test* adequately is not only more common than most people think, but a key factor in missing performance, availability, and SLA metrics post-Go-Live. Don't misunderstand; the organizations guilty of this usually believe that they have done plenty of testing (and the hours spent in the name of "testing" often bear this out). However, what these numbers fail to reflect is the lost productivity and poor response times suffered on behalf of the end-user community. And with perception being what it is, if the user community is not happy, the SAP implementation might well be perceived as less than successful despite your best efforts otherwise to mitigate the risks surrounding Go-Live.

▶ Failing to "lock down" the production system in time to conduct all pre-Go-Live testing represents another major implementation shortcoming. That is, failing to lock down a system invites the technical team to make last-minute changes. In doing so, the technical foundation itself becomes suspect, in that system availability, performance, security, and so much more goes untested. In the end, more unmitigated risk is introduced.

▶ Documenting not only the technology stack's "current state" but also the steps necessary to achieve that current state are critical. Use screenshots and other such methods of capturing as much detail as is required, so that your documentation is clear, concise, and irrefutable.

*By the
Way*

> Change control refers to the practice of first testing a suggested or potential
> change to a production system in a technical sandbox or other SAP system, and
> then "promoting" this change through the landscape (to the Development system,
> and then the Test/QA system, and so on), to ensure that none of the solution
> characteristics you required from the solution in the first place are compromised.
> Change control thus includes both technical and application-layer (functionality)
> change management.

Implementation Process Lessons Learned

Like high-level strategic milestones, process-oriented lessons learned can impact the
very nature of an implementation, as described next.

Start Small, Think Big

The longest journey starts with a single step. So it is with an SAP implementation.
Instead of biting off more than you can chew, avoid project-stalling points of con-
tention by starting small. Divide large tasks into smaller, more manageable ones. In
doing so, you will be positioned to make true progress, all the while working toward
your overall goal of implementing SAP.

This method of dividing and conquering has another advantage as well. By subdi-
viding tasks into more manageable pieces, it becomes possible to spread the work
out among more team members and in many cases complete high-level milestones
faster than otherwise possible.

Big Bang or Phased?

Another process-oriented lesson learned involves whether to deploy SAP "all at once"
in a big-bang manner, or to deploy SAP in phases (such as by geography, by business
unit, or by functional area). If you are leaning toward a big-bang implementation to
quickly transition the company from an old way of doing business, you might consider running the old system concurrently with the new SAP system for some period
of time. This helps to ensure no surprises with the new system will impact the business, for example. If your goal is to phase in different plants, facilities, or SAP components, though, a phased approach makes sense, as seen in Figure 9.1.

Weigh the alternatives against your specific implementation project's goals, make a
decision, and then work the plan.

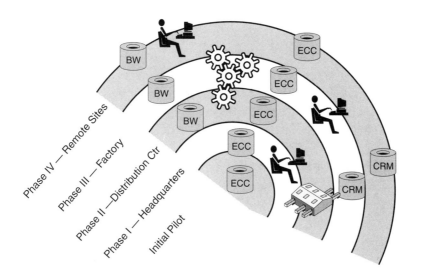

FIGURE 9.1
For complex organizations deploying multiple components, or those dispersed over wide geographies, a phased SAP implementation is most manageable.

Learn and Move On

Mistakes happen, and schedules can be impacted dramatically. Nonetheless, the lesson here is to learn from mistakes so as not to repeat them, and then move on. Implementing SAP is an iterative process, in that implementing the various system landscapes and working on the various development and test clients offers an opportunity to improve upon the IT and other processes already in place. The fact that SAP is deployed by first deploying Development, and then Test/QA, and then perhaps Training, and finally the Production system also lets you learn from your mistakes, so as to be prepared to circumvent known issues as each new implementation wave begins.

Beware of Long-Term Consultants

Relying too heavily on third-party consultants is problematic on many fronts. Whether technology or development-focused, this seemingly obvious problem is quite common. Third-party consultants and contractors serve a wonderful purpose, bringing much-needed expertise to bear. Keeping these same people engaged too long only wastes money, though. Keeping them in key positions or roles might not be the best idea, either—they hold too much knowledge and power, and therefore too much leverage. Knowledge that third-party consultants acquire during an SAP implementation needs to be documented and shared with the home team, not hoarded and carted away at Go-Live.

I have seen companies become "addicted to the spend" relative to employing consultants in an SAP implementation. This hurts the company in two ways. First, it costs more in the short term. Using consultants is naturally more expensive than migrating the support provided by a consultant to an in-house person, even a new-hire. Second, hanging on to expensive consultants prolongs a company's dependence upon these consultants. Without knowledge transfer to an in-house person, the company puts itself in the position of being unable to easily survive such a transition—and sadly, the longer the transition is put off, the more difficult it is when it's finally made.

Manage Scope Creep!

It is not reasonable to assume that no scope creep will occur in an SAP implementation. Priorities change, and scope must change in response to this. However, scope creep and bolt-on "madness" (adding extra features, bells and whistles, and other nice-to-haves to your originally trim SAP implementation project plan) has pushed many projects beyond their originally intended Go-Live dates. Not only does the add-on to the project lengthen time to implementation, configuration, and testing, it also impacts day-to-day operations as well as future support and maintenance needs. In all of this, then, the key is to stay focused as has been outlined previously throughout this hour; identify the critical path, establish priorities, and focus on executing against the project plan's tasks, taking care to document and transfer knowledge in the process.

Summary

In the end, an SAP implementation reflects the level of support given it by the business, by the technology teams tasked with designing, building, and supporting it, and by the end users asked to use it. Remember, if you don't have time to do it right, you will ultimately have to make time to do it over. The latter is obviously more disruptive to the business, not to mention much more expensive in terms of dollars and lost credibility. So set yourself up to do it right the first time, and learn from the lessons highlighted this hour.

Q&A

Q *What does it mean to work backward in the context of managing timelines?*

A If you identify the critical path tasks that need to occur to meet your overall implementation timeline, you might then fill in the gaps by identifying steps necessary to achieve these critical path milestones.

Q *What value does an understanding of the Adult Learning Model provide?*

A Understanding that adults learn by doing helps a training organization main-tain focus on effectively preparing end users for using a system, and IT person-nel for managing the same system.

Workshop

The workshop is designed to help you anticipate possible questions, review what you've learned, and begin thinking ahead to putting your knowledge into practice. The answers to the quiz that follows can be found in Appendix A, "Quiz Answers."

Quiz

1. What are two types of buy-in?

2. What is an execution window?

3. What is probably the most prevalent of all end-user lessons learned?

4. How does Technical Change Control differ from other types of change control?

5. Why is load testing important?

6. List two primary reasons for avoiding long-term consulting arrangements.

PART III

SAP Products and Components

HOUR 10

SAP NetWeaver

SAP NetWeaver has been likened to an orchestra in the past, a fair comparison. Each instrument plays a unique role in helping to assemble something larger than the sum of its parts. This hour I explore how the different instruments that make up SAP NetWeaver work and fit together. Highlights of this hour include

▶ A working definition of SAP NetWeaver

▶ A historical look at SAP NetWeaver

▶ A basic discussion of Enterprise Services Architecture and Web Services

SAP NetWeaver—A Working Definition

As I indicated in Hour 1, "Introduction to SAP NetWeaver and ECC," NetWeaver is essentially an umbrella term, encompassing a number of SAP products and technologies that combine to create a platform for building, extending, and integrating enterprise applications. The secret behind NetWeaver's success—and why it's something you need to pay attention to—is its built-in interoperability. With hooks into SAP-, Microsoft-, and Java-based technologies, NetWeaver eases integration with other applications like nothing else. This pays off at a high level in the form of a number of strategic benefits, outlined next.

Strategic Benefits of NetWeaver

SAP implementations based on NetWeaver benefit on several fronts, including

▶ Development cost is decreased.

▶ Integration is enabled, speeding up time to deploy as well as shrinking the time necessary to perform system upgrades and so on.

▶ Total cost of ownership is reduced significantly because maintenance and support costs are dramatically reduced.

▶ Thus, innovation is enabled; IT can spend more time meeting the needs of the business, and less time maintaining existing solutions.

SAP NetWeaver changed the enterprise applications playing field when it was introduced, as discussed next.

SAP NetWeaver Past and Present

When SAP NetWeaver was introduced, SAP AG's primary goal was to decrease the time necessary to implement and integrate diverse applications typically brought together to create enterprise-class solutions. This was to be accomplished by leveraging a common technology platform—SAP's Web Application Server, or WebAS—along with a common method of tying everything together, a common web-based front-end access method, and a method for both managing master data and enabling business intelligence.

Web Application Server

Although not originally envisioned as NetWeaver-specific, SAP's WebAS—a "new" and more comprehensive Basis layer—was designed to simplify installation, integration, and ongoing maintenance. Additionally, SAP AG wanted to give developers a choice, adding Java/J2EE support to SAP's mainstay ABAP/4. Finally, from the onset, SAP AG intended to integrate Internet Transaction Server into a common platform; this was finally accomplished with WebAS version 6.40.

WebAS also provides enhanced support for XML and Web Services technologies, including SOAP (Simple Object Access Protocol) and WSDL (Web Services Definition Language). With support for Unicode offered as of WebAS 6.30, the capability to standardize on a particular company-wide technology platform relative to matters as diverse as language support also makes a compelling argument for deploying what ultimately morphed into the platform undergirding NetWeaver.

By the Way

> *Unicode* refers to how the letters and numbers used by a particular language are encoded so they can be understood and used in a computing environment. Unicode unifies all characters of all character sets (that is, languages) into a single encoding scheme such that all letters, numbers, and other characters are uniquely represented. In other words, Unicode gives each character in each language its own unique computer-readable numeric representation. Doing otherwise requires transforming between different encoding schemes running on different computers, and therefore represents a potential risk in terms of data loss or corruption, as well as a performance hit. In SAP, non-Unicode systems use characters that are represented in binary (the lowest level of computer language) with only one byte, whereas Unicode systems represent characters in binary with two or four bytes (to make it possible to account for the many characters across all character sets). The downside for a system that has implemented Unicode is that the same data takes up more space—up to twice as much space in the database as a non-Unicode system. For more information, read SAP Note 79991 or visit http://service.sap.com/unicode.

SAP Exchange Infrastructure and Master Data Management

Issues surrounding system integration and data management are not new; IT has spent years applying what amounts to bandages to these severe problems. With this knowledge, SAP AG sought to simplify and modularize integration, enabling a hub and spoke middleware approach to tying systems together while consolidating master data into a single repository. SAP's Exchange Infrastructure (XI) and Master Data Management (MDM) products are the fruit of this vision, the products underneath the umbrella of NetWeaver.

Although deployment can be very complex, SAP XI itself is a model of simplicity and effectiveness. It enables process-centric collaboration of SAP and non-SAP applications alike, through the exchange of XML messages. In doing so, the business connectors are both standardized and straightforward, an elegant solution to the Enterprise Application Integration (EAI) issues faced by so many IT organizations today. To read more about XI, see Hour 13, "Other Enabling Technologies."

> SAP XI picks up where SAP's Application Link Enabling (ALE) technology left off, enabling simpler communication and the exchange of information between SAP systems and other enterprise systems.

By the Way

In the same way, SAP's solution for enabling data visibility between and within multiple applications is equally elegant. The need is certainly huge—managing the uncontrolled proliferation of part numbers, product descriptions, and so on adds considerable cost to the business. And such problems add unnecessary complexity to an otherwise solid supply chain or inventory management system, too. Finally, MDM answers the problem of poor customer management and an inability to conduct cross-business-group reporting—truly a better answer than trying to keep a number of ERP and other "systems of record" synchronized. To take a closer look at MDM, see Hour 12, "SAP BI, KW, and MDM."

SAP Enterprise Portal

If SAP XI represents the middleware portion of a solution, SAP Enterprise Portal (EP) represents the front-end. The vision of EP is simple—to enable portal-like access to SAP and non-SAP resources through the use of a web browser rather than SAP's proprietary user interface. SAP AG also tells us that Enterprise Portal is nothing less than the "People Integration" layer long used to describe how the various components of NetWeaver work together.

In a wise move, SAP AG has not required EP to play a part in a NetWeaver deployment. True, EP makes sense at a lot of different levels to deploy. By leaving the decision to a company's business units and IT organization, though, SAP has provided exactly the kind of flexibility promised by NetWeaver. To read more about Enterprise Portal, see Hour 13.

SAP Business Intelligence

A real-time enterprise application like SAP R/3 or ECC affords access to transactional information and to a lesser extent historical data. But these ERP solutions are decidedly (and purposely) single minded, not providing visibility into multiple ERP systems without a certain amount of special and therefore relatively costly integration work. For this reason, NetWeaver sought to include Business Intelligence within its umbrella of products and components, specifically the mature and capable SAP Business Information Warehouse (SAP BW).

Business Intelligence is a big word for a more common term—data warehousing. In a data warehouse, information is organized differently than in other database systems, so as to provide rapid access across different kinds of raw data, turning it into information useful in conducting analysis (hence another widely used term, analytics) in the process. The fact that companies can use this newfound valuable information to enable better decision-making is what helped coin the term Business Intelligence.

By including SAP BW in NetWeaver, the capability to conduct "roll-up reporting" across multiple systems provides great value beyond what can be provided otherwise. SAP BW allows visibility across the enterprise, from core transactional systems like ECC and R/3 to Supply Chain products, Customer Relationship products, Product Lifecycle offerings, and more. If Enterprise Portal is the "front-end" to NetWeaver, SAP BW represents a "back-end" that provides business insight into and across each standalone SAP application. For more information, refer to Hour 12.

The Evolution of SAP NetWeaver

In today's world, NetWeaver has been simplified to further ease administrative and maintenance support. Beginning in 2004, SAP adopted a synchronized approach to providing new versions of NetWeaver. Instead of requiring numerous technology-specific adapters to "connect" SAP's products to one another, NetWeaver '04 shipped with the same version of WebAS powering mySAP ERP, SCM, SRM, and so on. In doing so, a common technical foundation was facilitated. And the added advantage was that as this WebAS foundation matured, its new capabilities could be leveraged across the entire solution spectrum, not just in the case of a couple of leading-edge SAP components.

SAP NetWeaver '05

The same approach is true of SAP NetWeaver '05—as WebAS and all the other NetWeaver components continue to mature, provide greater flexibility, and reduce overall costs, SAP makes it possible to standardize on a single computing platform. And as NetWeaver and its components continue to evolve, it can only be expected that capabilities will continue to expand, all the while lowering costs.

NetWeaver '05 and its predecessor **NetWeaver '04** are labels that indicate that the fundamental WebAS platform underneath each of the SAP components within this NetWeaver release are essentially the same. In this way, it is easy to identify a particular "flavor" of NetWeaver with a particular version of WebAS.

ESA and Web Services

As NetWeaver evolves in response to a changing world, SAP has bet the bank on a number of technologies and approaches intended to further minimize integration headaches, total cost of ownership, and so on. These include

▶ ESA, or Enterprise Services Architecture

▶ Web Services, the backbone and enabler of ESA

Enterprise Services Architecture (ESA) provides the blueprint for designing and deploying SAP NetWeaver. It is SAP's adaptation of the more generic Service Oriented Architecture. SAP's ESA concept revolves around the vision of providing a roadmap for modeling and extending SAP NetWeaver. It acts as a blueprint for designing your SAP system landscape, much like three-tiered architectures helped organizations define their traditional SAP systems in the past.

Web Services represent the vehicle that makes ESA possible. They are beginning to become the new standard for interapplication communication. The idea is that Web Services are "open"; they're not tied to a particular type of technology or hardware or software vendor. This platform independence therefore makes it possible to communicate between vastly different technology platforms. At the end of the day, your developers have more time to focus on implementing valuable services, rather than spending their time figuring out the intricacies of technical communications protocols. This makes ESA and Web Services a valuable attribute of your NetWeaver solution.

Summary

From its inception, SAP NetWeaver was created to reduce the amount of time necessary to integrate disparate applications, reduce deployment and development time associated with new implementations, and minimize ongoing support and maintenance associated with in-place solutions. As NetWeaver has evolved, these goals have remained consistent. Sure, by folding in new approaches and enabling technologies, SAP AG's current release of NetWeaver looks very little like the original. But just as the NetWeaver platform and delivery vehicle has matured in the last few years, its mission has remained largely unchanged.

Q&A

Q *Why is Enterprise Portal viewed as the "front-end" to SAP NetWeaver?*

A Enterprise Portal provides seamless role-based access to the individual systems and components within the umbrella called NetWeaver. Thus, it acts as a single point of entry to the entire SAP system deployed by a company.

Q *What is the difference between NetWeaver, NetWeaver '04, and NetWeaver '05?*

A Version control relative to the enabling technical foundation (WebAS) varied with the original release of NetWeaver. In later releases, and presumably henceforth, this version control will be maintained via SAP's release strategy.

Workshop

The workshop is designed to help you anticipate possible questions, review what you've learned, and begin thinking ahead to putting your knowledge into practice. The answers to the quiz that follows can be found in Appendix A, "Quiz Answers."

Quiz

1. What is SAP NetWeaver?

2. What is the common technical foundation for the majority of SAP NetWeaver components and products?

3. What is Unicode?

4. What are Web Services?

HOUR 11

SAP ECC and R/3

SAP ERP Central Component, or ECC, and its predecessors R/3 and R/3 Enterprise, are online transaction processing (OLTP) systems—systems that by their very nature satisfy day-to-day transactional needs of typically many users. Within each of these products are a number of modules or submodules (in the case of R/3), or subcomponents (in the case of ECC, although for our purposes we'll stick with the term *modules*). At a high level, this includes finance, logistics, human resource management, customer service, and quite a few others. In this hour, I explore a number of these modules. I also kick things off with a discussion of the key differentiators between R/3 and ECC. Highlights of this hour therefore include

- ▶ An overview of core ECC and R/3 modules
- ▶ Differentiating between ECC and R/3
- ▶ A detailed look at SAP's Financials module
- ▶ A look at mySAP ERP's core solutions

> **By the Way**
>
> Although ECC stands for ERP Central Component, you will probably see the terms "ERP Core Component" and "Enterprise Core Component" incorrectly used across various websites, blogs, and pieces of literature. Rest assured we're all talking about the same thing—and you're the one in the know!

SAP R/3 Versus ECC

As I mentioned in Hour 1, "Introduction to SAP NetWeaver and ECC," the adoption of SOA and subsequently Enterprise Services Architecture by SAP AG changed forever how their software products were to be fashioned going forward. During this transition period, SAP R/3 morphed into R/3 Enterprise and finally ERP Central Component. Why? Strictly a client/server-based product, SAP's venerable R/3 offering was never intended or designed to support Web Services or a service-oriented architecture. Thus, in a nutshell, ECC represents the natural evolution of R/3 toward an architecture based on Web Services.

Beyond architecture, R/3 and ECC differ in other fundamental ways. Many of the differences reflect SAP AG's willingness to listen and learn from their customers. Changes to the technology stack, how it is installed, and perhaps most importantly how it is maintained account for most of the core differences between the two products; these and other differences are covered in the following sections.

Technology Platform Differences

The fact that ECC sits upon SAP's newest WebAS platform represents perhaps the most obvious technology difference between it, R/3, and R/3 Enterprise. Interestingly, R/3 Enterprise also sits atop a version of WebAS, albeit older (6.20). The differences between the two products are summed up in how these WebAS platforms differ. WebAS offered mature XML and HTTP support in version 6.10, but did not introduce support for Web Services and J2EE until 6.20. With SOA in its infancy, and only the initial framework for ESA being put together in Walldorf at the time, SAP AG needed an update to its R/3 solution, but at the same time wanted to hold a carrot out to customers to wait just a bit longer. With WebAS version 6.30, the Java stack and true Java development capabilities were introduced. Finally, with 6.40, both the ABAP and Java stacks were updated, and the entire platform was dubbed mature, ready to take on the world of Web Services, to enable Java development, and to host joint ABAP/Java deployments. Today, the entire NetWeaver '04 solution, including SAP ECC 5.0, is built on WebAS 6.40.

But what of plain old R/3? The vast majority of SAP R/3 customer installations today are getting up in age, to the tune of four to five years (ancient for an ERP solution). Although the tide is slowly turning, SAP R/3 versions like 4.6C, 4.6B, and even 4.5B greatly outnumber R/3 Enterprise and ECC deployments. These legacy installations (the term *legacy* is appropriate, I believe) sit not upon WebAS but rather SAP's original custom application server, coined *SAP Basis* or the Basis layer.

The Basis layer was SAP's extraordinarily successful attempt at hiding the complexities of multiple database and operating system platforms. And its three-tiered design solved problems of scalability and performance that other solutions in its day faced unsuccessfully. Basis was never intended to support the Web, though; indeed, the Internet itself represented the great unknown back when SAP Basis was introduced. To that end, when SAP finally first provided web support, it did so with a completely separate product, SAP Internet Transaction Server (ITS). And the SAP Basis platform merely served as the back-end to this decidedly front-end-focused solution geared toward enabling HTML-based web users with the opportunity to access SAP.

Installation Process Differences

That the installation process between R/3 and ECC differs is no surprise, given that the underlying platforms are different. SAP R/3 and ITS represented separate installations, each requiring specific hardware and tuning. A production R/3 and ITS system geared toward high availability might require eight different servers, in fact.

ECC, on the other hand, accomplishes everything SAP Basis and ITS ever did, and more. And you can accomplish its relatively simple installation process (given all that is offered) faster and with fewer hardware and OS-based costs. Case in point, you can deploy the same R/3 and ITS solution requiring eight servers across just two or four servers in the world of SAP ECC.

Support and Maintenance Differences

For many, the real beauty of ERP Central Component lies in how easy ongoing support and maintenance are. In the world of R/3, patches and fixes are often tied to specific functional releases and Basis versions. An adjustment or upgrade in one area therefore affects many other areas, necessitating additional testing to ensure nothing breaks after the change is made.

This mandatory testing is significantly reduced with ECC. ERP Central Component segregates functional business logic from the platform itself, including the kernel. And even within the platform, changes that must be made for a particular developer platform (like Java or ABAP) are independent as well. In this way, you can deploy specific changes and upgrades with confidence that other pieces of the technology stack will not break or degrade afterwards.

mySAP ERP Business Scenarios

SAP R/3 and ECC also differ relative to the business processes and full-fledged business scenarios each can support. ECC, boasting open Internet and Web Services standards alongside Microsoft .NET and J2EE interoperability, is much more powerful than its older R/3 siblings. And it is much more nimble to boot; embracing ESA makes ECC eminently more adaptable and agile than R/3. You can change business processes on the fly and turn around updated solutions in days and weeks rather than months or years.

Within the mySAP ERP umbrella, you can also quickly deploy ECC within four SAP-customized solutions, each of which is geared toward supporting essential business processes:

- ▶ mySAP ERP Financials, with built-in compliance for Sarbanes-Oxley and Basel II, takes financial reporting and corporate governance to another level. Admittedly, you can configure R/3 to do the same, but at a much greater investment in time and cost.

- ▶ mySAP ERP Operations takes logistics to the next level, too, introducing sales, warehousing, procurement, transportation, and distribution into the realm of collaborative business solutions. By extending these core business processes to include customers and suppliers, and enabling employees with Portal and even mobile access, ECC is truly at the core of a solution that R/3 could never so easily or inexpensively support.

▶ mySAP ERP Human Capital Management transforms an HR department into an organization well equipped to manage and retain the core of any successful business—its people. HCM pushes HR business processes out to the Web, enabling long-time mainstays of HR organizations like recruiting, training, and employee self-services to change and evolve with much greater velocity and agility than its predecessors.

▶ mySAP ERP Corporate Services wraps up a set of core services into a neat package. Processes ranging from Project and Portfolio Management to Environment, Health, and Safety (EH&S) Management, Real Estate Management, Travel Management, and Quality Management are unified and streamlined like never before possible.

The remainder of this hour looks at core business scenarios and business processes. It is interesting to note that the core business modules shared among R/3 and ECC are the same; only the arrangement and specific configuration of each module helps differentiate R/3's somewhat vertically oriented deployment methodology over ECC's more horizontally oriented and much-extended approach.

Core SAP Business Modules

ECC and R/3 are composed of many business modules. With SAP's architecture, a company deploying ECC or R/3 need not completely develop each module within their implementation. For example, if you are bringing in SAP to take care of financial accounting, controlling, and perhaps treasury cash management, there might be no need to develop SAP's logistics offering, HR module, and so forth. You likely have another system that takes care of these others needs. In that case, SAP might simply be constructed to interface (talk to) the other systems.

Because ECC and R/3 are such tightly integrated applications, though, it is a nearly impossible task to maintain a singularly focused implementation of one SAP R/3 or ECC module. Why? Because business processes still need occasional access to a certain amount of business rules, master data, and perhaps customer data *outside* of your core module(s), and you might find it easier to include that basic information within R/3 or ECC rather than building an interface to another system.

With that, a basic listing of many of SAP's ECC and R/3 modules is provided to give you insight into just how powerful—and potentially complex—such an implementation can be. The modules are arranged in the order they are found in the SAP Quick-Sizer and much of SAP's documentation. Again, note that ECC and R/3 are nearly identical in this regard.

- ▶ Financial Accounting (FI)
- ▶ Asset Accounting (FI-AA)
- ▶ Treasury (TR)
- ▶ Controlling (CO)
- ▶ Enterprise Controlling (EC)
- ▶ Sales and Distribution (SD)
- ▶ Materials Management (MM)
- ▶ Warehouse Management (LE-WM)
- ▶ Quality Management (QM)

- ▶ Plant Maintenance (PM)
- ▶ Customer Service (CS)
- ▶ Production Planning (PP)
- ▶ Project System (PS)
- ▶ Personnel Administration and Payroll Accounting (PA)
- ▶ Personnel Development (PA-PD)
- ▶ Basis Components (BC)
- ▶ Business Work Place (BWP)

Each of the modules listed previously represents a different area of your company's business; each module is designed to uniquely satisfy the needs of that part of the business. For the most recent list, visit SAP's Quick-Sizer link at http://service.sap.com/quick-sizer. A closer look at core R/3 and ECC modules follows.

mySAP ERP Financials

Within the domain of SAP Finance, FI and CO remain key modules as always. Combined with Enterprise Controlling and Treasury Management, mySAP ERP Financials transforms your accounting and other departments with its operational insight and excellent decision-making capabilities.

Financial Accounting

The Financial Accounting module gives you the capability to enhance the strategic decision-making processes for your company's financial needs. It allows companies to centrally manage financial accounting data within an international framework of multiple companies, languages, currencies, and charts of accounts. The Financial Accounting module complies with international accounting standards, such as GAAP and IAS, and helps fulfill the local legal requirements of many countries, reflecting fully the legal and accounting changes resulting from Sarbanes-Oxley legislation, European market and currency unification, and more.

The Financial Accounting module contains the following components:

▶ General Ledger Accounting, which provides a complete record of all your company's business transactions. It provides a place to record business transactions throughout all facets of your company's business to ensure that the accounting data being processed in your SAP system is both factual and complete.

▶ Accounts Payable, which records and administers accounting data for all vendors in your SAP system.

▶ Accounts Receivable, which financially manages your company's sales activities. It records and administers the accounting data of your customers through a number of tools specializing in the management of open items.

▶ Asset Accounting, which manages and helps you supervise your company's fixed assets. It also serves as a subsidiary ledger to the General Ledger, providing detailed information on transactions specifically involving fixed assets.

▶ Funds Management, which is designed to support you in creating budgets by way of a toolset that replicates your budget structure for the purpose of planning, monitoring, and managing your company's funds. Three essential tasks include revenues and expenditures budgeting, funds movement monitoring, and insight into potential budget overruns.

▶ Special Purpose Ledger, which is designed to provide summary information from multiple applications at a level of detail that you specify according to your business's needs. This function enables you to collect, combine, summarize, modify, and allocate actual and planned data that originates from SAP or other external systems.

By the Way

> Accounts Payable and Accounts Receivable subledgers are integrated both with the General Ledger and with different components in the Sales and Distribution module. Accounts Payable and Accounts Receivable transactions are performed automatically when related processes are performed in other R/3 or ECC modules.

Controlling

The SAP Controlling module provides the functions necessary for effective and accurate internal cost accounting management. Its complete integration allows for value and quantity real-time data flows between SAP Financials and SAP Logistics. It contains the following subcomponents:

- ▶ Overhead Cost Controlling, which focuses on the monitoring and allocation of your company's overhead costs and provides all the functions that your company requires for planning and allocation. The functionality contained within the Controlling module supports multiple cost controlling methods, giving you the freedom to decide which functions and methods are best applied to your individual areas.

- ▶ Activity-Based Costing, which enables you to charge organizational overhead to products, customers, sales channels, and other segments, and permits a more realistic profitability analysis of different products and customers because you are able to factor in the resources of overhead.

- ▶ Product Cost Controlling, used to determine the costs arising from manufacturing a product or providing a service by evoking a real-time cost control mechanism (capable of managing product, object, and actual costing schemes).

- ▶ Profitability Analysis, an effective tool useful in analyzing the profitability of a particular organization or segment of your market. In the latter case, these segments can be organized by products, customers, orders, or a combination thereof.

Treasury Management

The Treasury module contributes the functionality that your company needs to control liquidity management, risk management and assessment, and position management. Treasury Management includes the following:

- ▶ Cash Management, designed to facilitate an optimum amount of liquidity to satisfy required payments as they become timely and to supervise cash inflows and outflows.

- ▶ Treasury Management, used to support the management of your company's financial transactions and positions through back-office processing to the Financial Accounting module. It also provides a versatile reporting platform that your company can use to examine its financial positions and transactions.

- ▶ Market Risk Management, which quantifies the impact of potential financial market fluctuations on your company's financial assets. The Cash Management package, in combination with the Treasury Management package, sets the foundation for your database for controlling market risks, and includes interest and currency exposure analysis, portfolio simulation, and market-to-market valuation.

▶ Funds Management, designed to sustain your company's funds management processing from the planning stage clear through to the payments. Using this component, your company can create different budget versions, making it possible to work with rolling budget planning.

Enterprise Controlling

SAP's Enterprise Controlling module is divided into the following four components:

▶ Executive Information System (in R/3), which provides an up-to-the-minute overview of the critical information required in order for your company to effectively manage its resources. It collects and appraises information from various areas of your business, including financial information and information contained within your Human Resources Information System and the Logistics Information System.

▶ Business Planning and Budgeting, designed to assist in creating high-level enterprise plans that allow for the adaptable representation of customer-specific plans and their interrelationships. This also takes in to consideration the connections between profit and loss, balance sheet, and cash flow strategies.

▶ Consolidation, enabling you to enter reported financial data online using data-entry formats, and to create consolidated reports that meet your company's legal and management reporting mandates.

▶ Profit Center Accounting, used to analyze the profitability of internal responsibility or profit centers.

In SAP, a **profit center** is a management-oriented organizational unit used for internal controlling purposes.

mySAP ERP Human Capital Management

A company's Human Resources management system is arguably one of the most critical systems deployed. SAP offers a global human resources management solution including standard language, currency, and regulatory requirements, covering more than 30 countries. The innovative conceptual design of SAP Human Resources takes into consideration all the aspects of managing your company's human resources and corollary functions, including Recruitment, Training, and Organizational structure management.

SAP's Integrated Human Resources

Although extended HR business processes are made possible through NetWeaver, from an R/3 and ECC perspective, the Human Resources module is (still) divided into two modules:

- ▶ Personnel Administration (PA)
- ▶ Personnel Planning and Development (PD)

These HR modules are fully integrated within SAP R/3 and ECC. Each of these modules addresses different aspects of your company's Human Resource functions; the integration creates a well-oiled Human Resources machine that can also attach itself to other areas of your company's business through integration. Note that both PA and PD are also supported by the Human Resources Information System (HRIS), discussed later in the hour.

SAP Concepts Unique to Human Resources

Some concepts within SAP are unique to SAP's Human Resources products, making it stand apart from SAP's other applications. The most remarkable concept in the Human Resources component is its use of *infotypes*, detailed next.

Infotypes and Actions

In simple terms, an infotype is a screen in your Human Resources application that stores a particular set of information about an employee, such as payroll data or personnel data. There are hundreds of infotypes in the R/3 and ECC Human Resources modules.

SAP officially defines an **infotype** as a carrier of system-controlling characteristics such as attributes, time constraints, and so on.

Each infotype stores a group of relevant data. In the example shown in Figure 11.1, infotype 0002 from Personnel Administration (specifically, transaction /nPA30) is displayed. It stores the employee's basic personal data, including name, marital status, Social Security number, birth date, nationality, and so on.

When a series of infotypes are combined to complete a logical unit of work it is called an **action** (at one time, these were called events). For example, combining infotypes 0001 Organizational Assignment, 0007 Planned Working Time, 0008 Basic Pay, 0041 Date Specifications, and 0019 Date Monitoring yields most if not all the necessary infotypes (or screens) that you need in order to perform the Pay Change action.

FIGURE 11.1
Change
Personal Data
(Infotype 0002)
is a Personnel
Administration
infotype used to
hold employee
personal data.

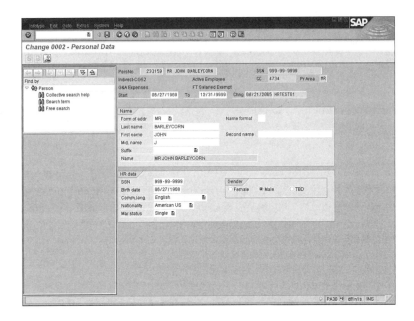

During your configuration, your company will decide which infotypes must be bundled together to create the actions necessary for your company. The Actions infotype (0000) controls the entry of HR master data and is automatically included as the first infotype for all actions. Your SAP actions are configured using your Implementation Guide during the initial configuration of your SAP system. Depending on the users' security access in the system, different actions are available for execution.

SAP Personnel Administration Components

The Personnel Administration module manages company procedures, including payroll, employee benefits enrollment, and compensation. This module's focus serves all the required Human Resource functions that most companies use. SAP's Human Resources Personnel Administration module contains the following components:

▶ Benefits Administration provides the functionality required to offer and enroll your employees into benefit plans. This includes the functionality to manage eligibility requirements, evidence of insurability, cost tracking and management, Flexible Spending Account (FSA) claims processing, benefit terminations, and COBRA.

▶ Compensation Management is used to implement your company's remuneration policies. Functions managed by the Compensation Management component include: salary administration, job evaluations, salary reviews, salary survey results, compensation budget planning and administration, and compensation policy administration. In addition, Compensation Management gives you the capability to create pay grades and salary structures to identify the internal value of the jobs and positions within your organization.

▶ Recruitment enables you to manage the process of employee recruitment. Recruitment initiates from the creation of a position vacancy through the advertisement and applicant tracking of potentials, concluding with the notification of successful and unsuccessful applicants and the hiring of the best candidate.

▶ Time Management provides a flexible methodology for recording and evaluating employee work time and absence management. Time Management is also integrated to other R/3 components that can make use of this data. A key benefit of the Time Management component is that it enables you to represent the time structures in your company in accordance with your actual conditions, using the calendar as a basis. Use it to address time models (like flextime, shift work, and normal work schedules), to plan work and break schedules, to manage exceptions like substitutions or business trips, and to meet regulatory requirements relative to absences, breaks, and holidays.

▶ Payroll efficiently and accurately calculates remuneration for work performed by your employees, regardless of their working schedule, working calendar, language, or currency. Payroll also handles fluctuating reporting needs as well as the constantly changing compliance requirements of federal, state, and local agencies.

SAP Personnel Planning and Development

In contrast to the Personnel Administration module, the Personnel Planning and Development module's functions are not necessarily required by your company but their functionality serves as a tool to better manage your Human Resource functions. Advanced organizational management and workforce planning are well-valued tools for your company, but are not required in order for your company's Human Resource tasks to function. The R/3 Human Resources, Personnel Planning and Development component, contains the following components:

▶ Organizational Management is designed to assist in the strategizing and planning of the comprehensive Human Resource structure. Through the development of proposed scenarios using the flexible tools provided, you can manipulate your company's structure in the present, past, and future. Using the basic organization objects in SAP, units, jobs, positions, tasks, and work centers are all structured as the basic building blocks of your organization.

▶ Training and Events Management assists your company in coordinating and administering attendance at business events, including conventions, seminars, and training. It contains functionality to plan for, execute, confirm, and manage cost allocations and billing for your company's events. It also features tight MS Office integration (and tighter integration on the horizon via Mendocino, discussed in Hour 22, "Integration with Microsoft Office").

Human Resources Information System (HRIS)

In the world of R/3, the Human Resources Information System (HRIS) can help you extract output from your Human Resources module. It also enables you to request reports from inside R/3's Structural Graphics. The HRIS offers reports that come from both the Personnel Administration and Personnel Planning and Development components of the Human Resources module. From the report tree in HRIS, you can view delivered (canned) reports that come preinstalled with SAP. Another tool found in the Human Resources Information System is the InfoSet Query tool used for Human Resources reporting (discussed in Hour 20, "Reporting Tools in SAP [SAP Query, InfoSet Query, Ad Hoc Query, and QuickViewer"]).

Employee Self Service

The number one complaint from HR managers tends to be that their teams spend an inordinate amount of time responding to employee inquires. Questions like "how many dependents am I claiming?" or "who is named as the beneficiary of my life insurance policy?" take up way too much of their time. SAP has developed a product that empowers employees to retrieve, and in some cases modify, their own employee data via web-based technology and interactive voice response functionality. Employee Self Service (ESS) is an effective means for providing real-time access and data upkeep capabilities to the employees.

With SAP Employee Self Service, employees can be responsible for the preservation of their own data and can get access to their information, on their own time, without requiring a PC connected to SAP, and without any SAP training. This saves time for the employees because they no longer need to stop work and visit the Human Resources department, and it saves time for the Human Resources professionals who otherwise need to stop their other important work to assist the employee.

Manager Self Service

A new addition, Manager Self Service (MSS), is a manager's equivalent to Employee Self Services. It is built within Enterprise Portal, and enables a manager to

▶ Manage the recruiting process

▶ Record and manage skills sets and other competencies

▶ Record and manage specific experiences

▶ Sort and conduct keyword searches of employees' records

▶ Manage annual budgets and the budget planning process

▶ Manage employee compensation planning

▶ Conduct the annual employee review process

MSS enables a manager to do his or her job well, and successfully manage a team—to grow it, care for and feed it, use it in the smartest way possible given any number of business or personal constraints and other factors, and retain the members of the team.

mySAP ERP Operations

Similar to mySAP ERP Financials, the mySAP ERP Operations area encompasses a large portion of your company's business. Essentially logistics, it encompasses all processes related to your company's purchasing, plant maintenance, sales and distribution, manufacturing, materials management, warehousing, engineering, and construction.

The Logistics module within R/3 and ECC enables you to arrange your business functions in a manner that encourages the creativity, competency, and flexibility that your company desires. Thus, mySAP ERP Operations is linked to, and must coordinate with, all or most of the following R/3 and ECC modules:

▶ Sales and Distribution

▶ Production Planning

▶ Materials Management

▶ Plant Maintenance

▶ Logistics Information System

Sales and Distribution

The Sales and Distribution module provides you with the necessary instruments to use a wealth of information relating to your company's sales and marketing. You can access data on products, marketing strategies, sales calls, pricing, and sales leads at any time to facilitate sales and marketing activity. The information is online, up-to-the-minute support to be used to service existing customers as well as potential customers and leads.

Also included within the Sales and Distribution module is a diverse supply of contracts to meet every type of business need. Agreements concerning pricing, delivery dates, and delivery quantity are all supported within this module. The subcomponents of the Sales and Distribution module include

▶ Master Data   ▶ Sales Support

▶ Basic Functions   ▶ Transportation

▶ Sales   ▶ Foreign Trade

▶ Shipping   ▶ Sales Information System

▶ Billing   ▶ Electronic Data Interchange

Some of the benefits of SAP's Sales and Distribution implementation include

▶ Automatic order entry via a simple user interface

▶ Automatic pricing in the sales order using price lists, customer agreements or pricing according to products, and product group or product cost

▶ Credit limit verification checks against credit, financial, and sales data to substantiate customers' credit limits

▶ Automatic product availability checks to verify sufficient quantities

Production Planning and Control

The focus of SAP's Production Planning and Control module is to facilitate complete solutions for

▶ Production planning   ▶ Production control

▶ Production execution

Production Planning and Control encompasses the comprehensive production process from its inception with the initial creation of master data through the production process, including control and costing. The Production Planning module includes a component called Sales and Operations Planning used for creating realistic and consistent planning figures to forecast future sales, and depending on your method of production, you can use SAP's Production Order processing, Repetitive

Manufacturing, or KANBAN Production Control processing. **KANBAN** is a procedure for controlling production and material flow based on a chain of operations in production and procurement.

One important benefit from the implementation of the Production Planning and Control module is its elimination of routine tasks for the persons responsible for production scheduling. The related reduction in time allows for additional time to be dedicated to more critical activities within your company. Several components of the Production Planning and Control module include

- Basic Data
- Sales and Operations Planning
- Master Planning
- Capacity Requirements Planning
- Material Requirements Planning
- KANBAN
- Repetitive Manufacturing

- Production Orders
- Product Cost Planning
- Assembly Orders
- Production Planning for Process Industries
- Plant Data Collection
- Production Planning and Control Information System

Materials Management

Your company's business processes are essential to the success of your company. The day-to-day management of your company's consumption of materials, including company purchasing, managing your warehouse and inventory, confirming your invoices, and analyzing your processes, are all part of the Materials Management module.

Savings of time, money, and resources are the three main benefits that you can derive from your Materials Management module. Its components include

- Inventory Management
- Warehouse Management
- Purchasing

- Invoice Verification
- Materials Planning
- Purchasing Information System

Plant Maintenance

The main benefit to SAP's Plant Maintenance module is its flexibility to work with different types of companies to meet differing designs, requirements, and work forces. The Plant Maintenance module also contains a graphical interface, which makes it very user friendly and enables it to cater to a larger population of your work force.

Different management strategies are supported within the application including Risk Based Maintenance and Total Productive Maintenance. Some benefits that your company will derive from the implementation of the Plant Maintenance module involve reduced down time and outages, optimization of labor and resources, and a reduction in the costs of inspections and repairs.

On the whole, the integration of the Plant Maintenance module supports your company in designing and executing your company's maintenance activities with regard to system resource availability, costs, materials, and personnel deployment. Components of Logistics, Plant Maintenance include

- Preventative Maintenance
- Service Management
- Maintenance Order Management
- Maintenance Projects
- Equipment and Technical Objects
- Plant Maintenance Information System

Logistics Information System (LIS)

In the world of R/3, the Logistics Information System maintains real-time information derived from multiple SAP modules/components, enabling you to evaluate actual data and then forecast future data using OLTP. You can use the Logistics Data Warehouse to customize and design your company's Information System to meet your company's unique requirements and use the Early Warning System, which targets weak or bottlenecked areas in Logistics.

In addition to these two components, the Logistics Information System contains a Logistics Information Library, which helps you to retrieve data via searches, enabling you to access key data when necessary. You use the Logistics Information Library (LIL) to record, classify, and retrieve key figures. The Logistics Information System is composed of the following information systems (see Figure 11.2):

- Sales Information System
- Purchasing Information System
- Inventory Controlling
- Production Planning and Control Information System
- Plant Maintenance Information System
- Quality Management Information System
- Project Information System
- Retail Information System (RIS)

LIS has been largely supplanted by reporting conducted via SAP's Business Warehouse, discussed in Hour 12, "SAP BI, KW, and MDM."

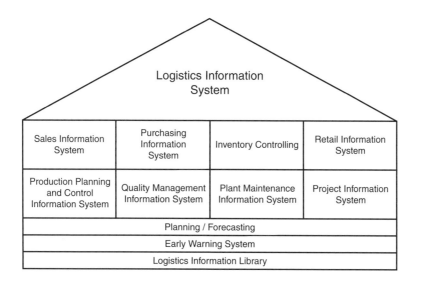

FIGURE 11.2
Overview of
R/3's legacy
Logistics
Information
System.

mySAP ERP Corporate Services

Corporate services include Real Estate Management, Quality Management, Project/Portfolio Management, Travel Management, and EH&S.

Real Estate Management

SAP's Real Estate module integrates real estate processes into your company's overall organizational structure. The Corporate Real Estate Management model is divided into the following two components:

▶ Rental Administration and Settlement

▶ Controlling, Position Valuation, and Information Management

> In order for your company to successfully use the Real Estate component, necessary configurations are required in your Plant Maintenance, Materials Management, Project System, and Asset Accounting modules.

Quality Management

The Quality Management module is directed at improving the quality of your products and to some extent processes. In order to produce high-quality products, a well-managed Quality Management system needs to be in place that assures the integrity of your products, which in turn helps foster good client relations while enhancing your firm's reputation relative to its products as well as the company in general.

The Quality Management module gives you the capability to analyze, document, and improve upon the processes in your company. Applications contained in the Quality Management module include

- Quality Planning
- Quality Inspections
- Quality Control
- Quality Notifications

- Quality Certificates
- Test Equipment Management
- Quality Management Information System

Project and Portfolio Management

Once simply called the Project System module, this important component of mySAP ERP Corporate Services assists your company in the management of a portfolio of projects. Such high-level cross-project insight allows for outstanding planning, execution, financial oversight, and it facilitates true project management. As such, it is centered on managing the network of relationships within your overall integrated system, establishing links between project management and other areas in the process.

You can use Project and Portfolio Management in many areas, including investment management, marketing, software and consulting services, research and development, maintenance tasks, shutdown management, plant engineering and construction, and complex made-to-order production. The components of the Project System module include:

- Basic Data
- Operational Structures
- Project Planning

- Approval
- Project Execution and Integration
- Project System Information System

Like always, the system is based on central structures called Work Breakdown Structures. A Work Breakdown Structure (WBS) is a structured model of work organized in a hierarchy format, to be performed in the course of completing a project.

WBSs are comprised of elements that represent the individual tasks and activities in the project. Elements include tasks, breakdowns of tasks, and work packages; see Figure 11.3 for an overview.

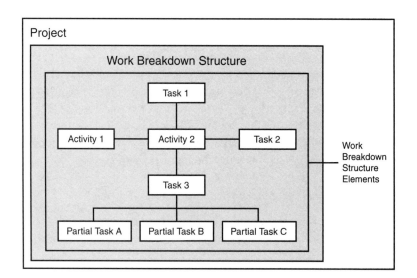

FIGURE 11.3
The project
structure
overview.

Travel Management

Although essentially a function of the Finance module, Travel Management is a key corporate service touching travel agencies, suppliers, global distribution systems, and your employees. SAP Travel Management also offers an integrated spectrum of procedures used for processing your company's business trip data. This includes entering receipts, approving reimbursement requests, and posting actual trip costs.

Summary

This hour gives you a very high-level overview of the primary business areas served by mySAP ERP: Financials, Operations, Human Capital Management (Human Resources), and Corporate Services. A set of side-by-side ECC and R/3 comparisons was also provided. Even at this level, it is easy to see why people say that nothing is easy when it comes to implementing an Enterprise Resource Planning application—business is necessarily complex, and this complexity must be modeled and reflected by SAP to create a useful solution. This introduction to these core modules provides familiarity and insight into this complexity, giving you an idea of the power and capabilities that R/3 and its newest successor, ECC, offer.

Q&A

Q *What are the major differences between SAP R/3 and SAP ECC?*

A SAP ECC represents the natural evolution of R/3 toward a service-oriented architecture. It reflects SAP's very own ESA rather than R/3's client/server architecture; SAP ECC sits atop WebAS, whereas R/3 sits atop SAP Basis; SAP ECC features a platform where functional/business logic and infrastructure technology underpinnings are separated, whereas R/3 lumps much more of this together, thereby complicating support and maintenance.

Q *Can you add your own functions to work with SAP Financials?*

A You can tailor Financials to suit the requirements of your company by adding non-SAP functions and developing your own solutions using R/3 and other SAP components.

Q *Does your SAP Financials system have the capability to link to older systems, like SAP R/2?*

A Application Link Enabling (ALE) technology permits the linking of your R/3 system to other R/3, mySAP ERP or Business Suite Components, as well as R/2 and even non-SAP systems.

Q *Is a preconfigured client available for the Financials and HR modules?*

A Yes, a preconfigured client is available for both of these modules, helping to minimize the time necessary to configure a workable solution.

Q *Is there a tool to assist in the transfer of data from a non-SAP system into SAP HR?*

A Yes. Since Basis release 4x, you can use the Data Transfer Workbench to assist in the transfer of data from a non-SAP system into SAP HR.

Q *If you are using SAP HR, is configuration required in any of the other SAP R/3 or ECC modules?*

A Configuration of a few items in the Financials module (cost centers, for example) is necessary in order for successful implementation of SAP HR—even as a standalone implementation.

Q *Can you use SAP HR with an external payroll or time and attendance system?*

A Yes, you can use SAP Human Resources to manage your company's human resources and organizational functions and still be connected to an external payroll system or a separate SAP-certified time/recording system.

Q *Can security in SAP HR be configured to prevent users from seeing sensitive payroll information?*

A Yes, there are many methods for restricting a user's capability to view sensitive data. For instance, you can use the SAP Profile Generator to develop and manage roles that allow only certain individuals access to sensitive payroll data.

Workshop

The workshop is designed to help you anticipate possible questions, review what you've learned, and begin thinking ahead to putting your knowledge into practice. The answers to the quiz that follows can be found in Appendix A, "Quiz Answers."

Quiz

1. Which Financials module is designed to support your company in creating budgets?

2. Which Financials module provides the functions necessary for effective and accurate internal cost accounting management?

3. In the Financials module, what subcomponent serves as a complete record of all your company's business transactions?

4. How does SAP define the term profit center?

5. What is the main benefit from the Human Resources, Recruitment component?

6. Define the SAP term *infotype*.

7. What are two methods you can use for SAP Employee Self Service?

8. Name the components available in the Materials Management module.

9. The focus of the Production Planning and Control component is to contribute solutions for which three areas?

10. Describe the types of data available to facilitate sales and marketing activity in the Sales and Distribution module.

11. Which component of the Production Planning module is used for creating realistic and consistent planning figures to forecast future sales?

Exercises

1. Execute /nST07 to review real-time how many different functional areas are being accessed by end users. Note the mix of users relative to each functional area.

2. List reasons why you might want to segregate your SAP HR system from your primary SAP R/3 or ECC system used to host logistics, financials, and so on.

3. If you are a current SAP R/3 customer, investigate reasons why SAP ECC might prove beneficial to your business departments. Then conduct the same exercise relative to your SAP IT organization. Weigh the pros and cons.

SAP BI, KW, and MDM

I touched on SAP Business Intelligence, Knowledge Warehouse, and Master Data Management briefly in Hour 10, "SAP NetWeaver," and elsewhere. This hour explores these three NetWeaver components—which enable what SAP AG calls "Information Integration"—more completely and from a number of perspectives. I highlight how each product fits into the grand scheme of all things NetWeaver, and the role or purpose of each, as well as discuss important subcomponents, legacy considerations, and real-world business benefits.

Highlights of this hour include

▶ Discover the business reasons for deploying MDM

▶ Uncover legacy considerations for MDM

▶ Discuss the IT challenges of implementing BI

▶ Share business benefits of deploying SAP KW

SAP Business Intelligence

I'm sure you have heard the expression, "If you can't measure it, you can't manage it." For this reason alone, SAP Business Intelligence and specifically SAP's Business Warehouse need to be on your radar screen. SAP BI lets you measure your business results, making it possible to then manage your business intelligently. If you're implementing NetWeaver, there's even more reason to deploy SAP BI—it serves as one of the core underlying components, providing a business intelligence platform for data warehousing, along with a suite of business intelligence tools. Use BW to combine data from SAP as well as external data sources; transform your data, consolidate it, and take care of all your reporting needs from this single repository underpinning NetWeaver and more.

Integration with Other SAP Components

Use SAP BW's BEx Information Broadcasting service to publish precalculated documents (or links to them) in SAP Enterprise Portal. And integrate content from SAP BW using tools like the BEx (pronounced "bex") Broadcaster, the BEx Web Application Designer, the BEx Query Designer, KM Content, the SAP Role Upload, and the Portal Content Studio. In this way, SAP users can actually use the data sitting across their NetWeaver enterprise, and make better decisions.

SAP Business Warehouse also has hooks into the SAP Knowledge Warehouse. Use it to manage your documentation, training materials, and other knowledge-management materials. Integrate SAP BW documents into SAP EP and KW using the repository manager. And use SAP XI to send data from SAP and non-SAP sources, including data marts built on any number of RDBMS platforms, to SAP BW. The possibilities are nearly endless.

Subareas of SAP BI

At a basic level, SAP BI consists of the BI platform and a Data Warehousing solution. The BI platform provides the technical infrastructure necessary to complete online analytical processing (OLAP) services, create planning applications, and conduct data mining. This includes

▶ Online Analytical Processing (OLAP), used to process and make sense of reams of operational as well as historical data. SAP's OLAP engine lets you slice and dice this data (SAP calls this multidimensional analysis) based on your particular organization's needs.

▶ SAP's Metadata Repository lets you access and use and report against the metadata (data about the data) associated with your BW data and its objects.

▶ BW's Business Planning and Simulation (BW-BPS, formerly found within SAP Strategic Enterprise Management, or SEM) is a generic planning module that lets you create planning applications that span an entire enterprise, complete with a web front-end to facilitate reporting.

▶ Analysis Process Designer (APD) can combine data from different sources and then help you "mine" it, essentially discovering new information in the form of trends, new developments, and so on.

▶ An easy-to-use Reporting Agent lets you schedule exception reports that run in the background; you can subscribe/unsubscribe to these reports, issue them based on alerts, forward them to delegates, and print them only when warranted (again, on an exception basis).

The second subarea of SAP BW, Data Warehousing, provides visibility to your data and then enables you to convert that data into useful information. You can segregate data by business units or other organizational entities, or aggregate it (combine it) across an entire enterprise—or both! SAP Data Warehousing supports real-time and historical SAP and non-SAP data sources, which can then in turn be

▶ Retrieved from source system(s)

▶ Transformed

▶ Consolidated

▶ Cleaned

▶ Stored

▶ Retrieved as needed for reporting and analysis

Use SAP BW's Administrator Workbench to manage this process (see Figure 12.1).

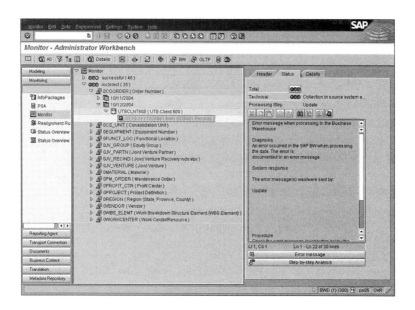

FIGURE 12.1
The SAP BW Administrator Workbench provides SAP's data warehousing tools.

Implementing BI

After you have determined the specific NetWeaver business scenarios you want to deploy, implementing SAP BI is straightforward:

▶ Prepare your SAP source systems (such as SAP R/3, R/3 Enterprise, or ECC).

▶ Install SAP WebAS ABAP, and then BW, and finally the BW content add-ons.

▶ Optionally, install SAP BW Java components (like the SAP BI Universal Data Integration or SAP BI Meta Model Repository options).

▶ Optionally, install SAP's Search and Classification add-on called TREX (necessary only if you want to be able to house and search for *documents* within BW, rather than data and data objects).

▶ Optionally, install SAP's BW Precalculation Service (required for SAP BW Reporting using the Business Explorer Analyzer).

▶ Install the SAP GUI with the SAP BW add-on on each desktop, laptop, or other host from which you want to connect to SAP BW.

▶ Optionally, install Internet Explorer 5.5 (or higher) or Netscape 7.01 (or higher) on each desktop, laptop, or other host from which you want to display SAP BW web applications.

▶ Optionally, install Crystal Enterprise SAP Edition Version 10 and Crystal Reports (useful for providing additional formatting in reports).

▶ Set up any remaining non-SAP data sources.

Legacy and Other Challenges

For companies that have already deployed a Data Warehousing or Business Intelligence platform for their enterprise, SAP BW might appear redundant. Truth be told, though, the capabilities that BW brings to the table sets it apart from other solutions you have already implemented. As one of SAP's most mature product offerings, it bears a closer look. In particular, BW's capability to proactively publish reports and provide access to BI through the Enterprise Portal makes it easy to use. Its capability to act as both a central warehousing repository and as a mechanism for consolidating information across SAP and non-SAP systems alike also makes it a valuable component for any company adopting NetWeaver.

Most arguments against deploying SAP Business Warehouse in favor of another data warehousing or business intelligence platform hold little water. For example, BW is highly scalable. It's very mature. It leverages SAP's standard WebAS (and previously Basis) layer, making it easy to initially install and support. It provides a wealth of technology options spanning all major operating systems and RDBMS platforms. Finally, it is highly capable. Compared to other solutions, with all these matters essentially a wash or decidedly in SAP's favor, combined with the SAP nametag, no other solution makes good business sense or IT sense like SAP BI.

SAP Knowledge Warehouse

SAP KW makes it possible for you create and manage your own enterprise-specific knowledge base replete with documentation, training, and manuals. With KW, you can create and update your own documents from a single interface, while leveraging SAP-provided documents and other materials to keep your development costs low. Documents in your Knowledge Warehouse are authored in traditional Microsoft Office formats like Word and PowerPoint. XML is supported as well. KW features an impressive translation capability, too—develop your documentation once, and present it to your global team in their local or preferred language by using the included TRADOS translation tools.

Role Within NetWeaver

You can use SAP Knowledge Warehouse (SAP KW) for many purposes; the following are common:

▶ To create and maintain documentation, the most common function of SAP KW.

▶ To create, manage, maintain, and distribute handbooks, that is, Quality Management Manuals (QMMs). SAP KW supports the creation of QMMs that meet ISO 9000 and 14000 standards.

▶ To create and manage training materials (course materials and instructor guides) for classroom or similar purposes. The training module is an optional package in KW.

SAP KW provides an authoring and translation environment that lets you create, edit, and translate the contents for any of the previously mentioned purposes. Microsoft Word, Excel, PowerPoint, and Microsoft Visio are already integrated in KW, along with an XML editor. The beauty of this approach is obvious, in that your documentation, manuals, and training materials are created and maintained using desktop products with which most users are already familiar.

Implementing KW

To install Knowledge Warehouse, a number of products and subcomponents are necessary:

▶ Install WebAS ABAP+Java (or make the determination to install the ABAP and Java components on separate WebAS servers).

▶ Install SAP KW Internet Knowledge Servlet.

▶ Install SAP Content Server.

▶ Install the SAP Gateway (if you do not use Search and Classification, TREX, and have installed SAP Content Server on the SAP WebAS host, you do not need to install this).

▶ Install Search and Classification (TREX).

▶ Install SAP Internet Transaction Server.

▶ Install the SAP GUI on any desktops or laptops from which you want to grant access to SAP KW; include the SAP KW add-on, and if you want to use Microsoft Office 2000 or Microsoft Office XP as your editing tool, be sure to register htmltidy.dll on each of these SAP GUI front-end clients.

▶ Install one of the following required editing tools (typically Microsoft Office 2000 or Microsoft Office XP, although you can use XML editors like Epic Editor 4.3.1 from Arbortext, Inc. and Authentic 2004 from Altova instead).

Benefits of SAP KW

SAP KW is designed to

▶ Provide a user-friendly authoring environment supporting multiple file and document types, as seen in Figure 12.2.

▶ Maximize use and reuse of documents maintained in the warehouse.

▶ Provide value in multilingual environments.

▶ Generate documents targeted toward specific groups or geographies.

▶ Provide the technical infrastructure necessary to share documents with users.

FIGURE 12.2
The authoring environment provided by Knowledge Warehouse provides for rich content and variety.

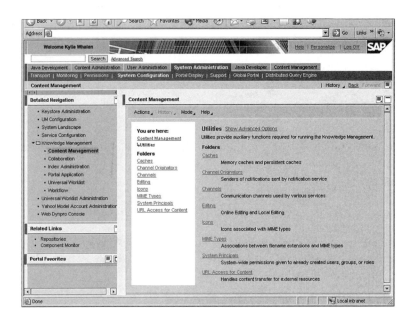

The fact that SAP KW supports rich search capabilities through the use of a web browser is another great benefit. You can search for documents and other content housed by the warehouse based on

▶ Full-text searches

▶ Attribute-based searches via "enhanced search" capabilities

▶ A combination of both full-text and attribute-based criteria

▶ A search for similar documents or other objects

You can also search for a document based on the area it is housed in within KW, or the language in which it is maintained.

SAP Master Data Management

As the final member of the "Information Integration" triumvirate, SAP's Master Data Management solution is the least mature of the bunch, but by the same token it holds perhaps the greatest promise for many companies—to collapse master data from many sources into one. By doing so, MDM appeals to nearly everyone, because it takes aim at consolidating and harmonizing master data across your heterogeneous SAP and non-SAP system landscape.

▶ Users of SAP will enjoy the consistent and easily maintainable data; "one version of the truth" is naturally appealing.

▶ The manager of the master data management team will suddenly find that the team has great bandwidth to tackle new projects.

▶ The CIO will deliver something that unequivocally provides quantifiable value, in the form of higher quality business processes and truly integrated data.

▶ The CEO will appreciate the reduction in headcount that he or she can realize inside the business units—the CEO can consolidate the teams tasked with data management and redeploy the "extra" people.

The only "downside" is that ultimately a company will need fewer data entry and data management clerks entering, manipulating, updating, synchronizing, and essentially fiddling around with master data. If you are one of these people, your position is at stake.

Subcomponents of SAP MDM

In most cases, you might find it necessary to implement a number of SAP components and products to deploy SAP Master Data Management. For example, to support Master-Data Consolidation and Master-Data Harmonization, the following are necessary:

▶ SAP ERP

▶ SAP Exchange Infrastructure (XI)

▶ An FTP server

▶ MDM server, the MDM workhorse

▶ MDM console, used to create catalogs and data models

▶ MDM CLIX (Command Line Interface), useful for scheduling batch jobs

▶ MDM client, used to review taxonomy results

▶ MDM Import Manager, used to import product data in different formats

▶ MDM Syndicator, used to export product data

In a rich product-content management scenario, SAP ERP, SAP XI, and an FTP server are not required.

Implementing MDM

Implementing the technical infrastructure for MDM appears time-consuming, given the number of steps involved, but it actually only amounts to perhaps a week or so. The steps include installing

1. The SAP MDM server

2. The MDM console

3. The MDM database (create it)

4. The MDM command-line interface

5. The MDM client and Catalog Manager

6. Optionally, the MDM Import Manager and Import Manager Batch

7. Optionally, the MDM Syndicator and MDM Syndicator Batch

8. Optionally, the MDM Language Selector

9. Optionally, the MDM Image Manager

10. Optionally, the Indesign or QuarkXTension plug-ins

11. Optionally, the MDM Layout Server

12. Optionally, the MDM ComObjects API

13. Optionally, the MDM Java API

After the specific components are installed to reflect your business scenario, it's a simple matter to put together the business process workflow. For example, the most popular MDM scenario—master data consolidation—follows a simple five-phase workflow that looks like this:

1. Phase I: Extract master data from each of your SAP ERP "clients" (islands of master data) via SAP IDocs.

2. Phase II: Import master data using SAP XI into the MDM repository.

3. Phase III: Consolidate the master data by merging it.

4. Phase IV: Enrich the master data as desired, or use it to support SAP BI analytics or catalog management.

5. Phase V: Export the master data back to SAP XI, and then distribute it back to the original ERP systems.

Note that the originating systems retain their master data, although at the end of the process it has been cleaned and made consistent. It is this simple process that saves companies so many hours of data entry and re-keying time.

MDM IT Deployment Challenges

Looking at MDM IT challenges from a technology stack perspective, the following areas might deserve up-front attention:

▶ The MDM server currently runs only on Linux and Windows platforms, which limits to some extent the scalability of MDM—if you're not interested in deploying high-end HP, IBM, or Unisys servers that support many processors, lots of RAM, and the Linux and/or Windows operating system, your hardware platform choices are limited.

▶ There are three excellent RDBMS platforms for MDM, including Oracle 9.2, Microsoft SQL Server 2000, and DB2 version 8.1 or later. This means that chances are good your SAP ERP database release is supported by MDM, too, helping you maintain IT standards. Unfortunately, mySQL MaxDB and Informix offerings are not supported.

> ► Given all the data moving back and forth between different systems, network bandwidth might prove troublesome when it comes to consolidating or harmonizing data spread out across a company WAN.

> I suggest you run through a number of basic network-testing scenarios in your test environment (assuming the test systems for the respective production systems are equally dispersed). Pay particular attention to systems connected over slow links.

> ► Finally, although MDM server-based components support both Windows and Linux, the MDM client and MDM administration components only currently support Windows XP, 2000, and 2003.

Legacy and Other Challenges

Given that the management of master data has not been traditionally automated (thereby representing such a compelling opportunity to reduce costs in the first place!), the real challenges in deploying MDM revolve around people and process considerations—not technology considerations. For example, for a company that has "always done it this way" (speaking to master data maintenance and management), the biggest challenge is in changing *how* master data is managed in a new NetWeaver-enabled world. Changing this process will no doubt impact how people spend their day, to the point of completely changing or even eliminating certain positions within the business units or potentially the IT department.

Benefits of SAP MDM

At the end of theday, SAP Master Data Management makes it possible to restructure operations, manage and consolidate master data, and synchronize diverse ERP systems and other repositories of master data. The biggest advantage to all this is in savings—people savings, savings related to making fewer mistakes related to master data, and savings resulting from streamlined processes.

Summary

This hour, you learned about three core components that make up many SAP NetWeaver implementations, core components that represent the Information Integration layer of the NetWeaver technology stack. SAP BI constitutes an important foundation for SAP NetWeaver solutions. Upon this foundation, cross-application reporting and true data warehousing is possible. And as the most central of the three "information integration" components, it enables smooth operation of business reporting functions across ERP, CRM, portal, and other NetWeaver components. In a similar manner, SAP Master Data Management provides a foundation for managing and maintaining consistent master data across multiple ERP and other systems, saving time and considerable money in the process. Finally, SAP's Knowledge Warehouse acts as the repository for training, documentation, and quality management manuals. These products and concepts help set the stage for additional components covered in the next hour.

Q&A

Q *When is Search and Classification optional for SAP BI?*

A Search and Classification, or TREX, is only necessary if your SAP BI system houses documents and you want to enable searching for these documents. Otherwise, TREX is optional.

Q *What is SAP MDM CLIX used for?*

A The SAP MDM CLIX component is usually deployed to support batch scripting.

Workshop

The workshop is designed to help you anticipate possible questions, review what you've learned, and begin thinking ahead to putting your knowledge into practice. The answers to the quiz that follows can be found in Appendix A, "Quiz Answers."

Quiz

1. List the three SAP components that comprise the Information Integration layer within the SAP NetWeaver stack.

2. Instead of using Microsoft Office, what are two other XML editors you can use for SAP KW?

3. List the required components of MDM.

4. What is SAP's BW Precalculation Service used for?

5. What value does Crystal Reports provide if you have already installed SAP BI?

6. By what mechanism does SAP KW support document translation?

7. How does SAP KW support searching?

Exercises

1. Obtain the XML editors discussed this hour and compare them in functionality to Microsoft Word.

2. In your own organization, research how many repositories or "systems of record" of master data you have. Are you a good candidate for SAP MDM?

3. Talk to an IT team who deployed or is considering deploying a data warehousing or business intelligence solution, and obtain from this team a list of non-SAP products and technologies they reviewed (presumably along with their evaluation of SAP BI).

HOUR 13

Other Enabling Technologies

Beyond the components discussed in Hour 12, "SAP BI, KW, and MDM," that make up SAP NetWeaver, a number of corollary yet very important additional components exist as well. These include SAP Enterprise Portal, Exchange Infrastructure, Mobile Infrastructure, and xApps. Although you can argue that some of these represent solutions in their own right, I take the approach that all these are enabling technologies—products that can stand on their own in some capacity, certainly, but tend to coexist with other components to augment or offer true end-to-end business functionality. This hour explores each of these NetWeaver components, including how they fit into constructing a NetWeaver-based SAP solution. Highlights of this hour comprise

▶ Discovering business benefits of xApps

▶ Finding out how XI extends SAP solutions

▶ Learning how Mobile Infrastructure enables your mobile workforce

▶ Uncovering legacy challenges relative to adopting Enterprise Portal

SAP Enterprise Portal

Undergoing a name change to *NetWeaver Portal*, SAP EP enables a user community or teams within the community the opportunity to collaborate—to work closely with one another by sharing applications and documents, communicating in a targeted fashion (through IM or online discussions), and working in a virtual team environment. EP does this through the use of iViews, Collaboration Rooms, and its single point of entry to back-end SAP and non-SAP systems.

▶ EP iViews are offered directly by SAP through their Portal Content Portfolio; others can be created through the use of SAP's portal content tools found in SAP NetWeaver's Visual Composer. An iView provides access to resources that can reside either within the portal or external to it. As such, iViews deliver business content to, and facilitate communication between, the portal's user community.

▶ SAP Collaboration Rooms host any number of applets, predefined content, and services geared toward a particular working group. They support groupware (like Microsoft Exchange and IBM Lotus Notes) and other kinds of collaboration applications like WebEx as well.

Enterprise Portal is deemed a required component of a Java-based NetWeaver solution; it is optional for ABAP-based solutions (where the SAP GUI for Windows user interface is often used instead). EP's deployment makes a lot of sense for many organizations, though, explaining why it is growing in popularity.

Implementing Enterprise Portal

To implement EP, use NetWeaver's Rapid Installer. Through the use of its configuration wizard, EP can be installed quickly. It is also used to set up connectivity between the portal and a mySAP ERP system, Business Warehouse, SAP CRM, and any system used to monitor the portal via SAP's Computing Center Management System (CCMS).

As Rapid Installer sets up EP on a single node (server), the system supports only 200 to 300 concurrent portal users by default (the exact number depends on the hardware platform). Scale the system with additional nodes to support more users.

IT Challenges

Because Rapid Installer does not support SAP applications before NetWeaver '04, it cannot be used to set them up. There are a number of technical limitations related to the operating system and database platform combinations as well—only the following are supported for Enterprise Portal within the context of NetWeaver '04, for example:

▶ Microsoft SQL Server 2000 Enterprise Edition running on Windows Server 2003 or Windows 2000

▶ The 64-bit version of Oracle 9.2.0.4 database running on Windows Server 2003 or Windows 2000

▶ The 64-bit version of Oracle 9.2.0.4 database running on Sun Solaris SPARC 8 or 9

As NetWeaver evolves, be sure to check for similar IT limitations early. The sizing process will uncover such limitations, of course, but a change of direction at this relatively late stage represents a lot of wasted time. Instead, try to uncover IT constraints and limitations in conjunction with your strategic discussions.

Because EP acts as a single point of entry for potentially all users of your SAP system, in many cases you will want to cluster this system to achieve high levels of system availability. Think about it—if EP is down, effectively everything else in the system is "down" for those users who rely strictly on Portal access. Clustering EP has its own challenges, too, in that you are effectively clustering Java instances.

Finally, the need to validate system scalability prior to deployment is just as important as deploying a highly available system. I suggest using a web-based load-testing tool like that offered by Segue or AutoTester, and conducting both real-world peak workload testing as well as maximum system capacity "smoke" testing. In this way, you can ensure that the system can meet your expected peak load, and can identify the maximum number of concurrent users that the system can handle "just in case." Note that SAP Support uses Mercury LoadRunner to execute a predefined load test in the course of conducting the Go-Live check for SAP EP; if you run a Mercury shop, the scripts found in SAP Solution Manager can provide an excellent starting point for EP workload testing.

Legacy and Other Challenges

You might find yourself retiring an older portal in favor of deploying SAP Enterprise Portal. Consider the following:

▶ Although more time-consuming, the opportunity to rebuild or modify your portal's content taxonomy can help make the new Portal more useful than its predecessor.

▶ In a similar way, you should look at deploying Single Sign On (SSO) if it's not already deployed; this makes for much more seamless access overall, and it eases transition to the new Portal.

▶ Both content (data) and applications need to be moved over, possibly constituting mini-projects.

▶ Access to the old portal is well established; users need to be trained not only on how to use the new Enterprise Portal, but also how to access it.

Although there are certainly challenges in deploying SAP Enterprise Portal, the benefits outweigh them considerably, as noted next.

Benefits of SAP EP

At the end of the day, a portal simplifies life for both an individual user and the team as they go about completing their work. The work itself typically doesn't change, but *how* this work is completed can change significantly.

▶ Collaboration helps a team make better decisions faster

▶ Collaboration provides the platform for SAP Knowledge Management, as discussed in Hour 12.

- ▶ The single point of contact that a portal provides simplifies where a user goes to gain access to existing reports, applications, and other information

- ▶ In the same way, the portal provides one-stop shopping for the latest and greatest information and applications, too, making for an efficient approach to completing work

In the midst of all this efficiency and streamlining, the work day might conceivably be shortened. More realistically, though, the team that uses SAP EP to its advantage is positioned to gain an edge in the business it conducts. And this can help it be successful.

SAP Exchange Infrastructure

Just as SAP Enterprise Portal provides single point of access to back-end applications and content, SAP Exchange Infrastructure provides single point of access between applications—possibly many applications. This simplifies integration, thereby improving the velocity with which new applications can be deployed and existing applications can be folded into your business processes.

Role Within NetWeaver

The role of SAP XI is straightforward—to connect or integrate two or more applications so that extended business processes can be deployed. To do this, SAP XI relies on the passing back and forth of XML messages (in the absence of native SAP-supported protocols). Thus, connectivity to SAP and non-SAP systems can be accomplished in many ways, such as

- ▶ Through the use of SAP Intermediate Documents, or IDocs

- ▶ Using SAP's Remote Function Calls (RFCs)

- ▶ Using SAP's BC (Business Connector) protocol

- ▶ Transferring files at a file system level

- ▶ Transferring files through the use of an FTP server

- ▶ Via XML using the Java Messaging Service (JMS)

- ▶ Via XML over plain HTTP

- ▶ Via Java proxy-based messaging, which uses XML and HTTP

- ▶ Using JDBC Data Access (which natively creates an XML message)

▶ Using web services, via the SOAP adapter

▶ Using a RosettaNet-compliant adapter for the exchange of messages (RNIF)

▶ Using the Mail Adapter, which exchanges messages from a mail server

▶ Via marketplace access using a standard Marketplace Adapter

With such inherent flexibility, the good news is that there's very few enterprises or other systems that *cannot* be melded into an SAP NetWeaver solution.

Subcomponents of SAP XI

SAP XI consists of much more than the basic Integration Server. SAP XI 3.0, for instance, comprises the following:

▶ Integration Server ▶ Runtime Workbench

▶ Integration Builder ▶ XI Adapter Engine

Further, the Adapter Engine consists of

▶ XI Adapter Framework

▶ XI Adapter Framework Core

▶ XI Connectivity XE (in the case of the Adapter Engine for J2SE)

There's also a Partner Connectivity Kit (XI PCK), which is used to allow secure access to your system by Business Partners. The XI PCK requires the same Adapter Framework components as described previously.

Implementing Exchange Infrastructure

SAP XI consists of potentially many components as outlined previously. This exacerbates implementation complexity, although in my experience this complexity comes slowly over time, not all at once. Therefore, it is still as manageable as complexity can be.

IT Challenges

IT challenges often relate to the specific technologies required to deploy SAP XI. That is, there is a certain amount of technology "variety" that comes into play.

▶ SAP XI requires a separate WebAS server from your other NetWeaver components. Normally this is not an issue, because your other components often dictate more horsepower than a single server can provide. But it is still something you need to consider.

▶ As usual, SAP often has specific minimum Support Package levels that are required to deploy XI. SAP's specially designed configuration templates for deploying SAP NetWeaver '04 scenarios based on WebAS Java, for instance, require Support Package 10 or higher.

▶ All the optional XI components add complexity when it comes to installing and (more importantly) maintaining the technology stack.

▶ If you want to provide Business Partner connectivity to your system, you have to deploy the SAP Partner Connectivity Kit (PCK). However, the PCK is currently supported only on Java-based WebAS solutions. Further, only the UNICODE version of WebAS is supported. Thus, you might well wind up with an SAP Web Application Server in your SAP system landscape that looks nothing like any of your other Web Application Servers.

Legacy and Other Challenges

If you have an integration scheme in place today, as most SAP environments have to some extent, you will find yourself in a quandary. Ripping out existing infrastructure and changing how data is moved and shared between applications usually amounts to disruption. But staying on the same course typically means spending a large chunk of budget money every year updating multiple integration points, especially when there's a one-to-many relationship between applications (as opposed to a hub-and-spoke design like that made possible by SAP XI). The easiest way out is to let the financial numbers do the talking—do the math—and put together a business case that quantifies your cost savings *over time*. Think about the cost of maintaining each software interface for each legacy system that talks to other systems. Think about the time and effort involved in connecting new systems. Think about the costs involved in upgrading and simply maintaining the interconnects (perhaps there are special hardware components involved that can be retired, for instance). And don't forget to consider the cost of lost opportunities—you probably have systems today that simply cannot talk to one another, resulting in costly duplicate data entry into different systems. SAP XI can change all this for the better.

Benefits of SAP XI

SAP Exchange Infrastructure enables you to integrate all kinds of SAP and non-SAP systems with one another. This makes it possible for you to design and deploy business processes that cross multiple applications, and include internal resources as well as business partner resources. And because SAP XI uses a hub-and-spoke design, it is simple to add new systems and maintain their single interface over time. The fact that XI supports so many connection technologies as discussed previously makes for a truly useful approach to building and extending business processes. Combined, these features make XI one of the least expensive and most powerful integration solutions on the market today.

SAP Mobile Infrastructure

Although not widely adopted yet, SAP MI promises great potential for SAP NetWeaver solutions in the coming years. SAP MI lets you SAP-enable applications that are not SAP-based, and it helps you extend SAP applications out to mobile devices that might otherwise require a proprietary and expensive alternative means of integration into your system.

Role Within NetWeaver

In your company, you probably have users who don't stay at their desk all day. They run back and forth between client sites, distribution centers, manufacturing facilities, and so forth. Maybe they office remotely, or out of their home, and need access to SAP when they're on the road. For these users, a truly "mobile" solution is necessary—SAP MI was developed expressly to meet such needs.

Subcomponents of SAP MI

SAP MI requires WebAS Java. MI functionality is built into the ABAP stack, however, making WebAS 6.40 ABAP+Java the minimum release level/configuration of Web Application Server supported for MI. The subcomponents of MI include the server and the client, outlined in the following two sections.

SAP MI Server

The SAP Mobile Infrastructure Server contains a J2EE server and an ABAP server. The SAP MI J2EE Server takes care of the Java requirement for MI, and comprises the following:

▶ Logic to determine what to install on the MI Client (applications as well as local device drivers)

▶ Administration component used to monitor the mobile device

▶ Administration component used to monitor the server (like how well synchronization is proceeding and how well load balancing is handled)

The SAP MI ABAP Server, on the other hand, is responsible for

▶ Deploying mobile applications to each mobile client device

▶ Queuing and acknowledgement of the data packages between the server and various mobile client devices

▶ Calling the SAP application logic

▶ Performing the actual data replication between the server and client

▶ Monitoring the state and status of data replication

Data replication for MI entails rationalizing what needs to be moved to the client in the form of a data package, defining the contents of each data package, packaging the data, moving the data, resolving any data version issues that crop up, and monitoring the overall process.

Not only data (in the classic sense) is replicated from the MI server to each mobile client device; mobile applications are deployed (and updated) in the same way. Your System Administrator determines which applications need to be replicated for each user based on the user's role or position.

SAP MI Client

The SAP Mobile Infrastructure Client takes care of how the application works with and on the client device. It serves a number of purposes and provides

▶ A framework for APIs from where services are defined and deployed, including data synchronization, data compression, data persistence, moving replicated data, support for peripherals like printers, and basic XML support

▶ A standard user-interface programming model based on Java Server Pages (JSP) and the Abstract Window Toolkit (AWT), among potentially older models

Implementing Mobile Infrastructure

Installing MI amounts to installing WebAS ABAP+Java, followed by installing the SAP GUI for Windows for any clients that need MI access. The next step is to install the SAP Mobile Infrastructure Client. Then, you can use the Mobile Development Kit (MDK) to develop a mobile application (using a well-stocked JavaServer Pages library provided by SAP). Or you can instead deploy a packaged mobile application.

Benefits of SAP MI

Because the SAP MI client component is installed locally on mobile devices and is *fully equipped* with its own web server, DB access layer, and application logic, it truly supports offline users. This is very different from other mobile solutions that offer only partial support for a particular application when offline. Thus, remote users can truly get their job done even when they are not connected to their SAP network; when ready, they simply need to connect and seamlessly synchronize their data. This is especially useful for a company's sales force (a classic example of why you deploy MI in the first place), although product engineers, project managers, and decision makers throughout an organization can benefit from MI. And because SAP MI supports PDAs, cell phones, pagers, and other mobile client devices that support Java, there's virtually no limit to your front-end mobile client options.

SAP xApps

The final component I discuss this hour is not actually a single component, but rather a collection of them. SAP AG tells us that NetWeaver is the technical foundation for xApps, a portfolio of existing and easy-to-create applications designed to facilitate business innovation. They work around and in conjunction with other applications. In essence, SAP xApps fill in the gaps in your NetWeaver implementation, delivering complementary services that help you build end-to-end SAP-native business processes. You don't implement the suite of xApps, though—most business units with such a need typically only implement one or maybe two xApps, for reasons that become more clear later in this hour.

Role Within NetWeaver

Again, SAP xApps fill in the gaps. They make it possible to quickly reconfigure and tweak business processes to accommodate new requirements. These requirements hail from everywhere: new corporate and other business structures and reorganizations, new customer or business partner requirements, and other changes that touch existing business processes.

To make this kind of business flexibility possible, xApps leverage the *SAP Composite Application Framework*, an application design that combines web services and open data access. In this way, xApps are consistent in architecture and approach, and inherently ready for future customizing—making it eminently easy to modify them when business requirements change yet again.

The **SAP Composite Application Framework** provides an environment for creating ESA-enabled applications. It includes a model-driven architecture, an object access layer that facilitates application snap-in to any NetWeaver landscape, built-in collaboration functionality, and easy-to-update user interface procedures.

Sample SAP-Provided xApps

SAP AG has developed quite a few xApps, with more on the way. Some of these include

▶ Cost and Quotation Management (SAP xCQM), which is used in the manufacturing industry

▶ Emissions Management (SAP xEM), developed for companies that need to manage compliance with environmental regulations

▶ Integrated Exploration and Production (SAP xIEP), used by the Oil and Gas vertical

▶ Product Definition (SAP xPD), useful to any entity tasked with developing successful, profitable, and innovative products

▶ Resource and Portfolio Management (SAP xRPM), useful to any entity interested in maximizing financial performance through the alignment of new product development with organizational objectives

▶ Global Trade Services (SAP GTS), used to automate, streamline, and mitigate the risks inherent to international trade (arguably the most popular xApp within the SAP Manufacturing industry vertical)

The development teams at SAP AG are not the only ones busy building xApps. SAP's large partner network includes a number of certified xApps partners as well.

Sample Partner xApps

SAP xApps are available from quite a few certified xApps partners, and the list grows every year. The applications are as diverse as the partners, including

▶ Accenture, the developer of composite applications *E&P Teamlink* and *Workspace B2B Retail Petroleum Portal*

▶ Answerthink, Inc., the developer of *PharmaConnect* for the pharmaceutical industry

▶ Bristlecone, the developer of *plannerDA*, which appeals to different industries such as apparel and footwear, consumer products, and high tech/manufacturing

- Digital Fuel, the developer of the ServiceFlow xApp useful to the service-provider industry

- Lighthammer Software Development Corp., the developer of the *Manufacturing Performance Improvement* xApp, which appeals to the aerospace and defense, chemicals, consumer products, industrial machinery and components, mill products, pharmaceuticals, and utilities verticals

- NRX Global Corp., the developer of *VIP* for the chemicals, oil and gas, and utilities verticals

- Vendavo, developer of the Pricing Analytics package, which appeals to the chemicals, distribution, forest products, high tech, industrial manufacturing, and metals industries

For details on these are other partner-provided xApps, refer to http://www.sap.com/solutions/xapps/partners/applications/index.epx.

Benefits of SAP xApps

SAP xApps fill in the gaps, providing important business services that help to optimize existing processes or fuel innovation through the adoption of new processes. Because xApps effectively snap in to the NetWeaver technology stack, deployment and infrastructure maintenance is a no-brainer. And through the growing portfolio of SAP xApps, other benefits to your company can include

- Realize improved short-term and long-distance visibility into its enterprise

- Capability to quickly formulate and execute against ever-evolving corporate strategies, business needs, and regulatory requirements

- Capability to collaborate on new product and service opportunities

- Capability to maximize efficiency and reduce costs through the melding of once-isolated business processes

- Capability to better analyze the marketplace and its competitive landscape, facilitating improved real-time decision making

By leveraging Enterprise Portal, SAP Business Intelligence, and SAP XI for access, analytics, and data exchange, respectively, the only real learning curve for an IT organization already running SAP NetWeaver lies in the ongoing development of the individual xApps solutions—not unlike any solution. But xApps pay off big in this respect, too. That is, you can reduce the *costs* of deploying new applications when you turn to SAP xApps. You can use the xApps framework and its accompanying tools and methodologies to quickly develop and turn out new applications. And then keep costs low by capitalizing on the fact that SAP xApps are not tied to the release cycles of the NetWeaver technology stacks underpinning them. This allows for leading-edge new business functionality to be both rapidly and cost-effectively introduced when it is needed, not months later.

Summary

The SAP EP, XI, MI, and xApps products and technologies represent key enablers or gap-fillers when it comes to constructing a well-oiled NetWeaver machine. The concepts covered in this hour are the key to understanding how these components work together to extend SAP's presence within your company, to bring together and rationalize islands of data, and to simplify access and changes to this data as well as their overarching business processes. By weaving together your SAP front-end with the back-end, and filling in the gaps with xApps, you can deploy a truly far-reaching and highly functional SAP system.

Q&A

Q *What framework makes it possible to create consistent xApps?*

A The SAP Composite Application Framework provides a consistent set of tools within a proven methodology for developing composite applications.

Q *What are two mechanisms or constructs within Enterprise Portal that not only facilitate, but also encourage the Portal's use?*

A SAP Enterprise Portal takes advantage of iViews and Collaboration Rooms to present data and applications and thereby facilitate work.

Q *What version and release of WebAS is required for the SAP Mobile Infrastructure Server component?*

A SAP MI must be deployed on SAP WebAS 6.40 ABAP+Java. That is, MI requires both the ABAP and Java stacks to function.

Workshop

The workshop is designed to help you anticipate possible questions, review what you've learned, and begin thinking ahead to putting your knowledge into practice. The answers to the quiz that follows can be found in Appendix A, "Quiz Answers."

Quiz

1. What is SAP NetWeaver's Rapid Installer?

2. What platform is used for SAP's Knowledge Management offering as discussed in Hour 12?

3. List several methods used by SAP XI to connect SAP and non-SAP systems together.

4. What is arguably the biggest factor in deploying SAP XI?

5. Describe the data replication process for SAP MI.

6. What is the minimum technical requirement for an SAP MI client device?

7. What is the core value of SAP xApps?

Exercises

1. Investigate whether any custom iViews or developer tips exist that might prove useful to your business or industry. Search SAP's main website www.sap.com, as well as the SAP developer network at https://www.sdn.sap.com/sdn/index.sdn.

2. Working with your IT organization, begin assembling a list of all the bolt-on and other applications that currently share data or communicate with your SAP ERP system manually (through duplicate data entry, typically). For each bolt-on or application, determine which one (or more) of SAP XI's communications protocols can be used to establish seamless automated links.

3. From http://www.sap.com/solutions/xapps/, review the list of xApps currently provided by SAP and its partners.

PART IV

SAP Technical Guide

HOUR 14

Technology Overview

In this hour, you take a look at some of the basic components of the underlying technology in an SAP system. Referred to by seasoned SAP technical veterans as "SAP Basis," the SAP technical foundation has expanded over the years to include a host of components that today make up SAP's Web Application Server, or WebAS. As such, this is a rather technical hour of instruction geared not toward the normal day-to-day end users of an SAP system but rather those tasked with installing and technically maintaining SAP. This hour will help you understand some of SAP's basic technical concepts in terms of how your SAP system operates and communicates.

Highlights of this hour include

- ▶ Learning about the different types of SAP work processes

- ▶ Understanding the concept of Enqueue processing

- ▶ Reviewing architecture and basic communications protocols

- ▶ Discovering Remote Function Calls (RFCs)

Application Architecture

In SAP "techno" speak, the WebAS or Basis system is the *middleware* or software that functions as a conversion or translation layer between the technology and business/ application layers of a computing solution and allows the various SAP applications to run on different hardware and system platforms. Some of these available platforms, as well as their technology and business-enabling layers, are displayed in Figure 14.1.

The WebAS/Basis layer manages all your application modules within your SAP system and ensures that these modules are integrated. This middleware enables platform independence as well. Some important functions of the WebAS/Basis System include

- ▶ Constitutes the runtime environment for SAP

- ▶ Represents the heart of the administrative core of SAP

- ▶ Enables management and distribution of your SAP technical components and resources

▶ Permits optimal integration of the various SAP applications into the overall computing environment

▶ Establishes a stable structural framework for system upgrades, enhancements, and so on

▶ Makes it possible to interface with third-party applications and products, thus extending SAP functionality beyond its own innate capabilities

FIGURE 14.1
SAP WebAS/
Basis available
platforms.

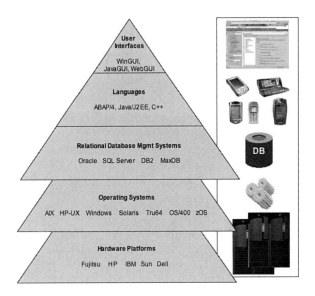

Basis Tools

The SAP WebAS/Basis system provides for the integration of software and technology through the use of the communications protocols or tools outlined as follows (see Figure 14.2):

▶ Remote Function Calls (RFCs)

▶ Common Program Interface Communications (CPI-C)

▶ Electronic Data Interchange (EDI)

▶ Object Linking and Embedding (OLE)

▶ Application Link Enabling (ALE)

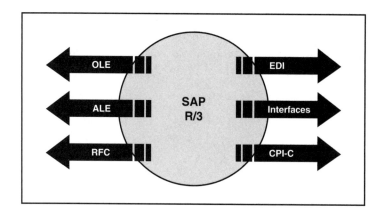

Remote Function Calls (RFCs)

Remote Function Calls, or RFCs as they are referred to in SAP, are the most common form of interface communication and allow for the simple programming of communication processes between systems.

In simpler terms, RFCs are used to pass communication throughout the SAP system and through interfaces into other systems. RFCs are also used for communication control, parameter passing, and error handling. RFCs are usually written in SAP's ABAP/4 language and, without getting too technical, are used to call and execute a program (see Figure 14.3).

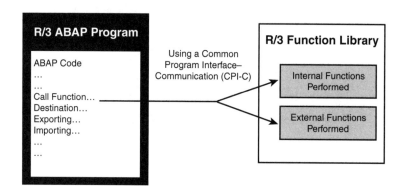

Common Program Interface Communications (CPI-C)

An SAP Common Program Interface Communications (CPI-C) is nothing more than a type of program interface communication that ensures a standard and consistent communication between two programs.

In nontechnical terms, CPI-C facilitates the communication (talking back and forth) and the processing of applications and programs within the system. CPI-C is a communications protocol that consists of a series of rules governing communication between programs. These rules can be divided into four discrete areas:

▶ Session setup

▶ Session control

▶ Communication

▶ End of session

The difference between RFCs and CPI-Cs is that RFCs allow other systems to call SAP functions and CPI-Cs allow program-to-program communications and exchange.

Electronic Data Interchange (EDI)

Electronic Data Interchange (EDI) is the electronic communication of business transactions electronically. EDI permits two different systems to pass information back and forth in a standard format (see Figure 14.4). If you have ever purchased an item off of the Internet, you have used some form of EDI. The EDI architecture consists of the three elements listed in Table 14.1.

FIGURE 14.4
Electronic Data Interchange (EDI) uses a standardized scheme for exchanging business data between different systems.

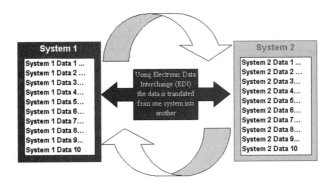

Electronic Data Interchange (EDI) is the electronic communication used to facilitate business transactions. EDI permits two different systems to pass information back and forth in a standard format.

TABLE 14.1   EDI Elements

Element	Description
EDI-capable applications	Applications that can effectively support the automatic processing of business transactions
EDI interface	Applications designed with an open interface and structure
EDI subsystem	Application that can convert the immediate structures into EDI messages

> The standard format for EDI is ANSI X12; it was developed by the Data Interchange Standards Association.

By the Way

Object Linking and Embedding (OLE)

Object Linking and Embedding (OLE) is used to integrate PC and other applications with the SAP system. OLE is the technology for transferring and sharing information among applications.

> In Hour 22, "Integration with Microsoft Office," you see how to use OLE to create SAP reports with the Microsoft Office family of products.

By the Way

OLE connects various PC-based and other applications to SAP as RFCs to your SAP GUI presentation layer (see Figure 14.5).

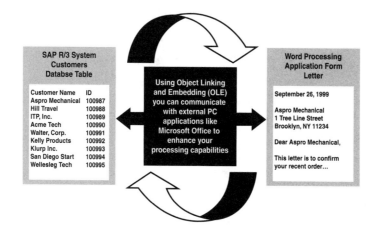

FIGURE 14.5
Object Linking and Embedding (OLE) enables the connection and incorporation of objects across platforms.

Application Link Enabling (ALE)

Application Link Enabling (ALE) is the creation and operation of distributed applications. In other words, ALE, which is closely related to SAP Work Flow, is the technology used by SAP to support distributed business processes.

Application integration is achieved not via a central database, but via synchronous and asynchronous communication. Synchronous transfer means that data is transmitted directly from program to program via a CPI-C interface. In asynchronous transfer, the sender and the receiver programs are independent of each other. This might sound a bit more technical than it actually is. An example of synchronous and asynchronous communication appears in Figure 14.6.

FIGURE 14.6
Application integration is achieved via synchronous and/or asynchronous data transfer.

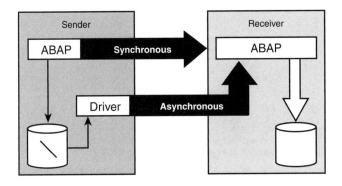

The following lists three types of data that are transmitted through ALE:

- ▶ **Control and customizing data**—Any data that is entered into the system as part of your configuration process, including user profiles, company codes, and business data.

- ▶ **Master data**—Any data that represents the organizational units of consolidation in the system, such as employee and vendor records.

- ▶ **Transaction data**—Records of transactions in the system: orders, shipments, purchases, payroll runs, and so on.

Work Processes

Several types of work processes execute behind-the-scenes in your SAP system, performing different types of functions—all of which can be customized. Work processes perform the bulk of the processing carried out by SAP, including performing dialog steps in user transactions, database updates, and record-lock management. If you are curious to see which work processes are executing at any given time in your SAP system, use the transaction code /nSM50. Check out the example in Figure 14.7.

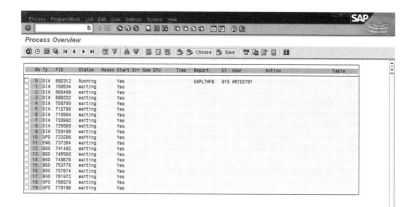

FIGURE 14.7
The SAP Process Overview screen displays a list of configured work processes (both active and inactive) for a particular application server.

Types of work processes include

- Dialog
- Background
- Synchronous Update
- Asynchronous Update

- Enqueue
- Message
- Spool
- Gateway

Dialog Work Processes

Dialog work processes implement requests in your active work session and are based on real-time or "online" synchronous communications.

Remember the Logical Units of Work (LUW) covered in Hour 1, "Introduction to SAP NetWeaver and ECC?" Well, a Dialog process is not complete until it completes a Logical Unit of Work.

By the Way

Background Processing (B)

As the name describes, Background processing tasks are usually executed in the background. These include tasks used to run reports or to process batch data loads. Background processing is based on asynchronous communications.

Update Processes (Vx)

Update work processes are requests to update the database, and these are broken into two categories: synchronous and asynchronous.

Synchronous Update (V1)

Synchronous updates are performed immediately. These are updates to the database that must be performed before you can proceed any further in a particular business transaction or process. Adding a new purchase order to the system is an example of a synchronous update, because this is information you immediately want reflected in your database.

Asynchronous Update (V2)

Asynchronous updates are not performed immediately; rather, they are performed in batch or "behind the scenes" and do not require a real-time update to the system. Many examples exist; your programmers often decide what must be "committed" to the SAP database immediately, and what can be committed when time permits.

Enqueue Processing (E)

Enqueue is another word for lock. In this particular case, I mean *lock management*. Lock management is meant to describe a sense of record management security in the system. In other words, if you have a record open (an employee record for instance) and you are changing important data on that record (employee salary for instance), lock management prevents another user from opening the same record and making changes to it while you both have it open.

> Function modules to lock (Enqueue) or release (Dequeue) records are generated from the lock objects that you define in your Data Dictionary.

Message Server/Processing (M)

The message server is responsible for message processing, which represents the communication between different application servers in your SAP system.

> Depending on your system's configuration, you might have only one application server. Not all companies have multiple application servers.

Spool Processing (S)

Spool processing concerns output requests that are sent to a spool, which stores them temporarily until they are output. Spool processing usually encompasses reports and output in your SAP system. See Figure 14.8 for an example.

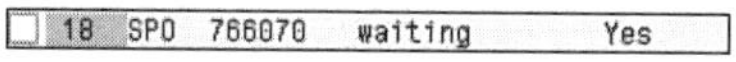

```
   18  SPO  766070    waiting      Yes
```

FIGURE 14.8
The SAP Process Overview screen displays your spool requests.

Gateway Process (G)

Last of all, a Gateway process is a communication among other SAP or other systems. An example of a Gateway process is between your SAP R/3 system and a mainframe computer system.

> If you want to see what the work process is doing behind the scenes (in SQL*Net), navigate to the Process Overview screen (transaction code /nSM50) and select an item in the list by highlighting it with your cursor. Then follow the menu path Process, Trace, Display File.

By the Way

Work Processes Review

The different types of work processes and the types of requests they manage are summarized in Table 14.2.

TABLE 14.2 SAP Work Processes

Work Process	Request Type
Dialog (D)	Dialog requests
Update (Vx)	Requests to update data in the database
Background (B)	Background jobs
Spool (S)	Print spool requests
Enqueue (E)	Lock management
Message (M)	Message management between application servers within an R/3 system
Gateway (G)	Requests between multiple systems, including external non-SAP systems

The basic processes that go on behind the scenes in SAP are similar to the very basic depiction illustrated in Figure 14.9.

FIGURE 14.9
Work processes
perform the
essential pro-
cessing carried
out by your SAP
System.

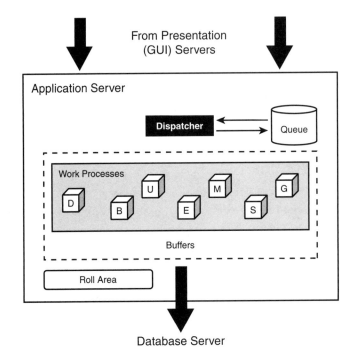

Summary

This hour provided you with a very elementary overview of some of the essentials of the SAP technology foundation known as SAP Web Application Server (SAP WebAS) or SAP Basis. These functions that go on behind the scenes in your SAP system are germane to hosting the workload driven by users and batch processes alike. This hour is a very basic overview; there are many additional functions and components of the Basis system that are not covered here. Some of these additional concepts are covered in Hour 15, "System Administration." Unless you are planning a career in an SAP technical discipline such as WebAS installation, performance optimization, or system administration, the technical terms and functions that are discussed herein should suffice in providing you with a basic understanding of the SAP technology platform.

Q&A

Q *Do all installations need to use the WebAS/Basis system monitoring tools?*

A Although not required, taking advantage of the system monitoring tools is an ideal way to ensure that your SAP system maintains a good runtime environment and is free of errors.

Q *Are you required to have an SAP technology professional specializing in Basis Administration implement your SAP system?*

A You will never have a successful installation and implementation without at least one knowledgeable SAP WebAS/Basis resource involved. By the same token, it is also useful to have an Administrator who is familiar with database management and OS platform administration that reflects your specific SAP environment.

Workshop

The workshop is designed to help you anticipate possible questions, review what you've learned, and begin thinking ahead to putting your knowledge into practice. The answers to the quiz that follows can be found in Appendix A, "Quiz Answers."

Quiz

1. With which type of interface do Internet communications usually communicate?

2. Which type of interface is used to communicate with Microsoft office?

3. What are the three types of data transmitted through Application Link Enabling (ALE)?

4. What are two types of update processes?

5. What does the term middleware represent?

6. What is a CPI-C?

7. What are the four areas of rules that govern CPI-C communications protocol?

Exercises

1. From your own SAP system, request authorization to execute /nSM50 and /nSM51. Compare these two transactions relative to breadth and depth. Note how SM51 provides access to SM50 simply by double-clicking a particular application server.

2. From your own SAP system, request authorization to execute /nST03 or /nST03N and look at your last week's workload. Drill down into the specific workload for each of the various types of work processes (dialog, background, spool, update, and so on) configured for your system.

3. Investigate your SAP IT organization and how it addresses SAP system installation and administration. How many resources are responsible for installing the system? Updating it? Managing it after installation? How do individual skill sets differ between these people?

System Administration

Administration, maintenance, and ongoing management of your SAP system are crucial. Administration includes monitoring for availability, user administration and basic authorizations, and other fundamental technical administrative functions of your system. Note that performance management is not covered here; an entire hour dedicated to optimizing SAP from a performance perspective has been composed (see "Hour 16, "Systems and Performance Management").

Meanwhile, highlights of this hour include

▶ Discovering system monitoring

▶ Introduction to the SAP System Log

▶ Introduction to SAP CCMS

▶ Reviewing basic authorization concepts

Monitoring the System

One of the tasks of the System Administrator is to perform general system maintenance on your SAP system. System monitoring designed to ensure the availability of SAP to its end users is the primary maintenance function. In the course of system monitoring, the System Administrator watches over a list of the active SAP *instances* and their services, looking to ensure that these resources are indeed "up" and available (see Figure 15.1); such fundamental oversight is performed by an SAP Basis Administrator. As you learned earlier, the term Basis is used by SAP AG to encompass management of SAP from a technical or technology-stack perspective.

You can view the SAP Servers System Monitoring screen following the menu path Tools, Administration, Monitor, System Monitoring, Servers, or by using transaction code /nSM51. This screen displays all available instances in your SAP system, including the core services (hosted by specialized *work processes*) provided by each instance—services earmarked for online users, batch jobs, performing database updates, and so on.

FIGURE 15.1
The monitoring
of your SAP sys-
tems is a task
performed by an
SAP System or
Basis
Administrator.

FIGURE 15.1
The monitoring
of your SAP sys-
tems is a task
performed by an
SAP System or
Basis
Administrator.

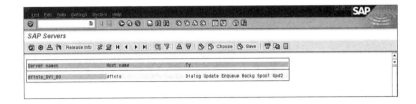

An **instance** is typically an administrative unit used to logically describe the set of SAP system components that together provide one or more services, for example, a "Production Instance" of SAP. An instance can also refer to the services provided by a single SAP server (for example, an SAP Application Server instance).

SAP System Log

SAP maintains a system log that records important events that occur in your SAP system. You can view the SAP System Log screen by executing transaction code /nSM21. The selection screen that appears—similar to the one shown in Figure 15.2—enables the System Administrator to sift through and select certain criteria from what can ultimately be a very large and very complex log of events and occurrences.

FIGURE 15.2
You can specify
certain system
criteria to be
displayed on
your system log
by using the
System Log:
Local Analysis
screen.

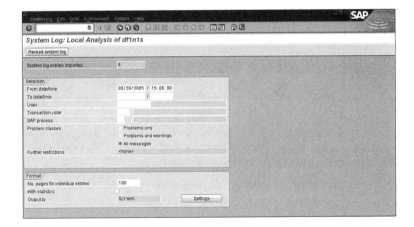

After the System Administrator identifies key search criteria such as dates, user IDs, and so on, the administrator then selects the Reread System Log button to generate the specified subset of the entire log. An abbreviated log like the one shown in Figure 15.3 is displayed.

System Monitoring with CCMS

SAP's Computing Center Management System (CCMS) is a built-in monitoring tool used for controlling, configuring, and managing SAP across much of the technology stack. This includes everything from the SAP application layer to the database, the underlying operating system, and even the servers, networks, and disk subsystems underpinning all of SAP. You can access the CCMS main screen by following the menu path Tools, CCMS (and in releases before R/3 4.6C, by using transaction code /nSRZL). CCMS covers a great deal; the following represent key capabilities of CCMS, relative to system administration:

- Systems management (called "Control/Monitoring")
- User/workload distribution and balancing (through "Configuration")
- Database administration
- Print management
- Background processing

You also use CCMS to monitor your installation. CCMS executes the SAP OS Collector, which collects basic performance and availability data via an SAP operating system service or daemon. You can then use CCMS to sort through and display this data, in text-based as well as graphic formats. Detailed information relative to the configuration and basic responsiveness of your SAP system can be displayed. Although traditionally limited to single instances, SAP CCMS has evolved over the last few years into a much broader and more capable systems-management tool—it serves as a key source of data for full-fledged systems management and other utilities, too, such as SAP Solution Manager, HP OpenView, BMC Patrol, and more. In this capacity, CCMS represents an ideal starting point to help you identify problems early on and characterize potential or existing performance bottlenecks. An example of an SAP CCMS monitoring screen is displayed in Figure 15.4.

FIGURE 15.4
CCMS can display and monitor the status of multiple SAP functions and parameters.

Workload Alert Monitor

Since SAP R/3 release 4.0B, CCMS has provided management-by-exception insight into the SAP technology stack through the use of the Alert Monitor. A capable and customizable tool, SAP's Alert Monitor features the following:

▶ Comprehensive, detailed status of any number of SAP systems, host interfaces, underlying database and OS layers, and more

▶ Easy-to-read color-coded status indicators (green, yellow, and red) for all your SAP components, interfaces, and so on

▶ Proactive alerts, based on whether the threshold of a particular status indicator has been exceeded

► Availability statistics useful in compiling and displaying reported alerts

► Alert tracking and management

I suggest you spend time getting comfortable with the CCMS Workload Alert Monitor—it is powerful, capable, and free (in the sense that it's paid for when you purchase your SAP license). To use this tool, follow the menu path Tools, CCMS, Control/Monitoring, Alert Monitor, or execute transaction code /nRZ20. A Workload Monitoring screen example appears in Figure 15.5.

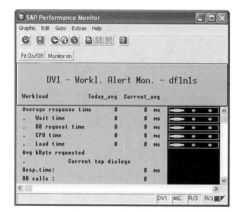

FIGURE 15.5
SAP CCMS provides a series of useful alert-driven graphical monitors and management utilities—the perfect starting point for the SAP System Administrator on a tight budget.

Other CCMS Tools

Many other monitoring tools prove useful in the day-to-day administration of an SAP system. At the high end is SAP's Solution Manager, a tool that among other things allows for cross-business-process monitoring (systems management encompassing multiple SAP and other systems tied together to execute complex business processes). However, SAP CCMS provides much in the way of administrative support as well. Run the following transaction codes to get a sense of the built-in management capabilities SAP offers:

► ST06, the Operating System Monitor, ideal for analyzing the performance of the entire SAP technology stack

► ST03N, the Workload Monitor, useful in drilling down into online and batch workloads, "top 40" transactions, peak workload details, and more executed over a particular time period

► SSAA, useful in conducting routine daily, weekly, and monthly systems-administration functions

▶ SMLG, to monitor how well SAP's logon load balancing is performing; use F5 to drill down into group-specific performance data

▶ AL08, useful in reviewing the end users logged into particular SAP application servers (and the transactions they are executing)

▶ ST07, useful in reviewing end users logged into the entire system, sorted by functional areas (such as SAP ECC FI, MM, PM, PS, SD, and so on)

▶ SM66, ideal for looking at system-wide performance relative to processes executing on every application and batch server within an SAP system

▶ ST22, to review ABAP dumps and therefore identify program errors (to aid in escalating such issues to the responsible programming team)

SAP Authorization Concepts

Although a detailed treatise on SAP security is out of the scope of the book, it would be unfair to not include a brief discussion on SAP authorizations and the role they play in securing your data. The data stored in SAP needs to be secure not only from outside intrusion, but also from within your end user organizations as well. Assume that your company has implemented SAP ECC Materials Management and Human Resources; you would not want individuals from your Materials Management department accessing confidential HR data, nor would you like to see HR employees mucking around in your warehouses. SAP uses the concept of "authorizations" to control access to data, based on logical relationships between user IDs and focused SAP system authorization rules.

User Authorizations

SAP user authorizations are stored in the master record of each user. Users in theory might be assigned one or many authorizations, depending upon their role in an organization.

The **master record** is a data record containing the principal employment and authorization data on a user that usually remains unchanged, including the user's system authorizations, standard printer settings, and transaction settings.

The following represent a number of the fields that a user master record contains:

User name	Company address
Assigned client	User type
User password	Start menu

Logon language   Authorizations

Personal printer configuration   Expiration date

Time zone   Default parameter settings

Activity group

Authorization Profiles

To simplify the administration of authorizations, *authorization profiles* are established. Such profiles are assigned to specific SAP user IDs (previously established by the SAP System Administrator, and discussed in Hour 2, "SAP Basics"). Your user ID is your user name in the user master record. Your user ID refers exclusively to profiles when designating access privileges in SAP. In turn, these profiles grant a certain level of system access to the user. Examples of ECC Authorization Profiles are listed in Table 15.1.

TABLE 15.1 SAP ECC Authorization Profiles

Authorization	Abbreviated Authorization Description Profile Name
SAP_ALL	All authorizations
S_ABAP_ALL	All ABAP programming authorizations
S_ADMI_ALL	All system administration functions
SAP_NEW	All new authorization objects added during an R/3 upgrade for functions that already exist in your R/3 system
S_A.ADMIN	System operator authorization without configuration authorization
S_A.CUSTOMIZ	All customizing authorizations
S_A.DEVELOP	All development operations within the ABAP Workbench
S_A.DOKU	Authorizations for Technical Writers
S_A.SHOW	Basis administration display authorization only
S_A.SYSTEM	(SAP superuser) All authorizations for a System Administrator
S_A.USER	Basis authorizations for a Basis user
S_ADDR_ALL	Authorizations for address administration
S_ADMI_SAP	Basic administration authorization except spool administration
S_ADMI_SPO_A	All spool administrations
S_ADMI_SPO_D	All spool device administration
S_ADMI_SPO_E	All extended spool administration
S_ADMI_SPO_J	All spool job administration
S_ADMI_SPO_T	All spool device type administration

You should develop your SAP user profiles specific to the job functions performed by individuals in your organization. For example, Human Resources Administrative Clerks require access to the basic data-entry screens to enter and maintain new employees' personal data (like PZ02 and PZ10); however, they might not need access to your company's organizational chart and reporting structure. Defining user profiles based on the roles individuals play in your organization is the key. Along the same lines, flexibility in refining and adding authorizations to existing roles will save you much administration time in the long run as well. Use transactions /nSU56 and /nSU53 to review authorizations you currently have and to check authorizations you are missing, respectively.

> Your SAP system contains some preinstalled standard authorization profiles. Although these might seem like a fast solution for security configuration, it is not a good idea to try to mold your organization into these limited standards. Creating specific profiles based on your organization's structure will serve you much better in the long run. Be prepared, though—such work can consume a significant amount of time.

SAP Profile Generator

The Profile Generator (PG) was introduced in SAP R/3 3.1G to assist in the implementation of your company's application-layer security model. Based on the concepts of authorization objects, authorizations, and authorization profiles, the Profile Generator is still key today. Using the Profile Generator, the authorization profiles that you develop are not typically (but might be) assigned to individual users (an activity that all too often would consume the bulk of an administrator's time); instead, users are assigned to one or more roles (called activity groups in the earliest releases of PG), and these roles are then assigned authorizations. With the roles, you assign to your users the user menu that is displayed after they log on to the SAP System. Roles therefore reflect the authorizations needed by users to access and run their reports, transactions, and web-based applications.

Combined, all of your various roles that are set up in SAP should map back to the various departments and teams spread across your user base. Authorizations can naturally become very detailed and complex; certain users might require additional capabilities based on their specific job within a department, for instance. As you can imagine, manually setting up these roles is very time-consuming, and managing and updating them as your business needs evolve is equally time-consuming. It was precisely for this reason that SAP developed the Profile Generator. For more detailed information, refer to SAP's online help (http://help.sap.com) or one of the many excellent texts on security administration and support.

An **authorization object** is a logical entity used to group a number of related fields that require "authority checking" within the SAP system.

Summary

SAP system administration is central to maintaining a highly available and well-performing system. As such, system administration in the broadest sense cannot exist in a vacuum—it must be tied to tools and approaches that facilitate proactive maintenance and management by exception. SAP's very own CCMS represents an ideal starting point for such system administration. This type of work is often performed by Basis Administrators designated within your IT organization to manage and monitor SAP. These individuals are critical in holding and managing the responsibility that comes with maximizing system availability day-to-day.

This hour was designed to provide an overview of some of the system administration tools and techniques used to manage your SAP system from a technical perspective. As a regular SAP end user or programmer/developer, such material provides grounding in what it takes to administer SAP; however, it is unlikely that anyone but an administrator will use the material found in this hour day in and day out.

Q&A

Q *At what stage of an SAP implementation should security issues be discussed?*

A Issues involving the security of your SAP system should be considered throughout each stage of your implementation process. Identifying the structure and configuration of your SAP security is a serious task that should be addressed initially and throughout the project—significant manpower will likely be required to implement a well-thought-out authorizations/security plan.

Q *Should you use the Profile Generator instead of manually creating user profiles?*

A With regard to this question, the right answer is to use SAP's Profile Generator or a similar third-party tool. Manually creating and managing profiles and roles invites inconsistency, which ultimately invites security breaches. With your company data at stake, even a single potential security breach is one too many.

Workshop

This workshop is designed to help you anticipate possible questions, review what you've learned, and begin thinking ahead to putting your knowledge into practice. The answers to the quiz that follows can be found in Appendix A, "Quiz Answers."

Quiz

1. Name three items that a user master record contains.

2. What is the name of the profile that gives you authorization access to everything in the SAP system?

3. What is the name of the SAP tool that helps administrators create user profiles based on standards?

4. What does the acronym CCMS stand for?

5. What is the menu path to reach the SAP Servers System Monitoring Screen?

6. Define an SAP instance.

7. Where are user authorizations stored in your SAP system?

8. List additional CCMS transactions useful in monitoring SAP.

Exercises

1. Take a look at your own user profile by following the menu path Tools, Administration, User Maintenance, Users, and typing your user name, and then selecting the Display (glasses) button from the application toolbar. Then execute a transaction for which you are not authorized (most users are unable to execute CCMS transactions like SM51, and most SAP technologists are unable to execute application transactions like FD32 or VA01, for example). Finally, execute transaction /nSU53. This enables you to view the authorization(s) that you are missing—the authorization(s) you need to be able to complete the transaction you just executed unsuccessfully.

2. As described previously in this hour, execute and review transactions /nST06, /nST03N, /nSSAA, /nSMLG, /nAL08, /nST07, /nSM66, and /nST22.

3. Navigate to the SAP System Log (/nSM21) to view the important and not-so-important events that are occurring both real-time and historically in your SAP system.

Systems and Performance Management

In Hour 15, "System Administration, "you learned the basics around how to manage and monitor SAP using CCMS. This hour builds upon that foundation and takes systems and performance management to the next level, addressing capacity planning and proactive performance tuning in the process. As such, this is one of the more technical chapters in the book, geared toward System Administrators as well as those tasked with deploying and maintaining a well-performing SAP system.

Highlights of this hour include

▶ Discovering useful management-oriented CCMS transactions

▶ Discovering useful performance-oriented CCMS transactions

▶ Identifying capacity planning methods and practices

What Is Performance Management?

No matter how much time you spend architecting and deploying an SAP system, in a matter of months you'll be revisiting system performance. Why? Because SAP systems, by their very nature, are not static. Operating systems and SAP kernels need to be patched. Hardware requires various firmware updates to improve stability or support new options. Databases are tweaked for improved performance as their various tables and other structures grow under the weight of daily transaction loads. SAP also changes as application-specific support packages, patches, and a host of functional and technical updates are applied in response to changing business requirements. In all this, the very foundation of the platform carefully constructed and tested prior to Go-Live changes; attention to performance management under the umbrella of systems management helps return balance.

Benefits of Performance Management

Too often, systems management is never fully addressed in the midst of an implementation. Many IT organizations supporting SAP spend hundreds of thousands of dollars on hardware, millions of dollars on database and SAP licenses, and then skimp in the one area that can save them more money in the long run than most anything else—proactive systems management geared toward performance optimization and intelligent capacity planning. Performance management

▶ Extends the life of the current technology stack.

▶ Assists in identifying pending performance bottlenecks, helping to justify when and to what extent an investment is required to stave off performance-robbing problems.

▶ Enables predictive capacity planning, helping an IT organization plan for potentially large capital outlays.

▶ Helps minimize IT headcount requirements.

Otherwise, the business suffers while IT gets its arms around performance issues. And without the luxury of shopping around for the best fit or best deal, a company might pay too much money too quickly in an effort to bandage performance problems. Finally, money not invested in tools instead grows to larger sums necessary to fund supplemental staff, expensive consultants, and even additional full-time Basis personnel, Technology consultants, and other Systems Administrators and resources.

Thus, without the economies of scale that performance management brings to the IT table, any innate growth in the number of SAP instances or servers necessary to support the business results in the need for incremental and usually expensive IT people.

SAP Performance Management is not a tool per se, but rather a proactive approach to monitoring and managing the performance of the individual and collective subsystems that make up an SAP solution—the hardware, OS, database, and SAP applications, along with third-party bolt-on systems that, combined, solve business problems.

Systems Management and Component-Level Tuning

Although systems management is intended to guide and direct performance tuning and capacity planning of your production system, it makes sense to engage in a certain level of *pretuning* as well. This involves testing and tweaking the individual technology stack layers such that they operate well in a "standalone" manner, to be later optimized together to reflect the prescribed balance of performance, availability, scalability, and so on. That is, after the hardware, operating system, and other technology stack layers are optimized, you can then more easily optimize the entire technology stack. This enables you to carefully build a cohesive well-performing solution of integrated components and technologies.

Testing the individual components or layers in your particular SAP solution stack is also often referred to as component-level or technology stack layer testing. Such testing saves you countless time and energy down the road as you apply the insight you gain to your performance tuning efforts. A number of reasons for component-level testing followed by performance tuning include

- ▶ To establish a baseline for individual component-level system performance today, to be measured every so often as you upgrade or change out these components.

- ▶ To understand where performance bottlenecks might lie in the future.

- ▶ To begin the process of capacity planning, or planning for upgrades.

- ▶ To identify where future budget dollars might best be spent; where you get the most "bang for the buck" relative to system or component upgrades.

Sources of Performance Data

Performance data comes from many places, first and foremost from tools or utilities specifically designed to support a particular piece of technology. For example, all operating systems come with tools designed to help you understand the performance of the CPU, memory, and disk subsystems. Similar insight is available for most hardware components, too. For instance, the manufacturers of most servers and disk subsystems provide tools designed to help you tune and tweak their systems; it's in their best interests, after all, for their gear to work well.

Automatically Collected OS-Acquired Performance Data

Tools that dump real-time performance data into a log or other repository, and then enable you to sort and sift through this, are important in performance management. Microsoft PerfMon or the various Unix OS-based performance-tracking tools are all effective. I recommend automating data collection by setting up the tool to take a snapshot every five minutes or so (less often is fine for less busy systems, more often for critical systems or in support of workload testing). This kind of data becomes especially valuable when you find yourself needing to correlate hardware, OS, and even database performance trends against a specific workload or against specific SAP throughput metrics.

Performance data is also available from software that sits atop hardware and operating systems, discussed next.

Leveraging Your Database for Performance Data

All databases supported by SAP include tools or utilities designed to help manage and monitor the database's performance. Oracle and Microsoft both offer "administrator" tools. And oftentimes the vendors of these RDBMSs include OS-specific counters, services, or daemons designed to provide greater insight into performance. SQL Server includes a host of performance counters available through the Windows Operating System—these counters can be tracked over time, like other counters, via Microsoft's Performance Monitor, or PerfMon.

SAP Computing Center Management System

With so much performance data available covering the operating system, network, hardware, database, and SAP application layer, it's no wonder that SAP CCMS is the simplest, most effective tool for uncovering and analyzing performance data. CCMS ships with various SAP products, and is quite consistent across different SAP releases and platforms. Beyond its capability to easily collect SAP data real-time, it also makes much in the way of performance data available over the course of time. CCMS is jam-packed with transactional, user-specific, and other performance data. The trick is simply getting to it. More about CCMS is covered later in this hour.

Performance Testing Tools

If you employ a load-testing tool for baselining and managing performance, you can typically gain a great amount of insight from it. After all, even the most basic of test tools uncover a certain amount of performance data. The simplest tools provide "snapshot data," which provides real-time visibility into the performance of a system. The best tools capture this real-time data and record or log it in to a file to be analyzed later.

Robust load-testing tools—especially SAP-specific tools such as those provided by AutoTester, Compuware, Mercury, and Segue—provide access to both real-time data as well as to easy-to-analyze historical data.

Did you Know?

I especially like Segue's one-tool approach to load testing and system monitoring; they enable you to analyze real-time or historical performance data with their SilkPerformer tool itself, dump your performance data into a database of your choice (such as Oracle or Microsoft MSDE or SQL Server), or even dump it into an Excel spreadsheet for further analysis.

Specific CCMS Transactions for Managing Performance

Although many SAP CCMS transactions can prove useful in managing performance, a number of these I consider fundamental, including

- ST07 and AL08
- SMLG
- DB02 and ST04
- SM12 and SM13

- ST02
- ST03N and ST03G
- ST06
- SM50 and SM66

User and Application Server Distribution

From a user distribution perspective, it's important to monitor not only the number of online and active users, but also the mix of users. You can do this by executing /nST07 and /nAL08 every so often. The former provides visibility into how many users are logged in across an entire system—including all application servers. The numbers are further broken down by functional areas, making it easy to track the growth in SD users or change in the ratio of MM to FI users, for example. See Figure 16.1, keeping in mind that wonderful historical data is also available via /nST07.

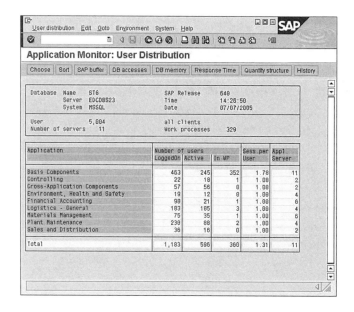

FIGURE 16.1
Transaction /nST07 provides visibility into both real-time and historical data relative to the mix of end users within various functional areas.

Transaction /nAL08 highlights similar information, in that the total number of logged-in end users are displayed. But /nAL08 divides users by logged-in application server, thus providing some insight into how balanced a system's application servers are. This transaction also reveals the individual transactions being executed by each end user, providing further insight into the kind of workload borne by a system in real-time. See Figure 16.2.

FIGURE 16.2
Transaction /nAL08 also provides visibility into the number of end users logged in to the system, although broken down by application server.

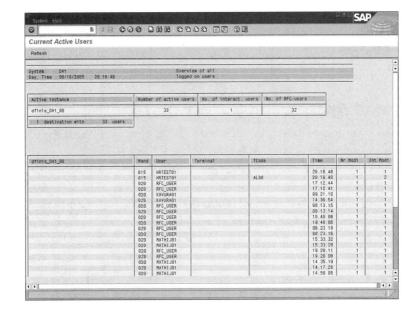

Managing Logon Load Balancing

Use transaction /nSMLG to review how well your particular logon load-balancing scheme is working. This transaction is not only used to set up logon groups, but also to monitor performance of each logon group. From the main SMLG screen, press F5 to view response-time statistics germane to each logon group, as seen in Figure 16.3.

Database Overview and Performance

SAP databases all grow over time, as users add new transactional data in the course of conducting their day-to-day business. This database growth eventually impacts performance, because table scans take longer and longer, indexes grow less effective with each new row of data added, and so on. Thus, tracking how quickly a database grows over time is very important. In the same way, tracking the number of indexes over time can provide insight into proactive tuning requirements. Both of these needs can be met with transaction /nDB02—it provides a summary of both data and indexes, and how they add up in terms of size, quantity, and historical growth. I like to track growth day-over-day, week-over-week, and especially month-over month (via the Database System *space statistics* button), as seen in Figure 16.4.

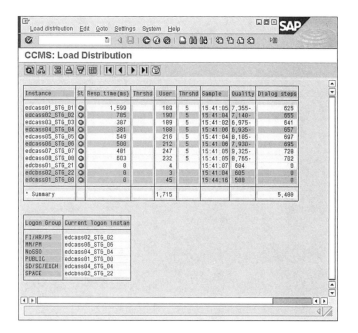

FIGURE 16.3
Transaction /nSMLG complements /nAL08 in that it shows the number of users logged in. SMLG provides the added benefit of displaying response times for each logon group, too.

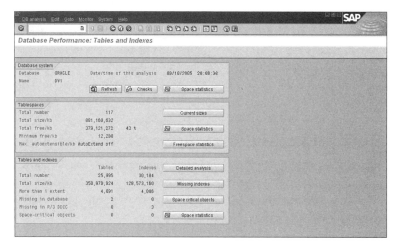

FIGURE 16.4
Use /nDB02 to track database growth month-over-month.

Although DB02 is very useful, it does not provide performance data per se. This is where transaction /nST04 comes into play. Called the "Database Performance Analysis" transaction, it affords real-time insight into cache hit-rate values, logical reads versus physical, critical "Buffer Busy Waits" values, and much more. See Figure 16.5.

FIGURE 16.5
The Database Performance Analysis transaction /nST04 provides very detailed real-time insight into SAP database performance.

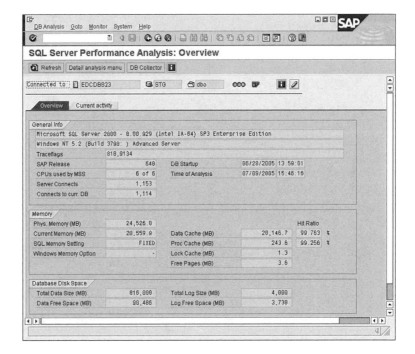

Note that these real-time statistics can be reset to determine the impact that a recent change has on database performance. Through the use of the Detail Analysis Menu, as seen in Figure 16.6, you can drill down into overall activity, exception events, resource consumption based on specific SQL requests or table accesses, and much more historical data.

Updates, Locks, and Disk Subsystem Performance

Understanding how well updates are applied or "committed" to the database, and whether lock entries are holding things up, can be accomplished by reviewing /nSM12 (Database Lock Entries; see Figure 16.7) and /nSM13 (Administer Update Records; see Figure 16.8).

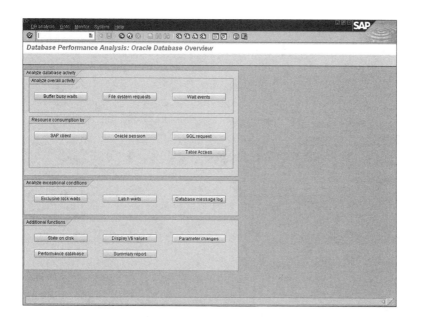

FIGURE 16.6
ST04's Detail Analysis Menu opens the door to detailed historical analysis.

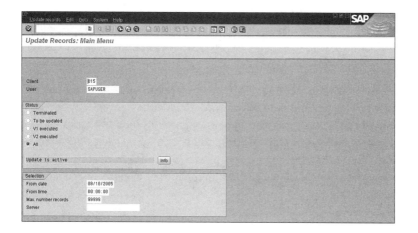

FIGURE 16.7
Use /nSM12 to review database lock entries related to a particular database table, user, or client.

FIGURE 16.8
Use /nSM13 to track and monitor database updates realtime.

Memory Management and the Tune Summary

The Tune Summary (or as I prefer to call it, "the red swap screen") provides real-time visibility into how well each SAP application server's memory and many buffers are performing. Buffers that are improperly configured or simply not optimal for a given load quickly mount up larger and larger values displayed in the Swaps column, highlighted in red to easily identify problem areas. See Figure 16.9.

FIGURE 16.9
The Tune Summary /nST02 helps you manage poorly performing application server buffers.

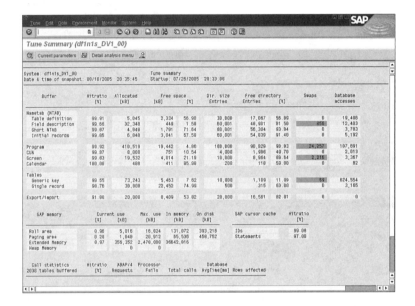

ST02 is not only for buffer management, though. Use it to help you track memory use per each application server. Pay particular attention to current percent of extended memory used (compared to peak). In the same way, verify often that the use of heap memory is minimized.

Heap memory is work process–specific. When a program uses a work process's shared memory, it must turn to privately maintained memory—PRIV mode. At this point, the executing program cannot be swapped to another work process, in effect tying up the work process until the program is finished executing. After the program is finished, the system restarts the work process, so that things return to normal (where programs can again be swapped in and out of memory as required, based on the needs of the SAP system).

Response Time and Workload Performance

Monitoring your unique workload is one of the most important components of performance management. Execute the Workload Monitor by running /nST03 or /nST03N. This enables you to display your workload in total, or broken down by dialog, batch, update, or other task-types. From each type, click the Transaction Profile button and then sort the results by *response time*. Here, you can analyze your top transactions—the programs that consume the most database time (DB Request Time), CPU time, and other core components of response time. You can also look at aggregate totals over various periods of time, from 15 minutes to a month's worth of data at a time. It's also common to view and track the total number of dialog steps processed each day, broken down hour-by-hour so as to get a feel for how each hour in a day holds up when it comes to workload (see Figure 16.10).

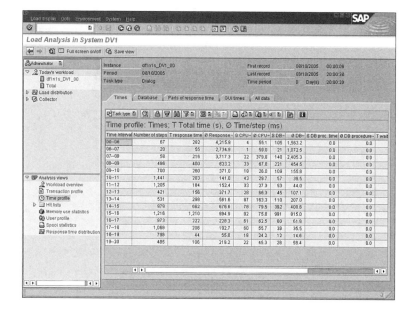

FIGURE 16.10
Using /nST03N, it's an easy matter to identify peak dialog steps executed per hour within the course of a day.

In addition, ST03N also makes it easy to track the number and ratio of direct reads, sequential reads, and changes (database updates or commits). The average number of bytes requested per transaction is also available. This makes it easy to characterize the disk load a particular system is currently supporting.

Beyond pure response time metrics, the Time Profile and Transaction Profile buttons available from ST03 enable you to quantify a system's load over a particular time period, or based on a particular work load—the most popular (top) transactions responsible for placing the greatest load on a certain hardware component are easily identified in this way as well.

Finally, ST03G gives you the capability to view and analyze the load associated with external systems, as well as the capability to analyze the performance of systems underpinning business processes that span multiple systems. It's a powerful addition to ST03. For SAP IT organizations responsible for multiple systems, ST03G has no equal.

The OS Monitor

The OS Monitor, /nST06, is another SAP transaction that displays much in the way of real-time performance data. This includes CPU utilization broken down by user, system, and idle time, the number of processes queued up in front of the CPU (called *CPU load count*), and memory/swap statistics.

The OS Monitor also allows for wonderful if not somewhat short-term historical analysis, too; click the Detail Analysis Menu to access a host of historical data divided by major hardware subsystems as well as by application server (see Figure 16.11).

FIGURE 16.11
The OS Monitor, as ST06 is known, provides both real-time performance snapshots as well as access to historical data.

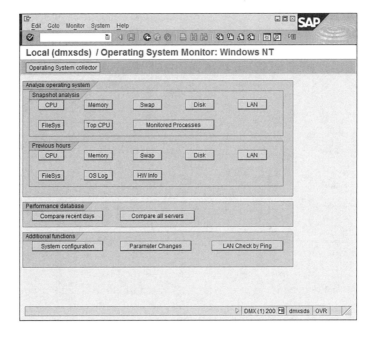

With this historical data, you can correlate disk performance metrics you have gathered at the OS and database levels with that seen by SAP. In the same way, the capability to review hourly CPU load over the last 24 hours makes it easy to not only identify peak times but also to monitor and analyze CPU performance relative to throughput (such as the number of dialog steps processed in a particular time period, as seen via /nST03N, discussed previously). In the same way, the hooks into the SAP performance database make it easy to launch additional server-wide or server-specific analyses from the OS Monitor. You can then compare and correlate these numbers to the results you glean from hardware- and OS-based performance tools.

Monitoring Active Work Processes

SM50 and SM66 are both useful in viewing the activity of work processes in the system. SM50 displays all work processes configured for a particular application server (the one you are currently logged in to, actually), whereas SM66 shows all active work processes across *all* application servers (see Figure 16.12). Transaction /nSM66 is particularly useful when it comes to correlating the number of active users or dialog steps processed for a particular server platform; presumably, the faster the platform, the fewer active work processes in any given time.

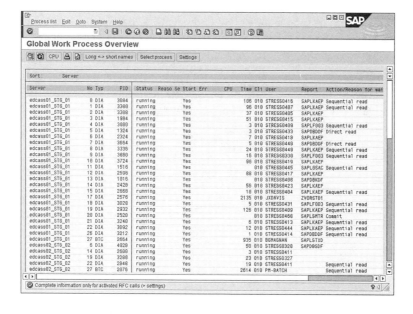

FIGURE 16.12
With SM66, you can view a system's end-to-end work process activity.

Analyzing Performance Data

Whether you use a single tool like SAP CCMS, or multiple performance management tools, all your performance data needs to be brought together and rationalized to be useful. My tool of choice is Microsoft Excel—it's easy to use, widely available, and is quite capable. Excel lets you convert data to and from many diverse formats, from text-based files to comma-delimited files, and more.

Loading Raw SAP GUI Output Into Excel

Capturing SAP GUI screen contents and saving them to a file varies between transactions. Some transactions, such as the Workload screen in /nSTAD, give you the capability to save the screen's contents to any number of file formats simply by clicking the Download button. In this way, unconverted (text), spreadsheet, rich text format (.RTF), and HTML format are all at your disposal instantly.

Many other transactions do not include a Download button, though. Fortunately, the SAP GUI gives you the capability to save *list-based* output easily, using %pc in the command line. Try it. Run transaction /nST07, /nAL08, /nST04, or any other transaction that generates a list. Then, to save this list-based output to a local file on your computer, simply type **%pc** on the command line and press Enter (see Figure 16.13). A window similar to the one you see in STAD after pressing the Download button pops up, defaulting to saving the screen's contents in an unconverted or XLS file format (depending on the component and release version). Choose the spreadsheet format (or any of the others as desired, keeping in mind that the XLS format is surprisingly the most compact one of all), press Enter, browse to the desired directory path, type the name of the output file you want to create, and then press the Save button to save the data to the filename you specified. It's that easy.

FIGURE 16.13
Use %pc to save
a SAP GUI's list-
based output in
a number of dif-
ferent file for-
mats on your
local computer
or file share.

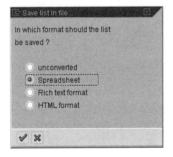

One-Stop Performance Management and Analysis Tools

Outside of Microsoft's Excel and the various SAP-aware test tools, a number of other tools are available for analyzing performance data. Vendors like Hewlett-Packard offer SAP-specific snap-ins to HP OpenView, for instance, which not only augment SAP CCMS but enable you to holistically view and manage a distributed and diverse SAP solution. With HP's technology-stack-specific software agents called

SPIs (pronounced "spies"), OpenView enables you to customize how you view performance data—by system, by instance, by business process, and so on. And by including additional SPIs, you can basically drill down as far as you want, gaining more insight into your SAP system's database, operating system, and hardware components through DB-, OS-, and HW-specific SPIs.

Other hardware and software vendors offer similar approaches, although some vary considerably when it comes to capabilities. You are probably familiar with names like BMC Software, Computer Associates, IBM, Microsoft, and NetIQ. Each of these companies offers SAP-aware performance-management suites designed to make managing SAP performance easier.

Summary

Performance management is a subset of what is broadly termed systems management. Performance management allows for intelligent capacity planning and helps an IT organization provide consistent service to its end users. In summary, with millions of dollars of budget money, tens of thousands of employee-hours invested, and your core business processes at stake, an SAP deployment or upgrade is not complete without proactive and predictive performance management.

Q&A

Q *What is capacity planning?*

A Analyzing a system with an eye toward identifying which subsystems are beginning to show signs of stress under load before the system itself fails to meet the needs of its business users.

Q *How does performance management differ from systems management?*

A Performance management is a subset of systems management, geared toward understanding and maximizing performance, whereas systems management seeks to balance performance and availability, scalability, security, and so on.

Q *Why is the SAP Workload Monitor, ST03 (ST03N), so valuable?*

A Transaction /nST03 shows workload statistics for a period of time, or broken down by a particular workload type (like online dialog steps, batch load, print load, RFC-based load, and more).

Q *Can one tool take care of a system's performance management needs?*

A Although enterprise management suites like HP OpenView, Microsoft Operations Manager, and BMC Patrol provide end-to-end insight into an SAP system, oftentimes a *set* of hardware, OS, and database-specific utilities are called for. Additionally, SAP-aware testing and performance characterization tools like Segue's SilkPerformer can make a huge difference in how well an organization tracks performance over time.

Workshop

The workshop is designed to help you anticipate possible questions, review what you've learned, and begin thinking ahead to putting your knowledge into practice. The answers to the quiz that follows can be found in Appendix A, "Quiz Answers."

Quiz

1. Which transaction enables you to view workload statistics collected over time?

2. What is the transaction code to see active users grouped by application server?

3. What is the transaction code to see active users grouped by functional areas?

4. What is the benefit of ST03G over ST03N?

5. Which transaction is used to validate how well your particular logon load-balancing scheme is working?

6. List two transactions that are useful in displaying work processes, and why each is useful.

Exercises

1. Using transaction ST07, determine the number of dialog steps processed over the last day, broken down by functional area.

2. Visit each company's main web page to search for and review the SAP load testing and performance optimization tools available from software companies such as AutoTester, Compuware, Mercury Interactive, and Segue.

3. Using transaction ST04, determine the mix of reads to writes in your SAP system.

ABAP Dictionary and Repository

In Hour 3, "Database Basics," you learned all about databases and how multiple tables store data that is related to data in other tables, making for a large relational database management system (RDBMS). In this hour, I take it a step further and show you the way in which SAP's database tables are arranged, followed by a closer look at SAP's Repository Information System or *repository*, which is a tool used in retrieving information relative to the objects in your SAP ABAP/4 Dictionary. I will discuss the features and functions of the Repository Information System, and you will learn why it is a useful tool in searching for information in your ABAP/4 Dictionary.

Highlights of this hour include

▶ A review of database structures, data elements, and domains

▶ A closer look at some of SAP's tables

▶ A review of ABAP Dictionary technical tricks and tips

▶ An overview of the basics of the Repository Information System

▶ Distinguishing the difference between Programming and Environment objects

Database Tables

The SAP Dictionary contains four types of tables (or structures): clusters, transparent, pooled, and internal tables, discussed next.

Pooled Tables

Pooled tables are a construct unique to SAP. They appear as separate distinguishable tables in SAP, but in fact they are really one colossal table. Pooled tables contain a one-to-many relationship with other tables in the database. An example of a one-to-many relationship is illustrated in Figure 17.1.

A *one-to-many* relationship between database tables means that a record in table A can have many matching records in table B, but a record in table B has only one matching record in table A.

FIGURE 17.1
In the ABAP
Dictionary,
pooled tables
reflect a one-to-
many database
relationship.

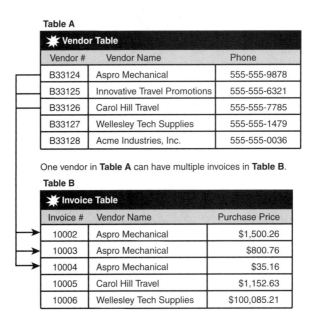

Table A

✳ Vendor Table		
Vendor #	Vendor Name	Phone
B33124	Aspro Mechanical	555-555-9878
B33125	Innovative Travel Promotions	555-555-6321
B33126	Carol Hill Travel	555-555-7785
B33127	Wellesley Tech Supplies	555-555-1479
B33128	Acme Industries, Inc.	555-555-0036

One vendor in **Table A** can have multiple invoices in **Table B**.

Table B

✳ Invoice Table		
Invoice #	Vendor Name	Purchase Price
10002	Aspro Mechanical	$1,500.26
10003	Aspro Mechanical	$800.76
10004	Aspro Mechanical	$35.16
10005	Carol Hill Travel	$1,152.63
10006	Wellesley Tech Supplies	$100,085.21

The term one-to-many with regard to pooled tables refers to the actual tables themselves. Just like in the preceding example in which the Vendor Name is the unique identifier, with pooled tables, the table name is the unique identifier. When you take a look at a pooled table in SAP, you will see a description of a table—but behind-the-scenes, so to speak, it is really stored along with other pooled tables as part of a *table pool*.

Cluster Tables

SAP cluster tables are a holdover from old versions of SAP R/3 and are similar to pooled tables in that they are also based on a one-to-many relationship with other tables in the database. Like pooled tables, many cluster tables are stored together in a larger table called a *table cluster*.

By the Way

Although the distinction between cluster and pooled tables can get quite technical, a major difference is that table pools hold a large number of tables, whereas table clusters hold only a handful.

Internal Tables

Internal tables are an interesting concept in SAP. They are structures that have defined fields yet do not store any long-term data. Instead, they are used only during the execution of a program. A simple way to define internal tables is to say that they are temporary storage holders of data during program execution and processing.

Transparent Tables

As explained previously, pooled tables and table clusters contain a one-to-many relationship with other tables in the database. A transparent table, on the other hand, represents a one-to-one relationship with a table in the database. An example of a one-to-one relationship is illustrated in Figure 17.2.

A *one-to-one* relationship between database tables means that every record in table A must have only *one* matching record in table B.

Table A

✹ Vendor Table		
Vendor #	Vendor Name	Phone
B33124	Aspro Mechanical	555-555-9878
B33125	Innovative Travel Promotions	555-555-6321
B33126	Carol Hill Travel	555-555-7785
B33127	Wellesley Tech Supplies	555-555-1479
B33128	Acme Industries, Inc.	555-555-0036

Every vendor in **Table A** can have only one address in **Table B**.

Table B

✹ Vendor AddressTable		
Vendor #	Vendor Address	Vendor City
B33124	111 Skillman Avenue	Brooklyn
B33125	30 Clearwater Ave	New Windsor
B33126	1400 Pearllink Drive Apt 5B	Friendly
B33127	2 Christopher Street	Maine
B33128	11793 Parkman Court	Wantagh

FIGURE 17.2
In the ABAP Dictionary, transparent tables reflect a one-to-one database relationship.

The term one-to-one relationship with regard to transparent tables, like pooled tables, refers to the actual tables themselves. Transparent tables, the database table, and fields therefore contain the same names as the SAP table definition.

Table Components

The basic elements for defining data in the Data Dictionary are

- ▶ Fields
- ▶ Data elements
- ▶ Domains

The three table elements contained in the ABAP Dictionary are outlined in Figure 17.3.

FIGURE 17.3
ABAP Dictionary
tables reflect a
relationship
between fields,
data elements,
and domains.

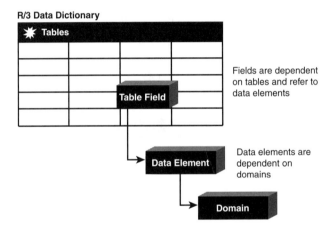

Database Fields

Step back for one minute to review exactly what a database field is. The database field is the column that stores data. If you have a table storing name and address information, the fields are name, address, and phone number. Now, depending on the data that you store in each field (whether they are text or numbers, for example), the fields require different formats—numeric, text, and so on. That's where data elements and domains come in.

Data Elements

SAP data elements contain the descriptive field labels and online documentation for a database field. Fields contain data elements, and in turn all data elements contain domains.

The data element description you provide for your field is displayed on any screens that show your field; see the example in Figure 17.4.

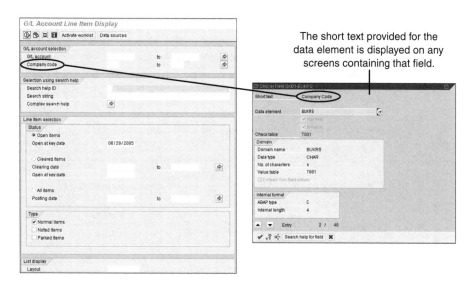

FIGURE 17.4
The data element contains the field labels for the field.

The short text provided for the data element is displayed on any screens containing that field.

Domains

A *domain* is an ABAP dictionary data object that describes the technical attributes of a table field, including the type, length, format, and values stored. For example, if you have a database field that contains employee salaries, the domain would specify that the field is of the type called currency and that it contains two decimal places.

Multiple fields can use the same domain. The domain I just described to store an employee's salary is also sufficient to store any currency value in your system that contains two decimal places. For example, this domain can also be used for Invoice and Purchase Order Amount fields.

Structures and Includes in the ABAP Dictionary

In addition to the different table types described earlier in the section "Database Tables," the ABAP Dictionary houses objects called *structures* and *includes*. Like tables, these objects globally define the structure of data used for the processing of programs or for transferring data between programs.

Structures

A *structure* is a group of internal fields that logically belong together. Whereas data in tables is stored on the database, structures only contain data that are grouped together for a specific purpose temporarily during program runtime. A structure is like a table in the ABAP Dictionary. It can be accessed from ABAP programs, but does not have a corresponding object in the database. Structures are commonly used in ABAP programming and follow the same naming conventions as transparent tables.

Watch
Out!

> You cannot have a table and a structure with the same name defined in your ABAP Dictionary.

Three main differences between ABAP Dictionary tables and structures are as follows:

▶ Structures do not contain a primary key.

▶ Structures do not contain any technical attributes.

▶ A structure does not have an associated database table.

Includes

Another component in the ABAP Dictionary is called an *include*. An SAP database structure can contain another structure, each nesting within one another to create larger structures. This nesting of structures eliminates redundancy and improves maintenance. If the same include is used in multiple structures, you need to change it only one time in order for that change to be effective in all structures that contain the include. Many of SAP's tables and structures contain includes because they are an ideal way to add fields, or a structure of fields, to a database table so that they are included into the table or structure definitions, without having to manually add these fields.

Exploring the ABAP Dictionary

You can access SAP's ABAP Dictionary main screen by following the menu path Tools, ABAP Workbench and then selecting the Dictionary button from the application toolbar. You can also access the ABAP Dictionary by using the transaction code /nSE11. The main screen is similar to the one shown in Figure 17.5.

The ABAP Dictionary is generally an area that only developers and other technical folks dive into. A review of the basics of the ABAP Dictionary might be helpful here, however. To get started, look at an actual SAP table. Navigate to the ABAP Dictionary main screen like the one shown previously in Figure 17.5. Type the

Database table name SFLIGHT and select the Display button. Your screen should appear similar to the one shown in Figure 17.6.

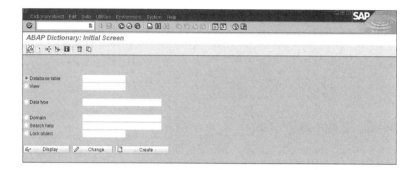

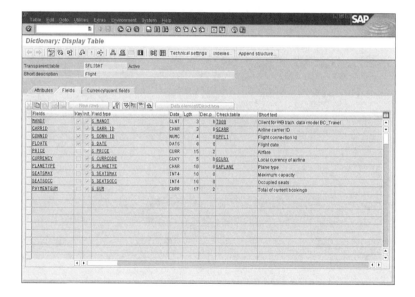

> The SFLIGHT table is a test table delivered with your SAP system that contains data for learning and testing purposes only; manipulating it will not affect the performance of your SAP system.

By the Way

You are viewing this table in Display Only mode. In this view, you are not permitted to make any changes; fields shaded with a gray background indicate that they are Display Only. If from the ABAP Dictionary main screen, you typed a table name and instead selected the Change button (assuming modifications to the table were permitted), the screen would not appear gray and shaded—you would be in Change mode.

From this screen's Fields tab, you can see

▶ Table name and type   ▶ Data type

▶ Short table description   ▶ Field length

▶ Field names   ▶ Check tables

▶ Key   ▶ Short text field descriptions

▶ Field type for each field

ABAP Dictionary Data Browser

The ABAP Dictionary contains a General Table Display function that allows you to view the actual data in the tables. To access the General Table Display function, execute transaction code /nSE16. The initial screen of the Data Browser appears similar to the one shown in Figure 17.7.

FIGURE 17.7
The Data Browser allows you to view the contents of your ABAP Dictionary tables.

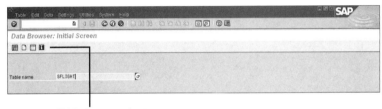

Display Table Contents button

From this view, you can take a look at the data in your tables. Navigate to the General Table Display screen, type your SFLIGHT table name, and select the Display Table Contents button (as previously viewed in Figure 17.7) from the application toolbar.

After selecting the Display Table Contents button, you are presented with a Data Browser: Table SFLIGHT Selection Screen like the one shown in Figure 17.8.

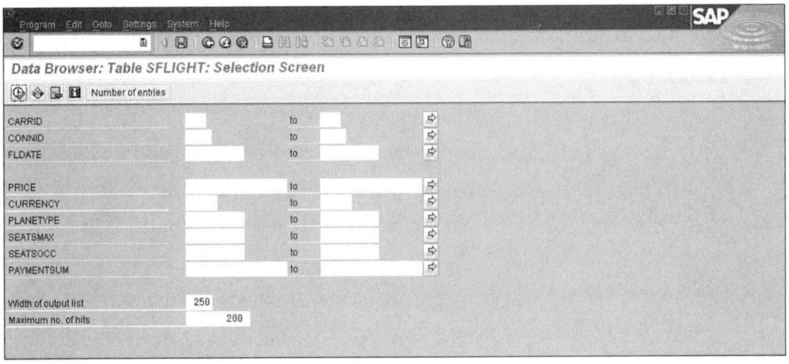

FIGURE 17.8
A selection screen appears after the execution of most SAP programs.

Selection Screens

The concept of selection screens is an important one for most SAP components. Irrespective of the R/3 module you are processing in, for example, you will be presented with SAP selection screens. Selection screens provide the opportunity to specify certain criteria. By way of example, look again at the SFLIGHT table. The selection screen gives you a chance to specify more precisely the data you want to view from the SFLIGHT table.

The first thing you will notice about the selection screen is that it contains all the fields that your table contains (with the exception of the MANDT field). First, take a look at the table without any special criteria defined. Do not fill in any fields on your selection screen and select the execute button (green check mark with the clock) from the application toolbar.

If you are not sure if the button you want to select is the correct one, place your cursor just under the button and simply hover over the button; do not click it. The description of its function, along with any keyboard shortcuts, appears.

By the Way

In this view, you can view all the records in the SFLIGHT table (see Figure 17.9).

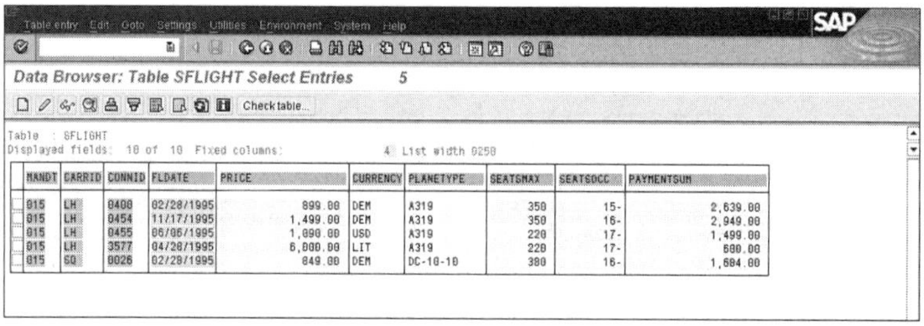

FIGURE 17.9
Table SFLIGHT output appears in a colored list format.

In this example, the SFLIGHT table contains five records (yours might contain a different number of records). Take a look at the FLDATE (flight date) column. It should appear similar to the one in Figure 17.9.

You learned that you can use the SFLIGHT selection screen to specify what database records you want to see, so give it a try. For example, to view data-specific records, use your green back arrow from the menu bar to return to the selection screen, which should appear like the one shown in Figure 17.8. This time, place your cursor inside the FLDATE field and enter the date. Keep in mind you can also select the Possible Entries Help button in the FLDATE field to access the calendar control, where you can use your mouse to select the date instead of typing it.

After typing your criteria, select the Execute button from the application toolbar to yield a set of search results that only displays the records you have specified on your selection screen (see Figure 17.10).

FIGURE 17.10
Selection
screens are a
useful way to
specify output
criteria in SAP.

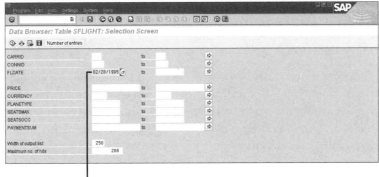

Fill in your selection criteria on the selection screen.

The selection screen is a great tool for helping you to pinpoint data. Note that you can also specify a *range* of values to be included in your output. For example, you can specify a date range, price range, plane type range, and so on.

You can practice using selection screens by viewing or changing the SAP predelivered test tables: SFLIGHT, SBOOK, and SPFLI.

By the
Way

> If for some reason your system does not contain the test tables, you can perform these exercises on real tables (like LFA1, for example). And, of course, always be careful when working with real SAP objects—obtain permission from your System Administrator before making *any* changes or modifications.

Client Dependence and Independence

As you know, your SAP system can have multiple legal entities or environments in which you can store data, called *clients*. Clients contain separate master records and their own set of tables, and reference tables shared across clients as well. Thus, some tables are client-specific, whereas other tables can be "seen" by all clients.

Client-Independent Data

Some tables in your system—for example, tables that store SAP error codes and messages—are the same in all your SAP clients. The data in these types of tables is the same regardless of the client you happen to be logged into. These types of tables are called *client-independent tables*.

Client-Dependent Data

Many of the tables that store your master data and your configuration data are unique to each client. For example, your test client might contain fictional vendors and purchase orders in your Vendor Master table (LFA1), whereby your real production client would store your actual data. Data that is specific to a particular client is called *client-dependent data*.

SAP database tables that are client-dependent always contain a MANDT field (abbreviated for *mandant*, the German word for "client"). The MANDT field stores the client number that the data is specific to. When you took a look at the SFLIGHT table through the ABAP Dictionary view back in Figure 17.6, the first field was a MANDT field indicating that the SFLIGHT table stores client-dependent data.

What Table and Field Is This Stored In?

In some situations, you might want to know where data that appears on your screen is stored in the database. This is easy to do. For an example, navigate to the Logistics, Batch Analysis Selection screen using the transaction code /nMCBR. Place your cursor in the Storage Location field and select the F1 key on your keyboard. This launches the selection-sensitive help (covered in Hour 23, "Support Overview") and typically provides a definition of the active field. On this dialog box, there is a button for Technical info (see Figure 17.11).

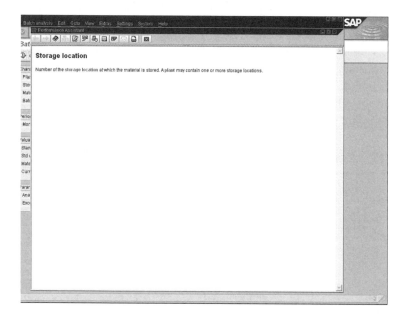

FIGURE 17.11
SAP field-specific help can be obtained on almost any SAP field by pressing F1.

Select the technical info box to bring up a Technical Information window like the one shown in Figure 17.12. This Technical Information window contains the table name and field name of the selected field.

FIGURE 17.12
The Technical Information window is available for most SAP fields.

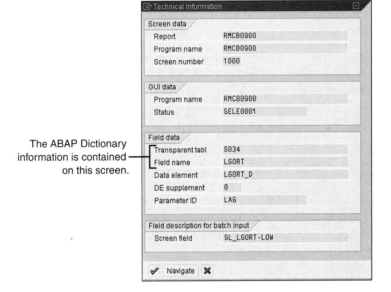

The ABAP Dictionary information is contained on this screen.

SAP Repository Information System

With the ABAP Dictionary behind you, I want to focus your attention now on the Repository Information System, or simply the Repository. The Repository is used as a tool to search for objects in the database—objects such as tables, views, fields, and domains. You access the Repository from the ABAP Workbench by executing transaction code /nSE84. The initial screen of the Repository Information System is shown in Figure 17.13.

FIGURE 17.13
Use the Repository Information System to search for objects in the SAP system.

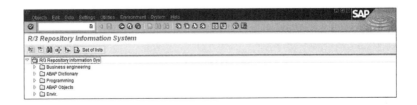

The main function of the Repository is to serve as a comprehensive cross-reference tool that enables a system developer to research SAP's development objects. In simpler terms, it serves as a technical encyclopedia for developers. As such, this tool is primarily used by your technical team to make requests like the following:

▶ **Search by an object's attributes**—For example, show me a list of objects that contain A but not B.

▶ **Research relationships between tables**—For example, show me the foreign key and check tables for table A.

▶ **Data review**—For example, show me all the data records in Table A that have attribute B.

▶ **Modified objects**—For example, show me all objects modified by user John Turner since last Thursday.

▶ **Where-used lists**—For example, show me all objects of type A that use objects of type B, or show me all ABAP programs that use Table A.

Like many SAP screens, the data presented appears in a tree structure. Use the menu path Edit, Expand Node to view what's available in the compressed tree structure. Your screen should appear similar to the one shown in Figure 17.14.

FIGURE 17.14
The expanded view of the Repository Information System screen shows each of the available nodes.

When expanded, the Repository Information System displays a hierarchical list of all the types of objects in your SAP system. The list varies depending on the version and release of the SAP product. Recent versions of SAP R/3 provide four or five cate-gories that reflect various available objects, a number of which are discussed next.

Modeling Objects

Modeling objects include the following three main subcategories:

▶ Data modeling

▶ Process modeling

▶ Business object browser

These subcategories can be further broken down. Data modeling includes data mod-els, entity types, and entity type attributes. Process modeling can be divided into application components, processes/functions, and events. And the business object browser encompasses business object types, business object attributes, business object methods, and business object events.

ABAP Dictionary Objects

ABAP Dictionary objects include those covered earlier in this hour, including

▶ Basic objects

▶ Other objects

▶ Fields

Basic objects include domains, data elements, structures, tables, views, and type groups. You should also recognize some of the objects contained under the other objects subcategory, including search helps, matchcode objects, matchcode IDs, lock objects, table indexes, and pooled/cluster tables.

By the
Way

> The final two object types available via the Repository require a bit deeper techni-cal explanations than the first two. Programming and environment objects are mentioned only to be thorough, and in case a developer uses this book as a basic programming reference. Do not be scared away by the technical lingo, nor worry about understanding most of it, though; it will be over shortly.

Programming Objects

Programming objects are not as familiar to nondevelopers. Object subcategories under the programming objects division include

▶ Function Builder

▶ Programming environment

▶ Program Library

▶ Program subobjects

The Function Builder subcategory contains your function groups and modules. The Program Library is a source for your programs, includes, dialog modules, and logical databases.

The programming environment subcategory contains message classes and numbers, SET/GET parameters, transactions, and area menus. Finally, program subobjects contain variants, global data and types, subroutines, PBO and PAI modules, macros, screens, and GUI status, title, and functions.

Environment Objects

The Environment objects contain the following four subcomponents:

▶ Development coordination

▶ Exit techniques

▶ Authorizations

▶ Automatic tests

The development coordination is composed of *change requests* and development classes, which are a group of logically related development objects. The authorizations group contains authorization objects, while automated testing tools such as SAP's Electronic Computer-Aided Testing Tool (eCATT) are contained in automatic tests. Finally, various exit techniques are provided as well.

A **change request** is an information source in the Workbench Organizer and Customizing Organizer that records and manages all changes made to Repository objects and Customizing settings during a development project.

The Repository Information System Window

With the Repository basics behind you, you can turn to the more interesting part: Actually working with the Repository Information System window. Follow along by executing transaction code /nSE84, and then expand all your subnodes so that your screen appears similar to the one shown in Figure 17.15.

In Hour 2, "SAP Basics," you learned that each screen contains an application toolbar. On this screen, the application toolbar provides functionality to assist you in working with the Repository Information System. The functions available on the application toolbar are as follows:

▶ **Expand Node button**—This button serves the same function as following the menu path Edit, Expand Node and expands all subnodes of the selected item.

▶ **Collapse Sub Tree button**—This button serves the same function as following the menu path Edit, Collapse Sub Tree and collapses all subnodes of the selected item.

▶ **Find button**—The Find button is probably the most useful button on your application toolbar; use it to search for objects in the Repository Information System. Selecting the Find button serves the same function as following the menu path Objects, Find.

▶ **Where Used List button**—This button serves the same function as following the menu path Objects, Where Used List and, like the Find button, is a search utility. The Where Used List function enables you to request and retrieve a list of locations where a specified object is used.

▶ **Environment button**—You can use the environment analysis function to determine the external references of an object—in other words, the referenced objects that do not belong to the object itself. This button serves the same function as following the menu path Objects, Environment.

▶ **Set of Lists button**—Selecting this button brings you to the Repository Infosystem: Work List screen where you can detail selection criteria for the objects you are looking for.

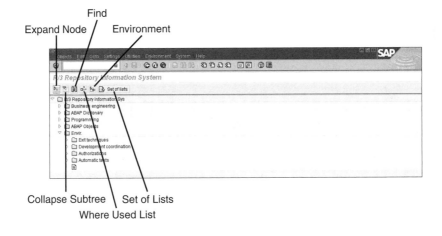

FIGURE 17.15
The Repository Information System application toolbar provides access to its functionality.

Summary

This past hour gave you a behind-the-scenes look at the ABAP Dictionary and Repository Information System. You should now be quite familiar with the components of SAP tables including the different types of tables and structures, fields, data elements, and domains. Also, you should now be able to take a look at any database table's contents and, by using selection screens, select and view table-specific criteria. Finally, with your broad understanding of the Repository, you are better positioned to understand how developers and programmers use the Repository Information System to configure and maintain SAP.

Q&A

Q *Which team members generally are involved with the maintenance of the ABAP Dictionary?*

A The maintenance of the ABAP Dictionary is performed exclusively by skilled ABAP programmers and is generally not modified by regular system users.

Q *If you make a change to a client-independent database table while you are connected to one client, when will the effect appear in the other clients?*

A Changes made to client-independent objects are reflected immediately in all clients.

Q *Do regular (non-technical) SAP end users use the Repository Information System?*

A The Repository Information System is primarily used by SAP developers and System Administrators as a tool for finding development objects within SAP.

Workshop

The workshop is designed to help you anticipate possible questions, review what you've learned, and begin thinking ahead to putting your knowledge into practice. The answers to the quiz that follows can be found in Appendix A, "Quiz Answers."

Quiz

1. What is the transaction code for the General Table Display function?

2. Define the term *structure*.

3. Name the three components for defining data in the ABAP Dictionary.

4. What are SAP selection screens used for?

5. Are pooled tables associated with a one-to-one relationship or a one-to-many relationship?

6. What is the major distinction between cluster tables and pooled tables in the SAP ABAP Dictionary?

7. Which type of tables contains a one-to-one relationship with tables in the SAP database?

8. ABAP Dictionary objects are broken down into what three components?

9. Environment objects are composed of what three subcomponents?

10. What is the Find button on the menu bar used for?

11. Describe what the SAP Repository Information System is used for.

12. Give an example of the types of queries you can request in the Repository Information System.

13. The Repository Information System displays a hierarchical list of the four types of objects in the SAP system: What are they?

Exercises

1. Use the Data Browser to view the contents of the SBOOK table.

2. Specify criteria on the selection screen for the SBOOK table to limit the number of records you retrieve.

3. Specify criteria on the selection screen using a range for the SBOOK table to limit the number of records you retrieve.

4. Use transaction code /nMB01 to navigate to the Goods Receipt for Purchase Order initial screen. Use the field-specific help to find out the table and field name of the Storage Location or SLOC fields.

5. Search for field CONNID and see whether you retrieve a listing for SPFLI-CONNID.

6. Search for the table SFLIGHT.

HOUR 18

Designing Screens and Menus

The SAP Screen Painter found in ECC and other SAP products is an ABAP Workbench tool designed for the purpose of creating and maintaining the elements of a screen. In other words, you can create your own SAP screens using the Screen Painter. It's most often used by SAP programmers rather than end users, though, because the mechanics of creating a screen, although straightforward, require a certain amount of programming knowledge. Called *flow logic*, this specialized knowledge is quite technical in nature.

However, an introduction to SAP is not complete without a bit of insight into the Screen Painter. Thus, the next hour provides a general overview as well as a certain amount of detail relative to the SAP Screen Painter and Menu Painter.

To this end, highlights in this hour include

- ▶ Introduction to the Screen Painter
- ▶ Introduction to the Menu Painter

SAP Screen Painter

The Screen Painter allows you to create user-friendly screens complete with pushbuttons, graphical elements, and table controls. Creating screens via the SAP Screen Painter is made possible by *Transaction Programming*. In Transaction (interchangeable with "Dialog") Programming, screens are merely static objects generated not by ABAP code, but rather through graphical design. The screens you design can be called from any ABAP program. They, in turn, can call ABAP processing blocks through the use of their *flow logic*. The nontechnical way to define transaction programming is to view it as special yet simple code written to allow you to execute your own transactions performed through custom SAP screens.

SAP screens are often referred to as dynpros. **Dynpro** is short for *dynamic program;* a screen and its accompanying flow logic combine to create a dynpro.

Creating or painting the screen is the easy part. It's the accompanying programming—code that allows the screen to function as expected—that gets complicated. The creation of new screens in SAP requires ABAP programming skills; hence, it is generally performed by an experienced ABAP programmer and is therefore usually reserved for SAP customizations deemed important enough to warrant a programmer's time. The four components of an SAP screen include screen attributes (or simply "attributes"), the layout of the screen, fields (one or more "elements"), and flow logic. Each of these is discussed next.

Screen Attributes

SAP screen attributes include the program the screen belongs to and the screen number. Recall from earlier hours that you can obtain the screen attributes from any SAP screen by selecting the menu path System, Status (see Figure 18.1).

FIGURE 18.1
The System: Status screen gives you useful information about your system as well as the screen attributes for the selected screen.

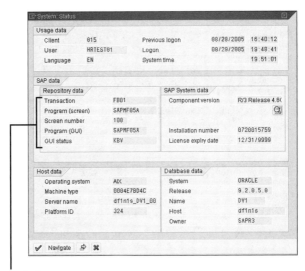

Screen attributes

Screen Layouts and the Layout Editor

Screen layout elements consist of the structures on your SAP screen with which the end user interacts, such as check boxes, empty input fields to be filled in, radio buttons, and so on (as illustrated in Figure 18.2). You took a closer look at the different types of screen elements in Hour 6, "Screen Basics."

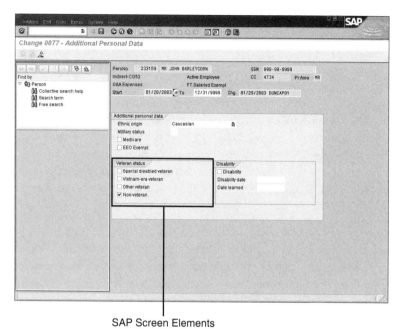

FIGURE 18.2
Screen layout elements consist of the different items represented on your screen, including check boxes, radio buttons, input fields, and so on.

SAP Screen Elements

Fields and the Element List

Fields are links to the SAP ABAP Dictionary. Fields on your screen correspond to actual fields in your ABAP Dictionary. When painting a screen, you will map to fields that are directly associated with and "known" by your actual SAP database (see Figure 18.3).

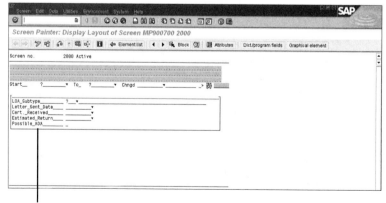

FIGURE 18.3
Fields that you add on to your screen will be connected, via ABAP programming code, to fields in your ABAP Dictionary.

Each of these on-screen fields
is connected or mapped to a field
in the SAP ABAP Dictionary

Field Validation

With Transaction Programming, screens allow you to both enter and display data. The fields on your screens can combine with the ABAP Data Dictionary to allow you to check the consistency of the data that a user entered.

An example is if you created a new screen for entering a new U.S.-based employee into your SAP HCM system. One of the required fields to do this is the employee's Social Security number. If you enter 123-45-123B, the system will check the validity of the entry and determine that the last character's value of B, for example, is not allowed as part of a Social Security number. The system would then halt and return the user to the Social Security input field, forcing the user to re-enter the correct value before proceeding.

In the same way, field checks based on data type and length can also be used to validate the integrity and authenticity of data being input into the system. Doing so significantly reduces the chance of data input errors. This behind-the-scenes integration found within the ABAP Data Dictionary is already inherent in the Screen Painter and requires no special coding from you.

Flow Logic

Here is where things start getting technical. Flow logic controls the flow of your program and is the programming code that makes the screen work or function as expected. Flow logic is written in ABAP code via the Flow Logic functionality found within the Screen Painter (see Figure 18.4).

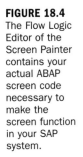

FIGURE 18.4
The Flow Logic Editor of the Screen Painter contains your actual ABAP screen code necessary to make the screen function in your SAP system.

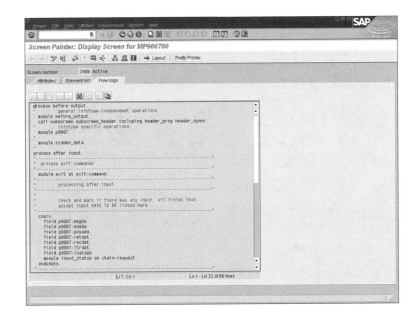

To start the Screen Painter and take a closer look at these features, execute transaction code /nSE51. The main screen of the Screen Painter is shown in Figure 18.5.

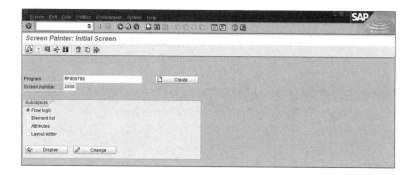

FIGURE 18.5
From the Screen Painter: Initial Screen, enter the Program and Screen number to display or change an existing screen, or select Create to make a new screen.

After selecting a program and screen number, you can then select one of the four subobjects discussed previously and click either the Display or Change buttons. In this way, it is easy to quickly drill down into the components that make up an SAP screen.

Layout Editor

The Screen Painter contains the Layout Editor (formerly the Fullscreen Editor), which is used to design your screen layout. The Layout Editor offers an easy-to-understand graphical mode featuring a "drag-and-drop" interface similar to a drawing tool. At one time, only a text-based interface was available to design screens—SAP is much improved in this respect, in that nearly any SAP GUI installation today supports Graphical Mode. If Graphical Mode fails to display, work with your SAP System Administrator to add this functionality to your user interface.

Selecting the Layout Editor displays a splash screen similar to the one shown in Figure 18.6 and launches the Graphical Screen Painter.

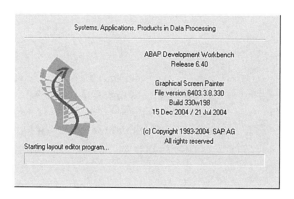

FIGURE 18.6
Selecting the Layout Editor launches a new window with the Graphical Screen Painter.

From this editor, you can maintain and update your screen's layout and graphical design.

The Element List Screen

The Element List view of the SAP Screen Painter is where you maintain the ABAP Dictionary or program fields for your particular screen (see Figure 18.7).

FIGURE 18.7
The Element
List view of the
Screen Painter
displays the
fields and their
attributes and
references that
you are using in
your screen.

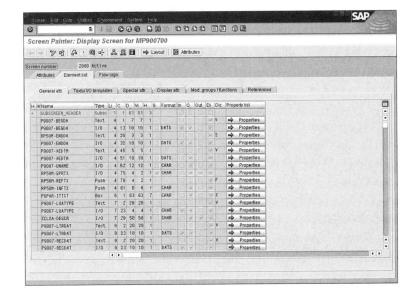

Screen Attributes

You can access the Screen attribute by selecting it from the Screen Painter Initial Screen. Selecting the Attributes subobject allows you to maintain a screen's fundamental attributes, including the name and short description of the program with which it is associated, the language, the screen's modification history, and more (see Figure 18.8).

Flow Logic

You can also access the Flow Logic view by selecting it from the Screen Painter Initial screen. Selecting the Flow Logic view launches the Screen Painter Flow Logic Editor discussed earlier. The Flow Logic Editor is where you define the flow logic of your screen, using ABAP to programmatically control how the screen functions. See Figure 18.9 for sample flow logic code that exists "behind" the main screen of the Screen Painter.

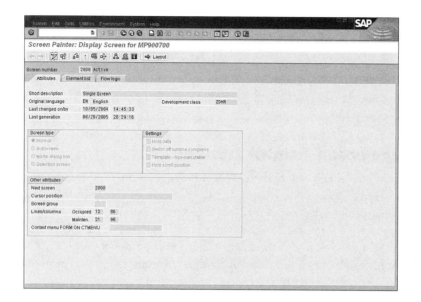

FIGURE 18.8
The Attributes view of the Screen Painter displays the high-level characteristics of your program.

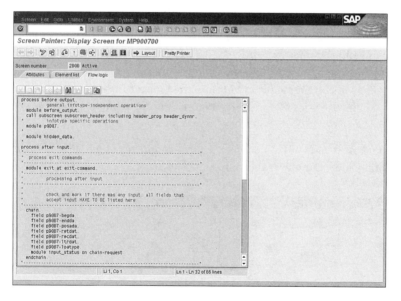

FIGURE 18.9
Flow logic code for most SAP screens is written in SAP's proprietary ABAP language.

When writing the flow logic for your SAP screen, you need to establish a *static sequence of screens,* which is a "what-happens-when" philosophy of how your new screen is going to function. SAP has two concepts used for this purpose:

▶ **PBO**—This refers to *processing before output,* and is the processing that occurs after a screen is called but before it is actually displayed on the screen.

▶ **PAI**—This term refers to *processing after input*, and is the processing that occurs after a screen has been displayed.

In combination, ABAP programmers use these two concepts when writing the code and sequence of their flow logic to determine how their newly created SAP screen will function.

Other Screen Painter Options

The Screen Painter is a very powerful tool in that allows you to determine where a particular screen is used and what "calls" it, as well as the hierarchy of a screen within a particular business process. The Screen Painter also provides a syntax checker, consistency checker, the ability to validate that a screen layout contains no inherent layout errors, and more. Right-click the background of the SAP GUI to obtain a list of additional functions and features germane to the particular SAP component or product in which you are working.

SAP Menu Painter

The Menu Painter is another ABAP Workbench tool with which you design user interfaces for your ABAP programs. In other words, using the Menu Painter, you can create your own custom menus in SAP. Like the Screen Painter, creating your own menus requires the skills of an ABAP programmer. You will take a look at the basics here.

You can access the Menu Painter by executing transaction code /nSE41. The main screen of the Menu Painter is shown in Figure 18.10.

FIGURE 18.10
The SAP Menu Painter is used to design custom user menus and toolbars collectively referred to as the *user interface*.

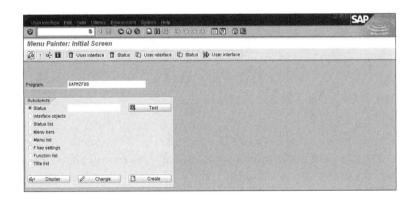

To use the Menu Painter, it's crucial to understand the term *GUI status*. An instance of the *graphical user interface* (*GUI*), consisting of a menu bar, a standard toolbar, an application toolbar, and a function key setting, comprise the GUI status. This differs from the GUI title, which includes the SAP title bar and menu bar.

The components of a user interface are shown in Figure 18.11.

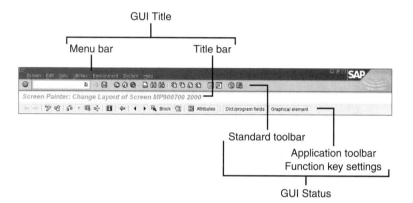

FIGURE 18.11
The components of the GUI title include the SAP title bar and menu bar, and the components of the GUI status include the standard toolbar, application toolbar, and function key settings.

Two of the components of a GUI status—the standard toolbar and the application toolbar—are covered in Hour 2, "SAP Basics." The Function Key setting refers to the 12 function keys that reside atop a standard keyboard, labeled F1–F12. The GUI status and GUI title define how the menu looks and performs in your SAP program. Note that different GUI statuses can refer to common components, and a program can have multiple GUI statuses and titles.

Menu Painter Object Components

From the Menu Painter Initial Screen, you can select the following options or subobjects to display, change, create or test:

- Status
- Interface Objects
- Status List
- Menu bars
- Menu list
- F–key settings
- Function list
- Title list

Status

Selecting the Status subobject from the main Menu Painter screen brings you to the Display Status screen. This tool is a little easier to work with than the Graphical Screen Painter, but it still requires ABAP programming skills. From the Display Status screen, you program the functions for the different items in the menu bar, application toolbar, standard toolbar, and function keys; see Figure 18.12 for an example.

FIGURE 18.12
You can modify the GUI status, menu bar, application toolbar, standard toolbar, and function keys by selecting the Status subobject from the Menu Painter window.

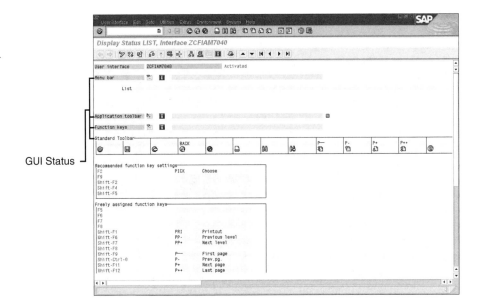

Interface Objects

The newest addition to the Menu Painter is this option to display any interface objects. In this way, an "object tree" can be displayed to visualize how dictionary structures, fields, events, subroutines, screens, and other various interface objects come together to form a menu.

Status List

Selecting the Status list subobject from the main Menu Painter screen brings you to the Display Status screen, which lists all the screens contained in your program.

Menu Bars

Selecting the Menu bars subobject from the main Menu Painter screen brings you to the Display Menu bars screen. This screen displays a list of menu bars sorted by status.

Menu List

Selecting the Menu list subobject from the main Menu Painter screen brings you to the Display Menu lists screen. This screen displays a list of menus (see Figure 18.13).

FIGURE 18.13
The Display Menu list screen displays a list of menus.

F-key Settings

Selecting the F–key settings subobject from the main Menu Painter screen takes you to the Display Function Key Settings screen. This screen displays a list of function key settings for use by your program (see Figure 18.14).

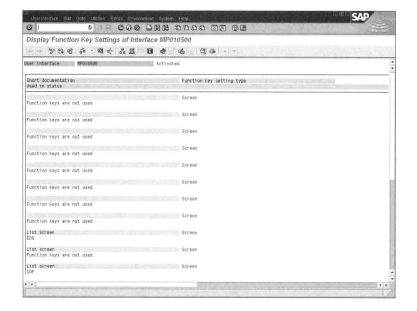

FIGURE 18.14
The Display Function Key Settings screen displays the status as well as a list of function key settings that can be used by your program.

Function List

Selecting the Function list subobject from the main Menu Painter screen brings you to the Display Function Lists screen. This screen displays a list of program functions; see Figure 18.15.

FIGURE 18.15
The Display
Function List
screen shows a
list of program
functions.

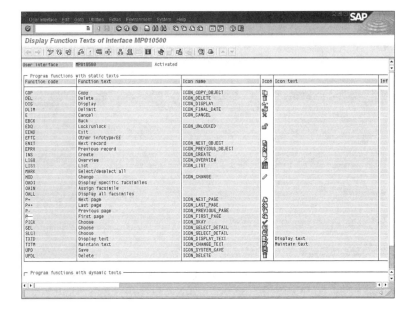

Title List

The final subobject available from the main Menu Painter, Title List, brings you
to the Display Title List screen. This screen displays a list of the words that appear
in the title bar of each of the screens in your program (see Figure 18.16).

FIGURE 18.16
The Display Title
list screen dis-
plays a list of
your programs'
titles.

Summary

In this hour, you looked at the SAP Screen Painter and Menu Painter tools. These
ABAP tools are very useful in designing and customizing your own screens and
menus. Although I have covered the basics here, there is much to learn when it
comes to implementing functional screens and menus. To that end, I recommend
that you enlist the assistance of an experienced ABAP programmer in order to create
screens and menus that not only look pleasing, but also perform well.

Q&A

Q *In what instances do you need to create your own SAP screens?*

A You typically create your own SAP screens only when you need to customize or enhance the functionality of your SAP system. Although SAP provides you with the tools to customize the system, it is recommended that you customize the system only when absolutely necessary.

Q *Is the Alphanumeric mode of the Screen Painter still used?*

A The Alphanumeric mode of the Screen Painter used to be the only tool available for customizing screens in versions of R/3 prior to 4x. Since the introduction of the Graphical Mode drag-and-drop Windows-based or Unix/Motif-based interface of the Screen Painter, its use has dropped significantly.

Workshop

The workshop is designed to help you anticipate possible questions, review what you've learned, and begin thinking ahead to putting your knowledge into practice. The answers to the quiz that follows can be found in Appendix A, "Quiz Answers."

Quiz

1. What is the primary mode of the SAP Screen Painter?

2. What are *dynpros*?

3. Give two examples of items considered as part of screen elements.

4. The programming code "behind the scenes" of your SAP screen that's used to make the screen function as expected is called what?

5. On which screen do you maintain the ABAP Dictionary fields for your screen?

6. What are the four components of a GUI status in the Menu Painter?

7. How can you view a list of all the title bars for each of the screens contained in your program?

Exercises

1. Locate the name of the program for the main SAP screen (Hint: refer to Figure 18.1).

2. Navigate to the Screen Painter Initial screen and type in the program name for the main SAP screen. Take a look (display only) at each of the four components.

PART V

Using SAP

HOUR 19

Reporting Basics

As you have seen in earlier hours, SAP has the capability to support and manage all your company's business processes and underlying data. Although this data is stored in the SAP system and can be presented to you on SAP screens, you might still want to produce printed or custom output from the system in the form of SAP reports. You can use reports to extract and manipulate the data from your SAP database. This hour, you take a look at some basic SAP reporting concepts.

Highlights in this hour include an

▶ Overview of reporting options in SAP

▶ Introduction to variants

▶ Overview of background processing

Reporting Tools

You can use several methods to generate reports in SAP, including

▶ ABAP List Processing (ABAP programming)

▶ ABAP Query Reporting

▶ Ad Hoc Query Reporting

▶ Structural Graphics Reporting

▶ Executive Information System

▶ SAP Information System (report trees)

In releases of SAP Basis 4x and above, there is also a web reporting tree that provides you with intranet access to canned SAP reports.

This hour covers the basics of reporting concepts and introduces the SAP
Information System, which contains the General Report Selection Tree. The other
reporting options are discussed briefly. The ABAP Query and the Ad Hoc Query are
summarized in this hour, but are explored in more detail in Hour 20, "Reporting
Tools in SAP (SAP Query, InfoSet Query, Ad Hoc Query, and QuickViewer)."

ABAP List Processing (ABAP Programming)

Custom reports can be created in SAP by writing ABAP code to generate lists. This
method is called *List Processing*. Using List Processing, ABAP programmers write
statements in the ABAP Editor that query the database and generate reports.
Writing reports using ABAP List Processing is therefore rather technical in nature
and subsequently relegated most often to the technical team.

This option becomes viable when you require a report that the canned reports cannot create. (*Canned reports* are created through the ABAP Query mechanism.) This
option is also used for creating interface files, or files that provide input to, and
therefore feed, external systems. For example, if you need your SAP system to connect to an external enterprise system such as an outside third-party bolt-on product,
you might consider using the ABAP List Processing method to write a report, the output of which is transmitted to the external system.

ABAP Query

You can create custom reports in SAP by creating queries using the ABAP Query
tool. ABAP queries are based on Logical Databases, Functional Areas, and User
Groups. Creating reports using ABAP Query is covered in more detail in Hour 20.

Ad Hoc Query

The Ad Hoc Query is a reporting tool that was borne out of the original SAP R/3
Human Resources functionality. Like the ABAP Query tool, it was initially based on
Logical Databases, Functional Areas, and User Groups. Ad Hoc Queries are used in
an "ad hoc" manner to query your SAP database. The output from the query can
then be formatted into a report. Creating reports using the most updated Ad Hoc
Query functionality is also covered in Hour 20.

Structural Graphics

Structural Graphics is an additional Human Resources tool used in the
Organizational Management application component. Structural Graphics enables
you to display and edit the structures and objects in your organizational plan and
to select reports directly from the graphical structure for an object.

Executive Information System

The Executive Information System is just as its name sounds: a reporting tool tailored for high-level decision-making. SAP also offers an entire mySAP component—Strategic Enterprise Management, or SEM—to cull executive-level information specifically from the SAP Business Information Warehouse (BW). EIS is still useful, however, for users who require quick access to real-time information found in R/3 and ECC (and does not require the time and expense necessary to deploy BW and SEM, the combination of which could easily consume a year's time and large budget). Using the Executive Information System Report portfolio, you call up a hierarchy graphic defined for access to your own report portfolio. You can also use Report selection, in which you call up either the general report tree of drill-down reports or your own custom tree. Or you can use the Report portfolio report, in which you enter the name of an individual report portfolio and then display it.

The Executive Information System provides you with information that presumably addresses key factors that influence the business activities within your company. It combines relevant data from external and internal sources, providing you with a view into real-time data that can then be quickly analyzed to make sound decisions.

SAP Information System (Report Trees)

Most of the reports you need are available within each ECC or R/3 module. That is, each module contains its own Information System that houses reports specific to that module. In earlier hours, you reviewed some of these module-specific Information Systems. One example is the SAP R/3 Human Resources Information System. Note that you can access all canned SAP reports via the general SAP Information System.

General Report Selection

SAP has many tools within R/3, ECC, and other components used to extract and then present data in the form of reports. Basic reporting capabilities are afforded through transaction code /nSART, or by navigating via the menu path Information Systems, General Report Selection. Note that in the newest SAP releases, SART is not available directly; instead, navigate through the menu paths to select a particular functional area, and from there select a particular report.

Report trees are hierarchical structures that can contain standard SAP reports, your organization's custom reports, and lists generated by executing certain reports. General Report Selection is structured as a hierarchy containing the following four levels:

▶ The top level contains the individual SAP System applications.

▶ The second level contains the work areas of each application.

▶ The third level contains the objects of each work area.

▶ The fourth level generally contains the reports and saved lists available for each object.

Your SAP R/3 and ECC systems ship predelivered with canned reports for all their functional areas. You can modify the general reporting structure according to your company's specific needs. For example, if you are installing and configuring only the R/3 Logistics and Financials components, you might want to remove the Human Resources reports from your General Report Selection screen.

You customize the General Report Selection reporting tree using the Implementation Guide (IMG). The IMG is discussed in Hour 8, "Implementation Tools, Methodologies, and the IMG." Reports specific to a particular ECC or R/3 module can be located through the module's Information System. Module-specific Information Systems are covered in more detail in Hour 11, "SAP ECC and R/3."

Executing Reports

You can execute reports directly from the General Report Selection screen. Depending on the modules currently installed on your system, different reports are available to you. To execute a common HR report within R/3, for example, drill down into the report tree as follows:

1. Expand the Human Resources node

2. Expand the Payroll node

3. Expand the Americas node

4. Expand the USA node

5. Expand the Payroll node

6. Double-click one of the reports, such as the Simulation or Start Payroll reports

Double-clicking the report icon launches the selection screen for the report. Selection screens are used by most SAP reports to enable an end user to clarify the output desired by entering precise input data (such as a payroll period, personnel number, reason for running a particular payroll cycle, and so on).

Once the input data is provided, you execute the report by selecting the Execute button from the toolbar. The Execute button is equivalent to the F8 function key on the keyboard. After you press the button or F8, the report will execute and output will appear on the screen. This output can be viewed, saved electronically in RTF or XLS formats by executing %pc in the transaction dialog box, or it can be printed in the more traditional manner.

> Depending on your system's configuration and your own set of authorizations or "permissions" within the system, different reports will be available to you. For example, if you have not installed and configured the Human Resources module, or are not authorized to work within the HR system, you will be unable to execute most of the Human Resources reports, if not all of them.

By the Way

Take a minute to practice executing different reports from the General Report Selection Tree. If you have trouble determining specific input criteria necessary to execute a particular report, work with the functional lead, developer, or power user associated with that functional area.

Report Attributes

To take a look at the attributes of a particular report in the General Report Selection Tree, select the report once using your mouse and then follow the menu path Edit, Node attributes. A window appears similar to the one shown in Figure 19.1. The window provides basic details about the report, including the report type, technical name of the underlying executable program, report description, and variants (if any).

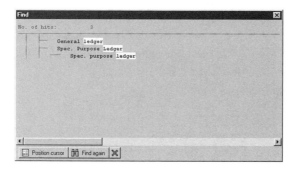

FIGURE 19.1
SAP's Report Attributes window gives you additional information about the selected report.

Searching for Reports

The General Report Selection Tree has a search function in which you can enter search criteria and search for a report based on its name. From any starting point in the tree, use the menu path Edit, Find, Node and you will be presented with an SAP Find dialog box like the one shown in Figure 19.2. Enter your search criteria; for my example, enter the word ledger.

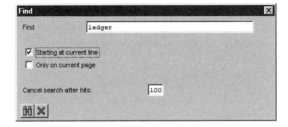

After typing your search criteria in the Find box and clicking the Find button, a new
Find window will display the results of your search. The new window includes **hot
keys** (sometimes referred to as hypertext in SAP documentation), which link that
text to the corresponding reports so that you can jump directly to the report. If there
were no reports matching your search criteria, you will receive a message box indicating something to the effect that the search has proven unsuccessful.

Selection Screens

As mentioned earlier, you will be presented with selection screens when you execute
an SAP report. The selection screens are quite useful in delimiting precisely which
output you are hoping to yield. Otherwise, the data processed in a report often
proves so plentiful that the report output becomes too large to be meaningful.

For example, if you wanted to generate a list of all open purchase orders in your
SAP system, you can execute a report listing your company's purchase orders and
indicate on the selection screen that you only want to display orders with the status
of Open. In some cases though, each time you execute a report, you are looking for
the same specific data. In this case, you would need to fill in the selection fields on
the selection screen for the data you desire. To assist you in this task, SAP makes use
of a concept called *variants*, discussed next.

Variants

A *variant* is a group of selection criteria values that has been saved to be used again
and again. If you want to run a report using the same selection criteria each time,
you can create a variant to save the data that you filled in on your selection screen.
The next time you execute the report, you only need to enter the variant name,
rather than re-enter the individual values in each of the selection criteria fields.

If you use variants, the selection screen for the report does not appear at all. The
report can also be preset to execute with the variant automatically so that no data
needs to be filled in at all. A report can have several variants, with each variant
retrieving different types of information. For example, a purchase order report might
have one variant to retrieve all open purchase orders for your company and another

variant used to display purchase orders for a specific vendor only. Use SAP's Save As Variant screen to save your selection criteria as a variant.

Variants are largely used for background execution of reports that tend to run a long time, and therefore are often scheduled to run behind the scenes. Variants are also used simply for convenience; if you tend to look at the same data day in and day out, but require a fresh view into this data, the use of variants can save a considerable amount of time. And with SAP's capability to schedule reports to run at certain times of the day, month, or year, executing a transaction using a variant is simple indeed.

Modifying Variants

From SAP's General Report Selection main screen, select a report that has variants available for it and then follow the menu path Goto, Variants. This brings you to the ABAP: Variants—Initial screen, similar to the one shown in Figure 19.3.

Indicates the report's program name

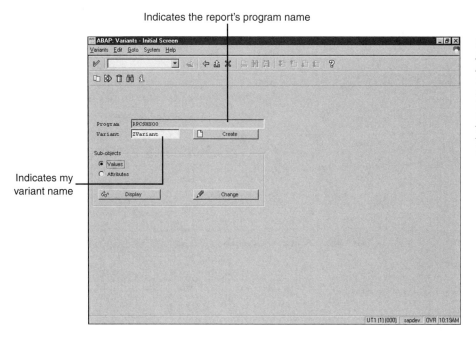

Indicates my variant name

FIGURE 19.3
Access the ABAP Variants Initial screen by selecting a report in the report tree and then following the menu path Goto, Variants.

From the ABAP: Variants—Initial screen, you can create new variants and modify existing variants. For example, you can enter the name of an existing variant and select the Values subobject and then click the Change button. This brings you to the selection screen for the report, which enables you to modify the selection criteria for your variant. You can also select the Attributes subobject and click the Change button, which brings you to the Save As Variant screen for the report. This screen enables you to modify the name, description, and attributes for your variant. On this screen, you can also specify additional variant criteria, some of which is displayed in Table 19.1.

TABLE 19.1   Additional Variant Attributes

Only for background processing	Reports can be generated in the background. Selecting this option specifies that the variant can only be executed in the background. Otherwise, if unselected, the variant can be run both in the background and in the foreground (online).
Protect variant	If you select the field Protect Variant, the variant can be changed only by the person who created or last modified it. This protects your variant from being modified by other people.
Only display in catalog	If you select this field, the variant name appears in the directory, but not in the general input help.
System variant	This box is reserved for system variants (automatic transport).

Background Processing

You can process reports in the background and, perhaps more important, schedule them to run in the background at predefined intervals. For example, you can have a scheduled background job that prints a list of all the new invoices issued through your Purchasing application at the end of each business day. A background job specifies the ABAP report or external program that should run, together with any variants for the report, including start time and printing specifications. The scheduling of jobs is a function of your System Administrator.

A key advantage of background processing is that the report or job is started in the background by SAP, and thus does not impact online users in the same way it otherwise might—many of the resources used to execute jobs in the background are distinct and different from those used to host online users. Thus, performance of both the batch job or report and the online users winds up being much improved (compared to executing a long-running report in the foreground).

Lists

After generating a report in SAP, you can save the output as a list. On all report output screens, there are List options available that enable you to save the file in Office, a report tree, or to an external file. Saving the report as an external file is covered in more detail later in Hour 22, "Integration with Microsoft Office." In that hour, I discuss how you can work with your SAP data using Microsoft Office products such as Excel, Word, and Access.

Saving the list using the menu path List, Save, Office enables you to save the report output in a folder. It also gives you the chance to email the output through SAP's email interface. Finally, you also have the option of saving the generated list to a reporting tree.

> It is important to note the distinction between a report and a list. A *report* generated at any time in the system contains real-time data at the time of generation. A *list* is saved output from a previously generated list and does not reflect the real-time data in your SAP ECC or R/3 system—lists are static, whereas reports are dynamic.

Summary

SAP offers a host of reporting capabilities, ranging from dedicated components like BW and SEM to built-in capabilities found in ECC, R/3, and other mySAP Business Suite components. This hour provided an introduction to the basics of reporting in SAP, including the concepts of variants and background processing. One of the biggest concerns of using a new system is your ability to retrieve output from the system in a manner that is relatively easy to do, in an equally easy-to-use format. Having all the data stored in your SAP system is good, but to be able to output that data into meaningful reports is crucial—SAP reporting makes this possible.

The information that you have learned this hour will be helpful in executing reports and creating variants for those reports. The next hour takes this instruction to the next level and drills down into reporting tools for SAP, including SAP Query, InfoSet Query, Ad Hoc Query, and QuickViewer.

Q&A

Q *Are there external tools available for reporting in SAP?*

A There are several products on the market that can be used for external reporting in SAP. Sample external reporting solutions hail from Microsoft, Monarch, Oracle, FOCUS, Cognos, Informatica, and many others.

Q *Can reports be made a part of SAP workflow?*

A Reports can be integrated with business workflow in your SAP system. For example, you can specify that a report be generated, saved as a list, and automatically sent to someone's email inbox on a predetermined and recurring schedule.

Q *Is there an ideal way to determine whether the canned reports in SAP can satisfy your reporting requirements?*

A During the implementation process, it is a good idea to compile a list (including samples of the reports that your company currently generates) and compare your current reports with the canned reports in SAP. In many cases, you will find that, because of the functionality available in SAP, many of your printed "hard copy" reports have quickly become obsolete, whereas in other cases many of your reports can be combined into a single SAP canned report.

Workshop

The workshop is designed to help you anticipate possible questions, review what you've learned, and begin thinking ahead to putting your knowledge into practice. The answers to the quiz that follows can be found in Appendix A, "Quiz Answers."

Quiz

1. What reporting mechanism is used to pose ad hoc queries to the database?

2. Which type of SAP reporting tool requires the user to write code in ABAP in order to generate reports?

3. What is the menu path to view a report's attributes from the General Report Selection screen?

4. What is the menu path used to search for reports in the General Report Selection Tree?

5. Define the term *variant*.

6. What does it mean to "protect" a variant?

7. Describe the primary advantage of background processing.

Exercises

1. In the General Reporting Tree, search for a report named Product Group Planning Evaluation.

2. Create two new variants for a familiar report, and then re-execute the report using each of the variants.

Reporting Tools in SAP (SAP Query, InfoSet Query, Ad Hoc Query, and QuickViewer)

In the earliest versions of SAP, two tools were delivered for end-user reporting. The ABAP Query was designed for all modules and the Ad Hoc Query was designed exclusively for the Human Capital Management module. Beginning with version 4.6, things have changed. The ABAP Query is now called the SAP Query and its features have been enhanced. Additionally, the Ad Hoc Query tool can now be used with all modules in SAP under the name the InfoSet Query (although in the Human Capital Management module SAP still refers to it as the Ad Hoc Query). Both reporting tools enable you to create reports within your SAP environment and neither requires any technical skills. Additionally, in version 4.6, SAP introduced another tool called the QuickViewer. In this hour, you learn how to create custom reports using these reporting tools, including the necessary configuration and administrative decisions to get you on your way.

Highlights of this hour include

▶ Learning the quick and easy steps to configure the query reporting tools

▶ Using the SAP Query to create basic and advanced reports

▶ Using the InfoSet (Ad Hoc) Query to create reports

▶ Using the QuickViewer to create QuickViews

The Structure of the Query Reporting Tools

The query tools (SAP Query, InfoSet/Ad Hoc Query and QuickViewer) are built upon the foundation of three main components:

▶ Query Groups (/nSQ03)

▶ InfoSets (/nSQ02)

▶ Administrative decisions (company specific)

Each of these components permits a user with no technical programming skills to create custom reports. The overview of the query tool structure is depicted in Figure 20.1.

FIGURE 20.1
The SAP family of query reporting tools gives users easy access to the database via Query Groups and InfoSets.

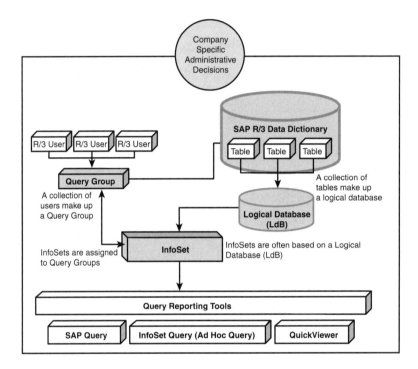

If you think about custom reporting in SAP in layman terms, you picture a programmer sitting down at a terminal and typing lines and lines of ABAP code that go to the core SAP database to collect the information needed for the report. The programmer also has to code to account for security access, output, formatting, and so on. The purpose of the SAP delivered query tools is that all the work is done for you behind the scenes. The use of the three main components holds it all together.

Query Groups

Let's start with the first component, Query Groups (formerly known as User Groups in earlier versions of SAP). The technical definition of Query Groups is a collection of SAP users who are grouped together. A user's assignment to a user group determines which queries he or she can execute or maintain. Additionally, it designates which

InfoSets (data sources) the user can access. Basically, Query Groups permit users to create, modify, and execute reports in a certain area within R/3. For example, you can create a Query Group for the Finance department that includes your Financial users; similarly you create a Query Group for the Human Resources department that contains reports specific to Human Resources. Query Groups are an easy way to group and segregate your reports.

Query Groups are often maintained by the System Administrator. Query Groups are created on the Maintain Query Groups screen, which you can access using the transaction code /nSQ03. Users can belong to multiple Query Groups and might, under certain circumstances, copy and execute queries from other Query Groups (only if the permissions are the same). Any user within a user group has authority to execute queries that are assigned to that group, but only users with the appropriate authorization can modify queries or define new ones. Users cannot modify queries from other Query Groups. Although the maintenance of Query Groups is usually a task for your System Administrator, you learn how to create a sample user group later in this section.

InfoSets

InfoSets (formerly known as Functional areas in earlier versions of SAP) are the second component of SAP reporting. InfoSets are created on the Maintain InfoSets screen, which you can access using transaction code /nSQ02. The technical definition of InfoSets are areas that provide special views of logical databases and determine which fields of a logical database or data source can be evaluated in queries. Basically, an InfoSet is the data source; it's where you get your data to use in your reports. InfoSets can be built on a variety of sources, but the most common is the use of what is known as a logical database (LdB). Recall that writing reports without Query tools requires a programmer to write code that goes into the main R/3 database and retrieves the records it needs. This is no easy skill. SAP's answer to this issue is the logical database.

Logical databases are rational prearranged groupings of data from multiple related tables that are indexed. In layman's terms, logical databases place all the fields you want to report in an easy container from which you simply select the fields you need to include in your report. An overview of the relationship between these different elements is shown in Figure 20.1. Although the maintenance of InfoSets is usually a task for your System Administrator, you learn how to create a sample InfoSet later in this section.

By the
~~Way~~

Depending on your SAP authorization privileges, you might need to request assistance from your System Administrator in creating a test Query Group, functional area, and query. It is also possible, if you are working with a newly installed SAP system, that you will receive a message saying you must convert objects first. If you receive this message, contact your System Administrator. He or she will be required to perform a standard administration function to convert the objects before you can proceed.

Administrative Decisions

As you see in just a moment, creating Query Groups and InfoSets is an easy task, but before you do so, you must first review the following administrative decisions to see which best applies to your organization.

▶ What is your client/transport strategy?

▶ Will you use the standard or global Query Area?

What Is Your Client/Transport Strategy?

With custom-coded ABAP reports written by programmers, the traditional methodology for report creation is as follows: A programmer accesses a development environment where the first draft of the custom report is coded. The report is then transported to a testing client where it is tested. Assuming it passes testing, the report then moves on to your production environment for use. This methodology differs from the strategy often used with the query family of reporting tools. The addition of the query tools to SAP enables end users to create reports in real-time with no technical skills. It is with this in mind that your organization has to make a decision regarding your transport strategy.

The creation of query objects can be performed in any client. However, there are some best practices you should follow. For starters, end users who will be using the query tools often only have user IDs in the live production environment. Therefore, many companies maintain Query Groups live in the production client.

Similarly, InfoSets can be created in any client; however, best practice dictates that InfoSets be treated inline with normal programming methodology. It's best to create InfoSets in a development environment and then transport them to a testing client, where they are tested and then moved on to production for use. The reason why InfoSets are treated differently is because a trained user has the capability to add special coding or programs to InfoSets (outside the scope of this book) that can have an impact on system resources or functioning and testing them is required in those cases. That leaves the reports (queries) themselves. Unlike custom-coded ABAP reports, query reports are designed to be made real-time in an ad hoc fashion, so the best practice is to create your queries live in your production environment.

Using the Standard or Global Query Area

Query Areas (formerly known as Application Areas in versions earlier than 4.6) contain your ABAP Query elements, queries, functional areas, and Query Groups. There are two distinct Query Areas in SAP: standard and global.

Standard Query Areas

Standard Query Areas are client-specific, which means that they are available only within the client in which they were created. For example, if you created a standard query in the production client, it exists only in the production client. You can transport query objects created in the standard area between multiple clients on the same application server via the Transport Truck function on the main InfoSets screen (SQ02). This bypasses the customary Workbench Organizer.

Global Query Areas

Queries designed in the *global area* are used throughout the entire system and are client independent. In Release 4.6, SAP delivers many of its standard reports in the SAP global Query Area. These queries are also intended for transport into other systems and are connected to the ABAP Workbench.

A common best practice is to allow SAP to continue to deliver reports via the global area and for end users to use the standard Query Area to create query-related reports. With your administrative decisions completed, you are ready to begin the configuration.

Creating a New User Group

To create a new user group, perform the following steps:

1. Navigate to the Maintain User Group screen using transaction code /nSQ03.

2. Ensure that you are in the standard Query Area by following the menu path Environment, Query Areas, and then selecting Standard area (client-specific).

3. Type the user group name that you will be creating, **ZTEST**, and select the Create button (see Figure 20.2).

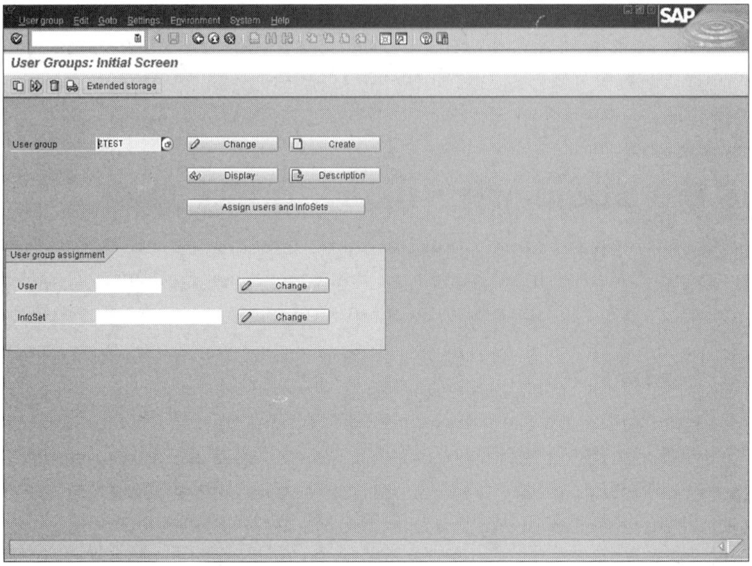

FIGURE 20.2
SAP Query
Groups are cre-
ated and modi-
fied using User
Groups: Initial
Screen.

4. Type a name for your user group on the User Group ZTEST: Create or Change screen, as shown in Figure 20.3 and select the Save button.

FIGURE 20.3
Enter the name
for your user
group in the
User Group
ZTEST: Create
or Change
screen.

5. A message appears in your SAP GUI status bar stating that the User Group ZTEST has been saved.

6. Select the Assign Users and InfoSets button. Type the SAP user IDs of any users whom you want to include in your test group. Be sure to include your own user ID (see Figure 20.4).

7. Save the entry by selecting the Save button from the toolbar. A message appears in your SAP GUI status bar stating User Group ZTEST saved.

Now that you have created a user group, your next step is to create an InfoSet.

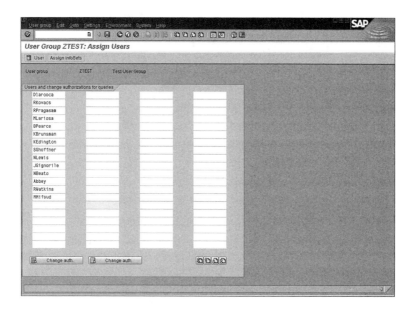

FIGURE 20.4
In your newly
created User
Group, be sure
to add your own
user name.

Creating a New InfoSet

To create a new InfoSet, perform the following steps:

1. Navigate to the Maintain InfoSets screen using the transaction code /nSQ02.

2. Ensure that you are in the standard Query Area by following the menu path Environment, Query Areas, and then selecting Standard Area (client-specific).

3. Type the InfoSet name that you will be creating, **ZTEST**, and select the Create button.

4. On the InfoSet: Title and Database screen, you are asked to input a description for your InfoSet. In this example, I used the name *Test InfoSet*. As mentioned earlier, you can create InfoSets using a variety of sources. The most common is the logical database. On this screen, select the F1S logical database from the drop-down box to be used as your data source (see Figure 20.5).

FIGURE 20.5
On this screen, select the F1S logical database from the drop-down box.

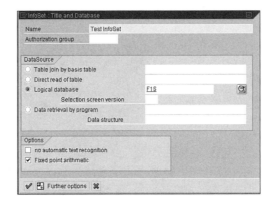

You can create InfoSets from various data sources, including logical databases, tables, table joins, and so on. The best business practice is to use the SAP delivered logical databases as your data source, because they were created for this purpose and there is at least one logical database delivered with your system for each module within SAP, including Accounting, Personnel Management, and so on. The F1S database used in this example is the training database that SAP uses in its training classes based on a fictional airline scheduling system. It is best to use this database for your test cases.

5. After entering a name and selecting the appropriate logical database from the drop-down list, F1S, select the green check mark to continue.

6. You are presented with a screen similar to the one shown in Figure 20.6. It lists the tables stored in the logical database F1S.

7. The logical database F1S selected is a test logical database containing three test tables: SPFLI, SBOOK, and SFLIGHT. To take a look at the fields in these tables, use the Expand Sub Tree button listed next to each table name (see Figure 20.7).

8. The next step is to assign fields to the Field groups (shown on the top-right of your screen) within your InfoSet. These field groups appear in your query tools while reporting. Only the fields that you include in your field groups are available for field selection in your query-reporting tools that use this InfoSet as its data source. By default, these field groups are empty (noted exception follows).

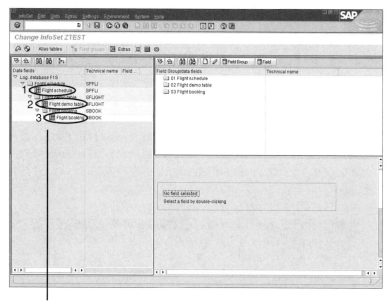

FIGURE 20.6
The Change InfoSet screen displays a list of all tables stored in your InfoSet.

Three tables are contained within the logical database F1S.

Table names   Field groups

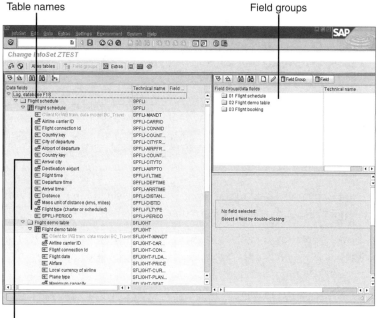

FIGURE 20.7
The Change InfoSet screen with expanded subnodes showing the fields available in each table.

Field names

By the
~~Way~~

> For nearly all modules in SAP, your field groups are empty and you need to manually move fields to them. This is true for all modules with the exception of the Human Capital Management module and the InfoSets that support it. The field groups in this module are created for you with a default set of fields; you can add additional information if required.

9. Place your cursor on the first field group, Flight Schedule. (You are going to select fields from the left side of the screen from the Flight Schedule table and add them to the Flight Schedule field group.) Place your cursor on a field on the left side of the screen, and right-click the option to Add Field to Field Group (see Figure 20.8).

FIGURE 20.8
The Change InfoSet screen with expanded tables showing the fields available in each table.

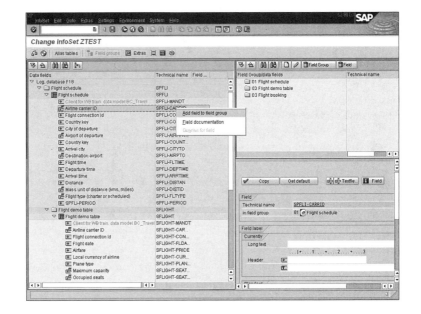

10. Your newly added field to the Flight Schedule Field group now appears at the top-right side of the screen (see Figure 20.9).

11. The next step is to add fields to your selected field group following the procedures outlined previously. Select the field group with your cursor and then move fields from the left side of the screen to the right using the procedure outlined previously. Be sure to add fields to the appropriate field group. For example, you can add the fields in the Flight Schedule Table to the Flight Schedule Field Group, or add fields from the Flight Booking Table to the Flight Booking Field Group.

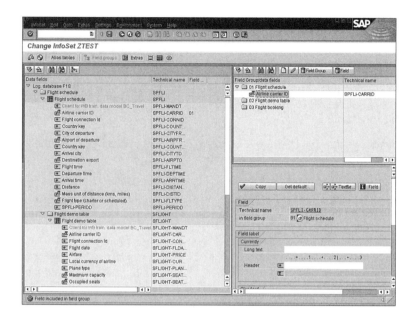

FIGURE 20.9
The Field Group, Flight schedule now has a field in it that is available for reporting with the query family of tools.

12. Now that you have added a series of fields to your field groups, select the Save button from the toolbar. A message appears in the status bar saying that the InfoSet ZTEST was saved.

13. Next, you need to generate the InfoSet by selecting the Generate button (the red beach ball) from the application toolbar. A message appears in the status bar saying that the InfoSet ZTEST generated.

> The process of generating your InfoSet determines whether any errors are present in the logic of the configuration of the InfoSet.

Did you Know?

14. The last step is to exit the Maintain InfoSet screen by selecting the green back arrow.

Assigning the InfoSet to Your Query Group

You have now accomplished the first two configuration steps. You have created a Query Group and you have created an InfoSet. The last step before you begin creating reports is to assign the InfoSet to your Query Group. This is an easy, two-step task:

1. From the InfoSet: Initial Screen (transaction code /nSQ02), make sure your InfoSet ZTEST is present in the InfoSet text box and select the User Group Assignment button.

2. From the InfoSet ZTEST: Assign to Query Groups screen, highlight your Query Group name by selecting the gray button to the left of it, and then selecting the Save button.

   A message appears in the status bar saying that the assignment of the InfoSet ZTEST was saved.

Note that some of the SAP screens and SAP Help text still use the "functional area" moniker instead of InfoSet or refer to Query Groups by their old name, User Groups. Just be aware of this. You can also assign the InfoSet to a Query Group by using the Maintain User Groups screen (SQ03) and by selecting the Assign Users and InfoSets button from the toolbar and selecting your InfoSet from a list.

SAP Queries

You create and maintain your SAP queries through the Maintain Queries screen. You can access the Maintain Queries screen by using transaction code /nSQ01.

Unlike Query Groups and InfoSets, which are often maintained by System Administrators, SAP queries are primarily maintained by trained end users (after the configuration steps are complete). Only users with the appropriate authorizations can modify queries or create new ones.

Security for managing query reporting is available on a couple of different levels. Besides the user group segregation, there also exists authorization group specifications. Security configurations are very customer specific; contact your systems administrator to learn more about your company's security configuration.

Creating an SAP Query

With the one-time configuration completed, the fun can finally begin. Creating an SAP query is a relatively elementary task. To begin creating your first SAP query, follow these steps:

1. Navigate to the Maintain Queries Initial screen using the transaction code /nSQ01. In version 4.6, a graphical version of the SAP query is available called the Graphical Query Painter. If you have not used the query tool, this will set

as your default. To turn it off and learn to create easy step-by-step reports, follow the menu path Settings > Settings and deselect the Graphical Query Painter check box.

2. The title bar will list the Query Group that you are currently in. For example, your screen might read Query of User Group ZTEST: Initial Screen. (If you are assigned to multiple user groups, you can see a list of the groups by selecting the Shift + F7 key.)

3. It is always a good idea to ensure that you are in the standard Query Area by following the menu path Environment, Query Areas and selecting Standard area (client-specific).

4. In the Query field, type a name for the query you are creating, **ZMYQUERY**, and select the Create button.

5. The InfoSets of User Group ZTEST window will list all the available InfoSets for your Query Group. Select the ZTEST InfoSet followed by the Enter key to proceed.

6. You are now presented with the Create Query Title Format screen, which enables you to save the basic formatting specifications for your query, including the name (title) and any notes you want to store for the query. The only required field is the title (see Figure 20.10).

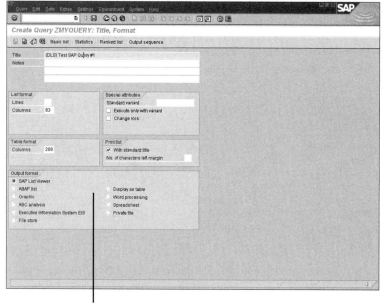

FIGURE 20.10
You enter the title, format, and processing options for your query on the Create Query Title Format screen.

The further processing options listed here are the same as the options that appear on the selection screens when you execute SAP delivered reports.

7. After entering a title, select the *Save* button on the toolbar. To navigate to the next screen in the SAP query-creation process, select the next screen (white navigational arrow) button from the application toolbar. You can use these navigational arrows to navigate between the different screens of the SAP Query.

8. A screen will appear listing all the field groups available within your InfoSet (in this example, you can see Flight Schedule [SPFLI], Flight Demo Table [SFLIGHT], and Flight Booking [SBOOK]). Place a check mark next to all field groups that you want to include fields from in your report. Select the next screen (white navigational arrow) button from the application toolbar.

9. A Select Field screen will appear (see Figure 20.11), giving you a list of all the available fields within the Field Groups you selected. Place a check mark next to all fields that you want to include in your report. You can use the Page Up and Page Down arrows to navigate between all the fields. Select the next screen (white navigational arrow) button from the application toolbar to continue.

FIGURE 20.11
You can use the Page Up and Page Down arrows to navigate between all the fields.

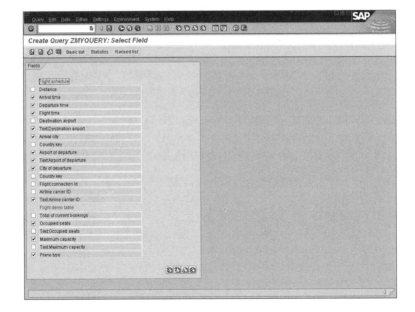

10. You are now presented with the Selections screen, which lists all the fields that you have selected. You can now add any of the fields to the selection screen that appears when you execute your report. This enables you to specify your report output when the report is executed. You can add any fields you want to

the Selection screen by placing a check mark next to each field. This is the last screen in the basic query sequence; to continue, select the Basic List button from the application toolbar.

11. The Basic List screen shows you a list of the selected fields that you want to include for your report. For each field, you can specify the Line and Sequence number as you want them to appear on your report. Additionally, you can use this screen to indicate sort order, totals, and counts, if needed. Start by entering the Line and Sequence numbers like the ones displayed in Figure 20.12.

Line corresponds to the line number the field appears on in the report.

Sequence determines the order the fields appear on for the line.

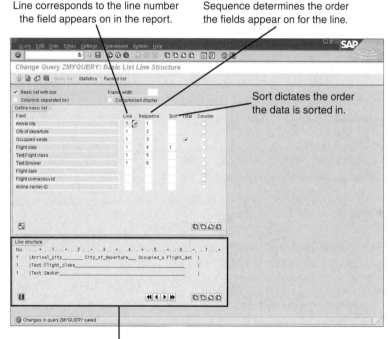

Sort dictates the order the data is sorted in.

FIGURE 20.12
Basic output options are defined on the SAP Query Basic List screen.

After selecting the Save button, a preview of the format appears in the Line Structure box at the bottom of the screen.

12. For this basic SAP Query example, you will proceed directly to the report. Select the F8 button from the application toolbar to execute the report.

13. You are presented with the report's selection screen. The selection screen gives you an opportunity to specify any criteria for the output of your report. Select the Execute button again to display the report. Your report output should appear similar to Figure 20.13. (The output of the report corresponds to the specification entered in the basic list screen.)

FIGURE 20.13
In version 4.6
and higher, your
report displays
in the SAP list
viewer, as
shown in the
picture.

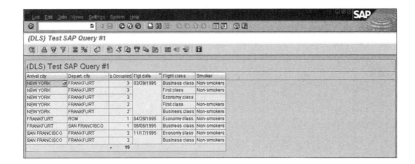

Advanced SAP Queries

You have created a basic query using the SAP Query tool. Before you start investigating the more advanced options available in ABAP Query, it's a good idea to try creating a few queries using different InfoSets (based on different logical databases). To do this, you need to start from the section "Creating a New InfoSet" earlier this hour, select a different logical database, and then assign it to your Query Group.

When you become familiar with the SAP Query tool, you will want to try some of its more advanced options. To investigate the advanced options available for processing your queries, follow these steps:

1. Navigate to the Maintain Queries Initial screen using the transaction code /nSQ01 and select one of your existing queries.

2. Select the Modify button followed by the Basic list button on the application toolbar from the Basic List screen.

3. You can use the next screen (white navigational arrow) button from the application toolbar to navigate to the additional seven screens that house the more advanced functions of the SAP Query. These include

   ▶ **Grouping, sorting, and subtotaling**—You can group, sort, and subtotal your SAP data onto reports and modify your subtotal texts. For example, you can create a report listing all open purchase orders and their amounts grouped by vendor and location with custom-named subtotals; see Figure 20.14.

   ▶ **Manipulating colors and texts**—You can manipulate the colors and text styles of the different data presented on reports. For example, your report can contain subtotals in yellow, group totals in green, and individual line items in boldface red text.

▶ **Alter the column widths, add colors, hide leading zeros**—You can manipulate the layout of the report output to be used in interfaces or flat file transfers; see Figure 20.15.

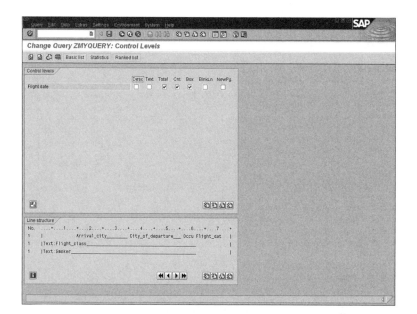

FIGURE 20.14
The Control Levels screen enables you to do sorting and subtotaling, as well as special formatting in your SAP Query report.

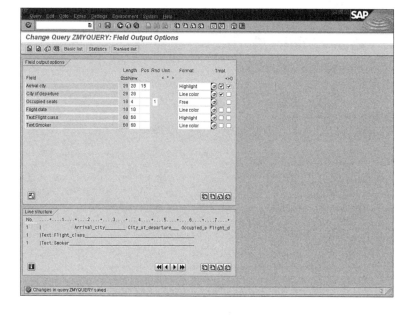

FIGURE 20.15
The Field Output Options screen enables you to vary the column width of your fields to prepare text spaced or delimited extract files or can be used simply to make your report output look better.

▶ **Custom headers and footers**—You can create custom headers and footers to be shown on each page of your printed reports. Your report can include the name of the report and the date and time it was created at the top of each printed page of the report; see Figure 20.16.

FIGURE 20.16
You can use special symbols to insert the current date, time, and page numbers in your custom headers and footers.

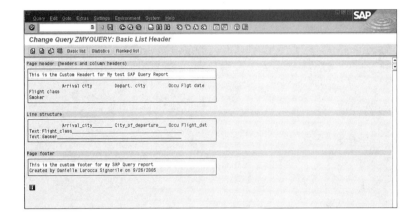

▶ **Charts and graphics**—You can include graphics and create charts of your SAP data on reports. You can create a bar graph displaying the open items currently available in your warehouse in comparison to the items sold; see Figure 20.17.

FIGURE 20.17
Charts appear in full color using SAP business graphics.

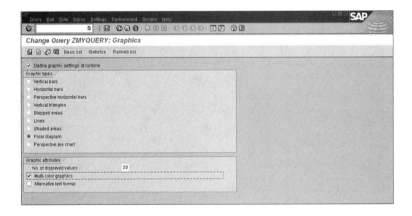

You can also create calculated fields in your queries to be used in your SAP Query reports. Calculated fields can be used to include variables that are not currently stored by SAP. Examples include a calculated field to store an invoice amount multiplied by a discount percentage or a calculated field to change output based on a number you enter on the Reports Selection screen. You can also create advanced calculated fields using "if-then" type logic. This is performed by using the local fields function on the Select Fields screen.

Understanding the InfoSet (Ad Hoc) Query

Unlike the SAP Query, which is a complete reporting solution tool, the InfoSet Query is designed for basic users to retrieve simple single-use lists of data from your R/3 database. Using this tool, (all query information) including the selection criteria is available on a single screen. In version 4.6, the Human Capital Management module-reporting tool, called the Ad Hoc Query, was combined with the technology of the SAP Query and made available for all modules. It's now called the InfoSet Query (although it is still referred to as the Ad Hoc Query when executed for HR reporting). This section refers to it as the InfoSet (Ad Hoc) Query; the functionality is the same regardless of its name.

Unlike the SAP Query (with the seven basic screens and seven advanced screens), all query information—including the selection criteria for InfoSet Query reporting—is available on a single screen.

You can use the InfoSet (Ad Hoc) Query to quickly answer simple questions, such as how many employees earn more than $100,000 annually, or to create a comprehensive report for printing or downloading to your PC. The InfoSet (Ad Hoc) Query is designed so that users can pose questions to the SAP system and receive real-time answers. Other sample questions you might pose using an Ad Hoc Query include

▶ How many employees are over the age of 40?

▶ Which invoices are charged to cost center 1234?

▶ How many widgets are available for delivery on 9/26/2007?

The InfoSet (Ad Hoc) Query is a very helpful tool that your functional users can use to retrieve important, comprehensive information in a quick-and-easy fashion.

Your System Administrator can control access rights to the InfoSet Query using Roles or SAP Query User Groups. Exactly one SAP Query User Group must be assigned to a role (an InfoSet must be associated with the User Group), although the user does not need to be listed in the User Group. If users want to save their reports, they need authorization object S_QUERY, field ACTVT, value 2; otherwise, they can only create and execute reports.

Like SAP queries, InfoSet (Ad Hoc) queries are built on the foundation of Query Areas, Query Groups, and InfoSets. Earlier in this hour, you created an InfoSet based on the test logical database F1S, which corresponds to SAP's test system. You can use the same data source used in earlier examples for creating an InfoSet (Ad Hoc) Query or you can create a new InfoSet using an HR logical database. The following example uses the one created earlier in the chapter.

Creating an InfoSet (Ad Hoc) Query

When the one-time configuration is completed, Creating an InfoSet query is a relatively elementary task. To begin creating your first InfoSet (Ad Hoc) query, follow these steps:

1. You can access the InfoSet query in three ways: through an application-specific role using the Easy Access menu, using the SAP Query (transaction SQ01) and then selecting the InfoSet Query button, or by using transaction code /nPQAH.

2. You are prompted to select your Query Group and InfoSet (data source) from a dialog box and then to press Enter. The main screen of the InfoSet (Ad Hoc) Query appears in Figure 20.18.

3. The main screen contains three areas: the actual InfoSet from which you select and choose your fields, the sample report display, and the Selection screen values.

4. To start creating your report, simply check the Output box next to each field you want to appear in the report. In this example, I selected only a few fields; see Figure 20.19.

5. Next, choose fields for the Selection screen by marking each field's Selection check box.

6. The Selections section works just as a standard Selection screen does, by enabling you to input values to specify your reporting output.

7. After selecting all the fields that you want to include, press the F8 key to execute the report. By default, your report displays in the SAP ALV grid from which you can easily drag and drop the columns and/or manipulate the look of the output.

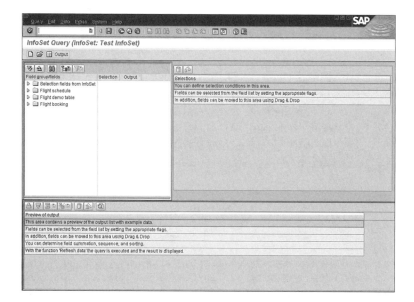

FIGURE 20.18
The main screen of the InfoSet (Ad Hoc) Query.

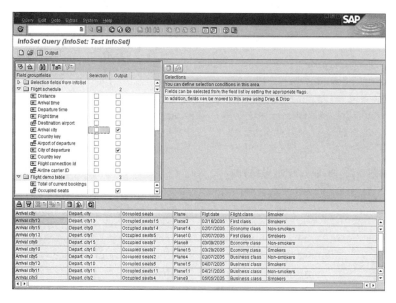

FIGURE 20.19
The three main areas of InfoSet (Ad Hoc) Query each perform a different function.

Did you Know?

The difference between reporting using the test logical database F1S and the Human Capital Management (HCM) module is that data in the HCM module is displayed by InfoType and not by table name. This makes it easier for the end users.

Understanding the QuickViewer

Unlike the SAP Query, which is a complete reporting solution tool, the SAP QuickViewer Tool delivered with a 4.6 system is a "what-you-see-is-what-you-get" utility for quick collection of data from your R/3 system. To define a report with the QuickViewer, you simply enter texts (titles) and select the fields and options that define your QuickView. Unlike with SAP Query, whereby you create *queries*, you create *QuickViews*. QuickViews are not queries and they cannot be exchanged among users. The good news is that they can be converted to queries to be used with SAP Query.

Like with the InfoSet (Ad Hoc) Query, you can use the QuickViewer to quickly answer simple questions.

By the Way

In contrast to using SAP Query and InfoSet (Ad Hoc) Query, you do not need to configure User Groups and InfoSets to use QuickViewer. However, if they have already created, you can use them. Users simply select a data source (table, database view, table join, logical database, or InfoSet) when building their QuickView.

Like SAP queries, InfoSet (Ad Hoc) queries are built on the foundation of Query Areas, Query Groups, and InfoSets. Earlier in this hour, you created an InfoSet based on the test logical database F1S, which corresponds to SAP's test system. You can use the same data source used in earlier examples for creating a QuickView or you can create a new InfoSet using an HR logical database. The following example uses the one created earlier in the chapter.

Creating a QuickView

After the one-time configuration is completed, Creating a QuickView is also a relatively elementary task. To begin creating your first QuickView, follow these steps:

1. Like the SAP Query explained earlier, QuickViews can be run in Basis or Layout (Graphical) mode. In Basis mode, the system automatically renders the report from parameters. In Graphical mode, a user can tweak the report's interface via a visual tool. Like the SAP Query, QuickViews are easier to work with in Basis mode.

2. You can access SAP R/3 QuickViewer in three ways: by using transaction SQVI, by using the QuickViewer button on the main screen of the SAP Query (transaction SQ01), or by using an application-specific role from the Easy Access menu.

3. On the main screen, enter a name for your QuickView followed by the Create button. You will be prompted to select a data source. For this example, I use the F1S data source.

4. There are three main tabs that you use to specify your QuickView. The QuickViewer appears in Figure 20.20.

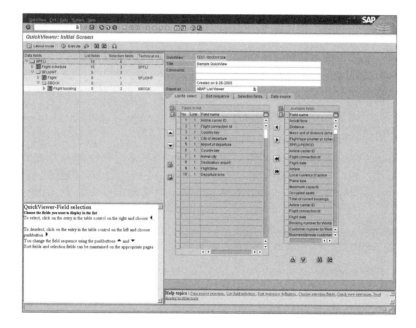

FIGURE 20.20
The main screen of the QuickViewer.

5. The first tab is your list of output fields. Simply select fields listed in the Available Fields column and select the arrow keys to move them to the output column. The second tab enables you to dictate the sort sequence for your selected fields. The third tab enables you to indicate selection fields for specifying your final output.

6. Note in the middle of the screen that you have different Export options for your QuickView. Select one from the drop-down box and then select the Execute button to see the Reports Selection screen. You can further specify your selections. Next, select the Execute button to see your completed QuickView.

If you have created a QuickView and you want to convert it to an SAP Query report, simply follow these three quick steps:

1. Navigate to the main screen of the SAP Query (SQ01).
2. Follow the menu path Queries > Convert QuickViews.
3. Select your QuickView from the drop-down box and press the Enter button. You are prompted to type a name for the query; press Enter again to convert the QuickView.

The Query family of tools contains a toolbar with functions to assist you in further processing your data, including

- Currency conversions
- Sums and totals
- Sorting

- Graphics generation
- Easy download options
- Expert mode options (increased report complexity)

Summary

In this hour, you reviewed how to perform the configuration necessary for the query tools and how to use each query tool. The skills learned in this hour might be the most meaningful to you as an end user because they will empower you with the skills to extract data from your own SAP system. Keep in mind that trial and error is usually the best method for getting accustomed to working with queries in SAP. To this end, seek to "test" your queries in nonproduction systems.

You have also read how to create Ad Hoc queries, truly valuable to those who otherwise must rely on the system administration and programming staff to generate reports from the system. Using the simple InfoSet tool, you can pose complex questions and enjoy the output you need in just minutes. You also have the capability to perform further analysis of the data within the query or by saving or downloading the report to a local spreadsheet.

Q&A

Q *Do users or System Administrators generally regulate the creation of Query Groups, InfoSets, and queries?*

A The use of different tools in SAP largely depends on the customer. In general, Query Groups and InfoSets are maintained by your company's technical users, although the creation of queries varies. In some organizations, users see it as a great means of creating their own reports without seeking the assistance of the technical users. On the other hand, depending on your company's security configuration, the creation of queries and QuickViews might be restricted to technical or super functional users only.

Q *What are the three main components of the Query family?*

A Query Groups, InfoSets, and administrative decisions (which are company specific) are the three main components of the Query family.

Q *When creating InfoSets in the Human Capital Management module, what is different about the configuration?*

A Unlike all other modules, the Field groups that are automatically created in your InfoSet contain fields based on InfoTypes automatically without the users having to add them.

Q *Out of the three query tools, which is the most robust reporting tool with the most features?*

A The SAP Query is the most robust.

Q *Does security restrict access in Query reporting?*

A There are several ways that security can influence the availability of data in Query reporting. Security depends on your company's security configuration, but if you use logical databases, the security is built-in and uses your standard security profile when determining what data you have access to.

Workshop

The workshop is designed to help you anticipate possible questions, review what you've learned, and begin thinking ahead to putting your knowledge into practice. The answers to the quiz that follows can be found in Appendix A, "Quiz Answers."

Quiz

1. What is the transaction code to access the Create Users screen?
2. What is the transaction code to access the Create InfoSets screen?
3. What is the transaction code to access the Create SAP Queries screen?
4. Are global Query Areas client-dependent or independent?
5. Name three different components of SAP queries.

6. What does a Query Area include?

7. What are the two different Query Areas?

8. What must you always do after creating or modifying an InfoSet?

9. What is the transaction code to access the QuickViewer?

10. In which R/3 application modules is the InfoSet (Ad Hoc) Query available?

Exercises

1. Make a cheat sheet of the transaction codes for each of the query reporting tools.

2. Create a new Query Group in the standard area called ZTEST2.

3. Create a new InfoSet in the standard area ZTEST2.

4. Open InfoSet ZTEST2 and peruse the different tables and fields available within it.

5. Assign the InfoSet ZTEST2 to the Query Group ZTEST2.

6. Create a new SAP query in the standard area called ZMYQUERY2 using the InfoSet ZTEST2.

7. Create a new InfoSet (Ad Hoc) Query called ZAHQUERY2.

8. Create a new QuickView called ZQVQUERY2.

SAP SCM, CRM, PLM, and SRM

Outside of mySAP ERP (which includes SAP ECC, NetWeaver, and many of the other SAP components discussed in earlier hours), SAP offers four additional components. These four components, along with mySAP ERP, constitute a family of tightly integrated business solutions under the umbrella of the mySAP Business Suite. In this hour, you learn about these four components, how they fit into the big picture, how they are used, and the value they provide.

Highlights of this hour include

- ▶ Discovering the business benefits of SAP SRM

- ▶ Learning how to use SAP CRM

- ▶ Understanding the components within SAP SCM

- ▶ Learning how SAP PLM can augment your business processes

SAP Supply Chain Management

By transforming your supply chain into a dynamic customer-centric supply chain network, SAP SCM enhances your planning–oriented business processes through streamlining their execution and coordination. SCM opens the door to cross-company collaboration as you partner with your suppliers, vendors, and customers to more intelligently and rapidly adapt to changing business scenarios. In the end, SCM empowers you. It makes it possible to be more proactive, to respond to changing business scenarios quickly, and to ultimately create a more predictable supply chain capable of capitalizing on circumstances and maximizing profitability through

- ▶ Improved responsiveness via real-time insight into your end-to-end supply chain

- ▶ Improved inventory turns made possible by synchronizing inputs with outputs (balancing supply with demand)

- ▶ Encouraging collaboration by providing visibility into trends via supply chain monitoring, analysis, and true analytics

Leveraging the SAP NetWeaver platform, SCM streamlines operations without taxing your IT team—the solution foundation and integration technologies are the same as those employed by other NetWeaver components, including WebAS, Web Services, and so on. This combination of capability and mature technology makes for a true win-win: better service, increased productivity, and improved profitability, all within the umbrella of standards-based and mature technologies.

Components of SAP SCM

As of SCM release 4.1, SAP supports creating and maintaining and adaptive supply chain network through three components—SAP Advanced Planner & Optimizer (SAP APO), SAP Inventory Collaboration Hub (SAP ICH), and SAP Event Management (SAP EM).

SAP APO

SAP's Advanced Planner and Optimizer supports supply chain network-oriented planning, decision making, execution, and optimization. By providing a flexible and adaptive engine for managing your planning processes, APO enables you to make smart decisions through central planning and execution. And because APO integrates supply planning with the other SAP components discussed this hour—CRM, PLM, and SRM—APO gives you complete 360-degree visibility of your supply chain network.

SAP ICH

SAP's Inventory Collaboration Hub enables you to collaborate with your suppliers, jointly approving and easily tweaking the best mix of inventory necessary to meet production demands. This is accomplished through supply chain visibility focused on your manufacturing facilities: knowing what each plant needs, what they consume and at what rate, and when each facility's stock needs to be replenished. With tight integration into your back-end ECC or R/3 system, ICH integrates naturally into your overall planning system and its subprocesses.

SAP EM

Through SAP's Event Management capabilities, SCM makes it easy to monitor your supply chain, including creation and escalation of alerts based on specific conditions and thresholds. This enables SCM's end users to identify and proactively resolve process exceptions and potential supply chain issues before they become show-stoppers.

Business Purposes and Benefits

Through APO, ICH, and EM, SAP Supply Chain Management impacts your bottom line. Benefits include

- Better supply/demand responsiveness, enabling your organization to see and respond to new opportunities.

- Improved customer satisfaction, given the improved underlying communication and collaboration made possible.

- Improved regulatory compliance, essential in today's world of Sarbanes-Oxley and EH&S requirements.

- Better coordination and synchronization between you, your suppliers, and your other business partners helps keep your supply chain working well—optimized and aligned with your priorities.

- Improved cash flows, given the reduction in inventory levels in conjunction with the improved number of inventory turns made possible.

- Enhanced profitability through lower costs, all made possible by timely planning, execution, and supply chain coordination.

Using SAP APO

Because the APO core interface back to R/3 or ECC is real-time, your supply chain network also becomes real-time. That is, real-time access to the most up-to-date master data and transaction data is enabled. In this way, the decisions you make that impact profitability, inventory turns, and the previously discussed benefits are truly real-time decisions; as conditions change in your back-end system or within your CRM, PLM, and other systems, they are reflected in SAP SCM. In the big picture, you can use SCM to enable

- Visibility across the supply chain. Use it to perform strategic planning, conduct day-to-day planning, and everything in between. Collaborate with your planning colleagues to analyze and tweak your supply chain. Monitor it, ensuring adherence to key performance indicators, and more.

- Supply chain modeling and planning. Model your existing supply chain and then begin the process of optimization: set production and other goals, forecast supply and demand, schedule time and materials, and so on.

▶ Supply chain execution. Maximize your return on assets while always remaining sensitive to potential efficiencies that might further increase profitability. Balance conflicting needs and then execute against the best plan, changing distribution, transportation, and other logistics factors as your real-time insight deems advantageous.

Because APO is the most well-known and mature component within SCM, it bears further real-world "use" examples. Typical applications of SAP APO include

▶ From the Supply Chain Cockpit (SCC), you can use APO to launch a query relative to any of your company-specific supply chain elements. This might include products, resources, locations, transportation lanes, and other variables. Display your query results in a map, in lists, or via tables or different graphical formats.

▶ Using APO's Demand Planning application, you can forecast market demand for your company's products or services, and follow this up with the creation of a *demand plan*. Work through different demand planning models, striving for the best balance between supply/demand, for profitability, for inventory turns, and so on. In doing so, feed not only your sales forecast, but also your sales analysis processes.

▶ From APO's Production Planning application, you can create a *production schedule* that balances and reflects your supply plan with your manufacturing capacity at a particular point in time.

▶ From APO's Purchasing Planning application, you can model and develop various plans for balancing your supply of raw materials and other resources against the demand for your products, and then generate a *supply plan*.

▶ Leveraging APO's Transportation and Handling capabilities, you can plan for, optimize, and manage the transportation and handling surrounding a particular product group.

▶ Using APO's SNP Planner, you can schedule the people, products, and other resources that need access to your company's internal facilities.

Through these sample real-world scenarios, you can see how using SAP SCM can help to maximize your company's return on assets, increase your profitability, and help your business unit become more competitive than ever.

APO Demand Planning includes a data mart used to store and maintain your company-specific demand planning data. Combined with user-defined planning layouts and interactive planning books, APO DP enables you to bring together people and resources from across your organization and others. Then you can leverage the APO DP library of statistical forecasting and advanced macro techniques to model and create forecasts. Afterwards, fold in marketing intelligence and then enable management to make their own adjustments to create a demand plan that reflects your real world of constraints and unique advantages.

By the Way

SAP Customer Relationship Management

SAP's Customer Relationship Management component has found great acceptance in the CRM marketplace in the last few years. In its traditional role, SAP CRM is used to support customer-related processes end-to-end. It enables you to obtain a 360-degree view of your customers and their various touch points into your organization. SAP CRM also augments typical back-end functions such as order fulfillment, shipping, invoicing, and accounts receivable. And it folds in and enables enterprise-wide *customer intelligence*, or business intelligence specific to your individual customers and their unique needs.

By bringing this functionality together, CRM facilitates better and faster decision making, lending itself to improving profitability per customer while helping you address your business's strategic priorities and realize your business objectives. Exactly how this is all accomplished is covered in the next few sections.

How CRM Extends mySAP ERP

Through the functionality mentioned previously, SAP CRM effectively extends mySAP ERP and SAP ECC in particular. It brings together and integrates your industry-specific processes to better support your customers; customer-facing organizations within your company benefit from insight obtained across many different touch points, from marketing and sales to service, support, back-end financials, and more. And because SAP CRM is tied to these essential touchpoints, the solution collapses all your field interactions, Internet-based transactions, and even channel and partner-based transactions into a single power view into each customer. Within this view lies the true power of SAP CRM—powerful analytics let you capitalize on what you know so as to not only *retain* your customer but maximize *profit* per transaction and expand your *revenue* base as well.

Features of SAP CRM

A number of the core features and support for specific business processes outlined previously are worth exploring further:

▶ **Marketing support**—Use SAP CRM to enhance your marketing effectiveness, maximize resource use, and empower your team to develop and maintain long-term profitable customer relationships. From a user's perspective, this includes marketing resource management, campaign management, trade promotion management, market segment management, lead/prospect management, and marketing analytics.

▶ **Sales support**—Maximize your sales efforts by removing barriers to productivity and working with your customers in a consistent manner. CRM Sales is geared for your sales force, empowering them and providing the tools they need to close deals. For example, territory management, account and contact management, lead and opportunity management, and sales planning and forecasting help your sales force identify and manage prospects. Then, by leveraging quotation and order management, product configuration, contract management, incentive and commission management, time and travel management, and sales analytics, you can retain customers all the while growing sales volume and margins and managing the expenses associated with sales.

▶ **Service support**—Through CRM service you can maximize the value both you and your customers obtain from post-sales services. This enables you to profitably manage a broad range of functions geared toward driving successful customer service and support, including field service, Internet-enabled service offerings, service marketing and sales, and service/contract management. After they are entrenched, customers benefit from improved warranty and claims management, and effective channel service and depot repair services. Your service team benefits from service analytics, enabling the team to maximize profit per touchpoint.

▶ **Internet-based e-commerce**—For both your sales/marketing force and service team, use the Internet to drive profitable sales and post-sales support. From e-marketing to e-selling, e-service, and e-analytics, SAP CRM delivers a well-thought-out set of Internet-enabled offerings and methods for acquiring and retaining customers.

▶ **Interaction Center (IC) management support**—With support for marketing, sales, and service vehicles such as telemarketing, telesales, customer service, e-service, and interaction center analytics, SAP CRM IC complements and arms your field-based sales force.

▶ **Channel management support**—SAP CRM users can also benefit from this indirect channel support mechanism, which provides sales and service support for your channel partners. Combined with channel-based marketing, sales, service, commerce, and partner/channel-specific analytics, Channel Management support rounds out SAP CRM.

The Latest CRM Enhancements

SAP AG is unwilling to stand still, as evidenced in their continuing efforts to add substance and value to SAP CRM. Most recently, this effort has been aided through close cooperation and collaboration with many of SAP's very own CRM customer accounts. In this way, the CRM development team at SAP identified and incorporated enhancements to CRM that are truly warranted, authentically desired, and able to provide true business value. Some of the latest enhancements include

▶ The introduction of new high-impact value-oriented industry-specific processes across many different industries

▶ Optimized business practices that reflect CRM best practices in marketing, sales, services, and interaction channels

▶ Highly evolved and easily adaptable analytical content and enterprise customer intelligence, complementing the SAP NetWeaver analytics platform (and ready to be deployed and tailored for specific business user needs)

▶ A great number of platform enhancements relative to deployment, optimized user interfaces, and updated navigation procedures

CRM Industry-Specific Processes

CRM processes are typically very customer-focused, built around the needs of a particular business unit or organizational entity. SAP CRM takes these fundamental capabilities and kicks them up a notch, helping you manage and deliver customer-focused value within your unique industry vertical. And because SAP CRM is easily adapted to different industries, it's uniquely positioned to service multiprovider organizations.

SAP CRM offers much more than a couple of extra CRM features or cosmetic usability changes, though; indeed, SAP CRM delivers the kind of holistic end-to-end industry-specific solution that meets all the needs of many industries. SAP worked with a large number of their installed base to make this so. Examples of the power that SAP CRM delivers relative to industry-specific CRM processes include

▶ **Professional services industry**—Use SAP CRM to manage prospects, opportunities, client relationships, project resources, and the development of client deliverables.

▶ **Automotive industry**—Use SAP CRM to manage the automotive sales cycle from start to finish, including vehicle market planning, sales, financials, distribution, and post-sales management.

▶ **Leasing entities**—Use SAP CRM's SAP Leasing capabilities to address end-to-end lease management, from identifying financing opportunities for new leases or loans to remarketing existing leases, to lease termination.

▶ **Consumer products industry**—Manage customer trade promotions, including brand management, activity planning, demand planning, budgeting, program execution, evaluation, and subsequent analyses of each phase.

▶ **Media industry vertical**—SAP CRM can manage intellectual property (IP), help you leverage this IP to your financial benefit, and manage any resulting royalties or other payments.

▶ **Utilities vertical**—Manage both commercial and industrial customers from a sales perspective, including opportunity and quotation management, cross-system contracts, and key revenue-producing accounts.

▶ **High-tech industry**—From managing and measuring business volume to viewing customer demand, managing channel inventory, and splitting commissions, SAP CRM addresses all your high-tech partner and channel relationship needs.

▶ **Public sector**—Through constituent services and tax and revenue management, SAP CRM can help you manage all "citizen-driven," tax administration, and similar tasks.

▶ **Pharmaceutical industry**—Use SAP CRM to manage and support the stages of drug commercialization, from strategy definition through sales planning and execution, on to measuring the success of each drug's respective sales and marketing programs.

▶ **Manufacturing vertical**—Manage orders, the manufacturing process, fulfillment, and more through SAP CRM's lean batch-management capabilities.

Business Benefits of CRM

Given the variety inherent to more than 20 industry verticals for which SAP CRM provides a solution, it's no surprise that SAP's business benefits are as far-reaching as they are diverse. SAP CRM provides support for end-to-end business processes covering 300 discrete processes across more than 400 points of integration.

What does this mean for a CRM user? First, it means you benefit from true enterprise-wide customer insight. With visibility across customer data effectively spread across your enterprise (from financial systems to supply chain, ERP, and HR repositories), sound decision-making is naturally expedited.

Next, CRM enables you to prioritize competing initiatives and balance your strategic objectives against tactical needs, all the while helping you achieve measurable return on investment (ROI). Finally, along the same lines, SAP CRM enables you to manage and support customers while enjoying a low total cost of ownership. That is, you can deploy CRM and bring it up to speed quickly, which means it pays for itself in short order as your sales increase and costs of doing business diminish.

SAP Product Lifecycle Management

One of the lesser-known components in SAP's suite of business solutions is SAP PLM, or Product Lifecycle Management. PLM is focused on helping companies develop new products by helping those organizations embrace and facilitate creativity and innovation. Further, SAP PLM helps companies identify and remove productivity-robbing organizational constraints. It serves as the foundation for successful *new product development and introduction* (*NPDI*). Using NPDI, you tie people and information together, effectively interconnecting your sales, planning, production, procurement, maintenance, internal service provider, and other organizations together. And outside of your own company's organizations, PLM enables you to bring together partners, suppliers, contract manufacturers, external service providers, and even customers under the umbrella of developing better products.

PLM's IT Platform

PLM is built upon the NetWeaver technology stack. In this way it takes advantage of industry-standard communications protocols to maximize its capability to connect and operate with other solutions. Specifically, PLM's use of HTML, XML, and the Wireless Application Protocol (WAP) enables you to access your PLM system from your desktop or laptop as well as by using handheld and mobile devices. Its open architecture also means you can customize PLM for your specific company and industry vertical, allowing anytime, anywhere access regardless of industry business process specifics.

Business Insight Through PLM

PLM facilitates rapid development and delivery of the products upon which your business depends for its revenue. PLM's technology platform sets the stage for usefulness, but in itself does not solve any business problems. Only by affording a holistic view into the processes and resources that come into play during a product's lifecycle does PLM become a comprehensive problem-solver. With it, you can take care of your product conception, design, engineering, production ramp-up, product change management, post-sales service, and maintenance needs. In this, the benefits are many:

▶ Enjoy a faster time to market as a result of rapid development capabilities.

▶ By tying together your supply chain with procurement and PLM, manufacturing operations are streamlined; delivery and production are sped up.

▶ Capitalize on core competencies while outsourcing noncore tasks, thereby minimizing your overall costs.

▶ Measure and evaluate the progress of discrete product-oriented projects across different product lines.

▶ By integrating with your operational systems, lower your total cost of ownership relative to planning for and deploying a new product.

▶ Leverage PLM's modular approach to product development and ramp-up, so as to incrementally meet your product's needs as it evolves through the product lifecycle.

▶ Realize improved product quality.

▶ Maximize your product worker's productivity through the use of a role-based enterprise portal front-end.

▶ Reduce the waste and inefficiency that surrounds typical product lifecycle management processes.

▶ Make better and faster business decisions, taking advantage of powerful analytics across the product lifecycle (portfolio management, quality, occupational health and safety, maintenance management, and others).

Ultimately, the greatest business benefit of PLM is found in the improved business results you'll enjoy as a result. PLM enables you to pursue and develop new products; innovate, explore, and analyze new markets; penetrate those new markets; gain a higher market share in existing markets; and increase your customer's satisfaction throughout the entire product lifecycle.

Using PLM

At the end of the day, SAP's comprehensive solution for product lifecycle management aids your company in the day-to-day execution surrounding product management. Use PLM to enable collaborative product development, engineering, and associated project and quality management. Plug in your partners as you all seek to meet environmental, health, and safety requirements. Gain visibility across your enterprise by extending PLM via the entire mySAP Business Suite—from CRM and SCM to mySAP ERP and more. In doing so, you can tie in every inter-company and partner-provided department or organization, which enables you to optimize communications, strengthen marketing and sales efforts, and include the necessary post-development service and support organizations. Through all this, you maintain a low cost of ownership as you push new products through their development and engineering phases into manufacturing, and ultimately into the hands of your customers—reaping better margins and faster turnarounds than ever possible.

SAP Supplier Relationship Management

SRM is SAP's solution for managing the procurement and support of the goods and services a company needs day in and day out. Just as SAP CRM manages the relationship between a company and its customers, SAP SRM helps to optimize and manage the relationship between a company and its suppliers.

As another one of SAP's more mature offerings, it's no surprise that SAP's Supplier Relationship Management is well integrated with other mySAP Business Suite components. For example, SRM integrates seamlessly with PLM, enabling a high degree of collaboration between product buyers and parts suppliers. Bidding processes are streamlined as well. All this naturally impacts mySAP ERP as well, because financial and logistics data are updated and shared between systems. SRM also ties into SAP SCM, extending and enabling tight integration with your supply chain while leveraging the open standards-based SAP NetWeaver platform.

Integration Benefits with PLM

With this tight integration into NetWeaver, the mySAP Business Suite, and specifically PLM, SRM users benefit in terms of

- Improved design collaboration and therefore time-to-market
- Streamlined access to engineering documentation and other materials useful in optimizing product quality, manufacturing processes, and more

- ▶ Better visibility into ERP back-end data, like materials management processes, financial documents, and bills of materials (BOMs)

- ▶ The capability to mark up and "redline" computer-aided drawings

By the same token, SAP PLM users benefit from

- ▶ PLM's tight integration with SRM's sourcing capabilities

- ▶ A high degree of collaboration made possible during the design and engineering phases of a product, because workers focus on technical specifications and the development of requests for proposals (RFPs) and requests for quotes (RFQs)

How SRM Impacts Your Enterprise

Beyond PLM, SRM lowers your total cost of ownership through its integration with the other components found in the mySAP Business Suite. This is especially so with your "operational" systems, such as ERP, CRM, computer-aided design, and supply chain systems. Through this integration, Supplier Relationship Management enables you to improve product and sourcing strategies, shorten sourcing cycle times, and effectively reduce your procurement costs.

Business Benefits

By reducing the costs of goods sourced and used throughout your company, yet improving supply efficiencies, SRM enables you to manage your bottom line. The business benefits are many:

- ▶ Sourcing strategy improvements, which includes improved access to each supplier's performance, improved management of supply, and therefore decreased supply-related risk

- ▶ Compressed cycle times made possible through faster RFP-to-receipt processes, use of online approvals to speed up the procurement cycle, and improved supplier responsiveness

- ▶ Reduced process costs facilitated through simplification, process automation, low-cost integration and connectivity with other systems, and the elimination of maverick buying

- ▶ Lower overall unit prices in light of the consolidation made possible for all your departments, along with reduced costs for carrying inventory and as a result of competitive bidding

Using SAP SRM

With your understanding of SRM from a business benefit and technology perspective, a final look at *how* you can use SRM is in order. Most obviously to those who have already deployed it, SRM is used by those responsible for *internal procurement*. This includes

▶ Employee-driven self-service, whereby employees are empowered to procure materials and services necessary to the completion of their organization's goals. Administration and processing are accomplished through one interface using web-based tools that not only make the process a simple one, but also facilitate corporate spending and procurement compliance.

▶ Automated materials procurement performed as part of an organization's supply-chain workflow (essentially integrating your purchasing function with your supply chain management system).

Second, SRM enables strategic purchasing and sourcing by supporting a host of management, development, and analysis functions. Use SRM to

▶ Manage contracts relative to overall compliance with each contract's terms and conditions and more.

▶ Create, manage, and administer your procurement catalog, using built-in tools to import new product detailed data from external sources, to manage your product hierarchy or schema, and to index your products so that search capabilities are enabled.

▶ Manage your supplier-selection process, thereby creating a base of supply and inherently improving process repeatability. Use electronic auction and bidding tools to analyze each supplier's performance, to collaborate with your suppliers, and to minimize procurement risks.

▶ Develop strategies for supply, again using built-in tools to aggregate the demand for particular materials and services across your enterprise. In the same way, manage and analyze your product portfolio, conduct product management tasks, and control the purchasing process.

▶ Analyze your spending patterns through global spend visibility; conduct analytics related to your products and suppliers, and then share this data across your enterprise (populate data warehouses, data marts, other procurement systems, as well as electronic catalogs, supply chain management systems, and other internal systems).

Third, collaborate with your suppliers to streamline procurement processes, provide better information access to your company's purchasers, make better sourcing decisions, and

▶ **Collaborate with product developers**—Share data between trading partners and your own purchasing team to enable faster product development cycles.

▶ **Collaborate with your suppliers**—Give them access to your inventory and replenishment data so they can help you maintain your minimum required inventory levels.

▶ **Connect and integrate your suppliers with your team**—Use standard XML-based document exchange technology to gain real-time access into the lowest prices, best volume discounts, and so on.

By using SRM's breadth of capabilities, you can optimize, integrate, and automate your own procurement processes into your day-to-day workflows, helping your organization to never miss a beat.

Summary

As you can imagine, the complexity of the SAP business solutions discussed in this hour are much greater than reflected here. Each SAP component within the broader mySAP Business Suite umbrella constitutes an SAP implementation in its own right, after all. However, the skills and knowledge you have gained in the past hour have equipped you with a wide-ranging understanding of how each solution can benefit you and your company.

Q&A

Q *Which features in SAP CRM augment your capability to support new customers?*

A Three support-oriented features of SAP CRM include marketing support, sales support, and service support.

Q *How does SRM's tight integration with PLM benefit your SRM users?*

A Benefits are derived on four fronts—improved design collaboration (and therefore time-to-market); streamlined access to engineering documentation and other materials useful in optimizing product quality, manufacturing processes, and more; improved visibility into ERP back-end data (such as SAP ECC or R/3 MM processes, financial documents, and BOMs); and through the capability to mark up and "redline" computer-aided drawings.

Workshop

The workshop is designed to help you anticipate possible questions, review what you've learned, and begin thinking ahead about putting your knowledge into practice. The answers to the quiz that follows can be found in Appendix A, "Quiz Answers."

Quiz

1. List three ways in which SAP Supply Chain Management can maximize profitability.

2. What are the three components of SCM?

3. How does SAP CRM maximize your profitability?

4. Which three communications protocols used by PLM enable access to your PLM data?

5. What are four business benefits of SRM?

6. What is the technology used to connect and integrate your SRM-enabled suppliers with your procurement?

HOUR 22

Integration with Microsoft Office

Integration between SAP and Microsoft's products is nothing new. Using object linking and embedding (OLE), a concept introduced in Hour 14, "Technology Overview," it has long been possible to drop your SAP data into a Microsoft application. In this way, additional analysis of your ECC, R/3, APO, and other list- and simple report-based SAP data sources can be easily accomplished through Microsoft Excel, Access, and so on. And with the latest joint announcements between SAP and Microsoft—code-named *Mendocino*—this integration continues to grow deeper and more valuable, adding Microsoft Exchange, Outlook, other database sources, and more to the list of Microsoft products that afford better integration with SAP.

Highlights of this hour include

- ▶ Using SAP's %pc functionality to save SAP data
- ▶ Moving SAP data into Microsoft Excel, Word, and Access
- ▶ Review of Mendocino
- ▶ How Mendocino impacts end-user productivity

SAP and MS Office Integration Architecture

Integration between SAP and Microsoft products hinges upon the use of OLE, a common and standard technology for transferring and sharing information among applications. With OLE, you can take data out of your SAP system and place it into another system, all the while maintaining the format and integrity of the data. For example, you can view data residing in any number of SAP database tables as a series of columns and rows in Microsoft Excel—an easy way to view and manipulate data otherwise trapped in the SAP database.

The SAP Assistant is the OLE interface used for calling SAP functions and transactions from other non-SAP applications. The SAP Assistant exposes both ActiveX controls and OLE object classes, for logging in to SAP, managing data and tables, calling functions and transactions, and more. SAP systems are therefore designed today so that you can share data with any OLE-compatible application. Sample OLE-compatible applications include

▶ Microsoft Office, including Visio and other products

▶ Corel Office, including Paradox

▶ Star Office

▶ Lotus Smart Suite

▶ Many Web Server development environments, such as Microsoft FrontPage

Additionally, nearly all modern application development languages in use today support OLE. This includes the old-school C++ programming language as well as the latest and greatest Microsoft .NET Visual Basic offerings, to IBM's WebSphere Information Integrator and PowerBuilder by Sybase. In this way, the developer of a non-SAP application can create objects that can access information in SAP.

Using %pc to Download Data

There are many ways to share data between SAP and Microsoft. As I briefly mentioned in previous hours, executing %pc in the transaction dialog box is an excellent and expedient way of moving data from SAP lists into other formats. Transactions that display their data via OCX controls—in various panels, each with its own data sources, constructs, and so on—are generally not good candidates for %pc. That is, OCX-based output typically does not lend itself to being downloaded into a PC format such as XLS, RTF, and so on. But transactions that are displayed in list format—most of them, to some degree—are excellent candidates for this method of downloading SAP data into Microsoft Office–based formats.

To save SAP list-based output to a file on your desktop or the network, enter the characters **%pc** in the transaction dialog box and then press Enter. A print window pops up (see Figure 22.1), defaulting to saving the screen's contents in an unconverted file format. Choose the format most appropriate for your immediate needs, press Enter, browse to the desired directory path, type the name of the output file you want to create, and then press Save to save the list data to the filename you specified.

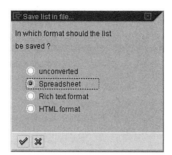

FIGURE 22.1
Saving SAP data
in a number of
formats is easi-
ly and quickly
accomplished
by using %pc.

Exporting SAP Data to Microsoft Excel

Microsoft Excel provides a user-friendly format and helpful tools to assist you in the
process of analyzing and presenting data. To get your SAP data into Microsoft Excel,
you can employ several methods. The most basic method involves the System List
function, which enables you to save lists displayed on your SAP screen.

> If you want to save your downloaded SAP list in Microsoft Excel, be sure to select
> File, Save As and then select the Microsoft Excel Workbook (*.xls) option in the
> Save As type box or your spreadsheet; otherwise, by default, it is saved in a text
> format.

By the Way

You can also use the SAP Query tool to export data to Microsoft Excel, as follows:

1. Execute an SAP Query, as discussed in Hour 20, "Reporting Tools in SAP (SAP
   Query, InfoSet Query, Ad Hoc Query, and QuickViewer)."

2. The options listed on the selection screen enable you to designate the type of
   output you want for your report. For a basic transfer to a Microsoft Excel
   spreadsheet, select the Display As Table radio button.

3. From here, select the List, Save, Local File to download this table into Microsoft
   Excel. A Save As box appears, enabling you to select the download file format.
   Be sure to select the spreadsheet option.

4. After the download is complete, start Microsoft Excel and open the data you
   have just saved (see Figure 22.2).

5. Return to your SAP Query output screen displaying your table.

> You can use the same method detailed previously to download InfoSet or other
> "ad hoc" queries, as covered in Hour 20.

By the Way

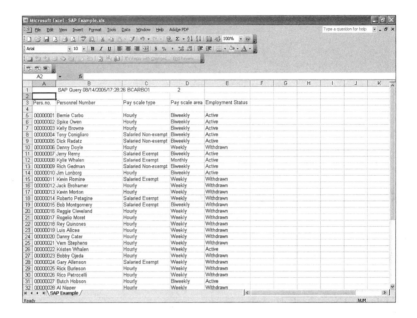

Creating SAP Form Letters in Microsoft Word

SAP has a great interface for creating form letters using Microsoft Word. This tool has endless possibilities for your company. For an example, let's assume you need to output SAP Human Resources employee data into Microsoft Word so that you can create a form letter to all employees.

1. Select a query to execute.

2. From the selection screen, use the Display As Table option and then execute your report.

3. When the output appears, rather than saving this file to Microsoft Excel, select the Word Processing button at the top of your Query Output. Doing so opens the Word Processor Settings dialog box shown in Figure 22.3. Press Enter to continue.

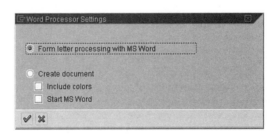

4. The dialog box that is displayed presents you with a number of options. You can designate whether you want to create a new Word document, use a current Word document (one that is currently "open" on your system), or use an existing Word document (one that is saved on your computer). Click the green check mark to begin the merge between SAP and Microsoft Word. Upon execution, SAP opens Microsoft Word (see Figure 22.4).

The mail merge toolbar containing a link to your SAP fields

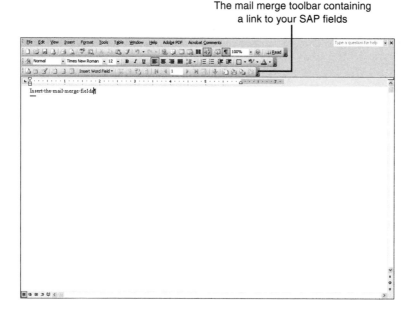

FIGURE 22.4
A Microsoft Word application launches with a new document.

5. An important thing to note is that your Microsoft Word application now contains a new mail merge toolbar that gives you the capability to insert your SAP fields into your Microsoft Word form letter. In Microsoft Word, press the Enter key to begin at a new line, and then select the Insert Merge Field button on the toolbar. In the drop-down list (or the Insert Merge Field pop-up window, in the case of Microsoft Office 2003), shown in Figure 22.5, you see all the SAP fields contained in your original SAP Query.

6. As appropriate for your needs, select one of your SAP fields. It appears in brackets in your Microsoft Word document. Press Enter and insert another SAP field. Type some text into your Microsoft Word document, and then insert another SAP field (see Figure 22.6).

FIGURE 22.5
The Microsoft Word Insert Merge Field button contains the names of your SAP fields from your SAP Query.

SAP fields appear in brackets

FIGURE 22.6
Your Microsoft Word form letter contains the inserted fields from your SAP Query in addition to any text you typed manually.

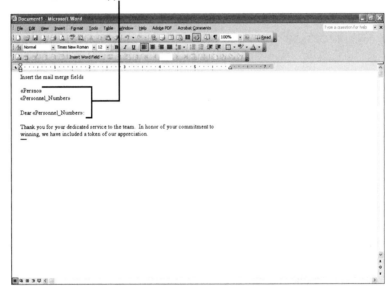

7. To preview the output of your form letter, click the ABC (View Merged Data) button from the mail merge toolbar, shown in Figure 22.7.

8. Use the Record selectors (forward and backward) buttons on the mail merge toolbar to view the various records.

View Merged Data button
Actual SAP data | Record selectors

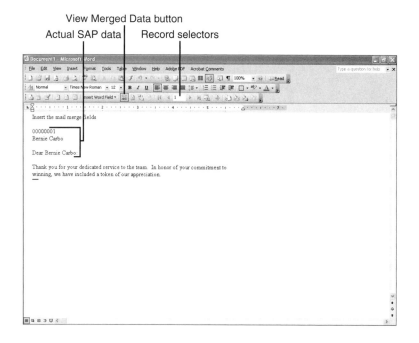

FIGURE 22.7
A sample
Microsoft Word
form letter containing the SAP
fields from your
SAP Query, in
the View
Merged Data
view.

You can save your Microsoft Word merge document for repeated use. Next time
you want to use the same form letter (but with the latest data from SAP), you
need to reopen the SAP Query that serves as the source of the document, select
the List, Word processing option from the menu, and then select the existing Word
document radio button. You are then prompted to enter the name of your Word
document where you saved the file. Microsoft Word will launch, displaying your
existing form letter containing the latest data from your SAP system.

*Did you
Know?*

Exporting SAP to Microsoft Access

As you have seen, exporting SAP data to Microsoft Excel and Word is useful when it
comes to performing further offline manipulation of your data, for creating reports
and graphs, or for drafting form letters. Exporting data to a Microsoft Access database is quite useful, too, when it comes to general reporting.

Exporting to Microsoft Access is helpful as well when you want to compare data
among multiple systems. For example, if your company stores your vendor master
data in SAP and it also stores vendor master data in a non-SAP application (and
you have not implemented SAP Exchange Infrastructure with Master Data
Management), you can use Microsoft Access as a tool to quickly compare the two
sources relative to overall data consistency.

*By the
Way*

The initial steps to export data into Microsoft Access are the same as the steps to download a file into Microsoft Excel—the idea is to get the data into the Excel XLS format. Verify this is the case before proceeding.

Depending on your Microsoft Excel configuration, you might have to perform a few extra steps here:

1. Launch Microsoft Excel and open the spreadsheet you saved earlier.
2. In Excel, use the menu path File, Save As—as if you were going to save the file again.
3. Take a close look at the Save As Type box; ensure that the file is saved as a Microsoft Excel Worksheet and not any other format.

Alternatively, view and verify the extension of the file using Microsoft's Explorer.

Importing SAP into Microsoft Access

After the XLS file resides on your local system or an accessible file share, you need to import this file into Microsoft Access (the following steps assume Access has been installed on your system; given that Access is not included with all versions of Microsoft Office, this might not be the case by default):

1. Launch Microsoft Access on your system.

2. From this initial window, select the Blank Database option, and then click OK. You are prompted to create a name and to select a location for your database. In this example, I selected the C:\My Documents directory and named the database MySAP.mdb, as shown in Figure 22.8.

FIGURE 22.8
The Microsoft Access File New Database window prompts you to create a new database file.

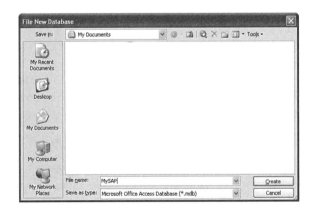

3. Click the Create button; you then see the main Microsoft Access window, which appears in Figure 22.9.

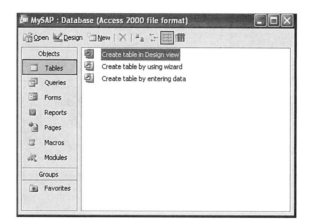

FIGURE 22.9
The Microsoft Access data-base main win-dow displays the different database ele-ments.

4. To bring the SAP data into Microsoft Access, use the Microsoft Access menu path File, Get External Data, Import. You are then prompted with a window similar to the one shown in Figure 22.10. This is where you have to input the location and filename of the output file you saved earlier. By default, the Files of Type box lists Microsoft Access (*.mdb). You have to change this to Microsoft Excel (*.xls).

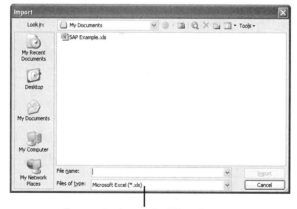

FIGURE 22.10
Select your import file loca-tion in the Microsoft Access Import window.

Be sure to change the Files of type
drop-down box to reflect Microsoft Excel

5. After changing the Files of Type box and selecting your file, click Import. Just as in the Microsoft Excel import, in Access you are presented with an Import Spreadsheet Wizard similar to the one shown in Figure 22.11.

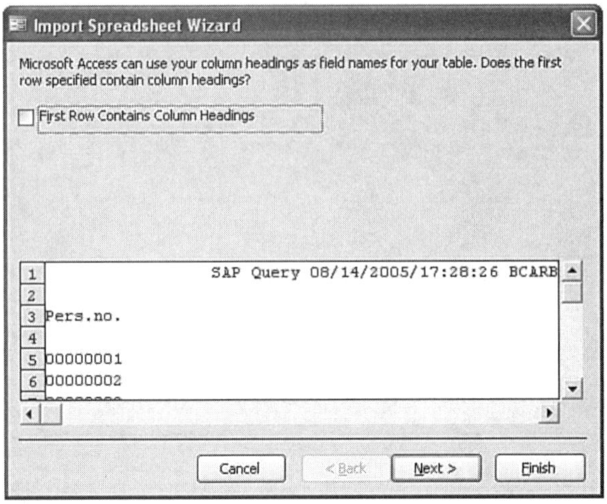

FIGURE 22.11
The Microsoft
Access Import
Spreadsheet
Wizard assists
you in importing
your file.

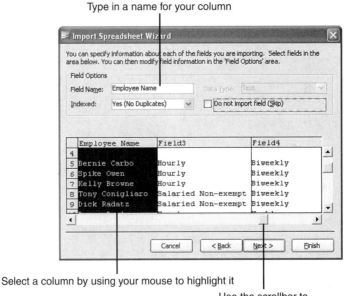

6. On the first screen of the Import Spreadsheet Wizard, click the Next button to continue. On the second screen, it asks whether you want to create a new table or add the data to an existing table. To create a new Access database table containing your SAP data, click Next. The next window, shown in Figure 22.12, gives you an opportunity to name each of your fields.

Type in a name for your column

FIGURE 22.12
The Microsoft
Access Import
Spreadsheet
Wizard field
enables individ-
ual field specifi-
cation and
more.

Select a column by using your mouse to highlight it

Use the scrollbar to
navigate through your file

7. By selecting each column (use your mouse to do so), you can type a field name for each. After you have named all your fields, click Next.

8. The following screen enables you to assign a unique identifying number for each of your records, to be used as a primary key (primary keys are discussed in Hour 3, "Database Basics"). Click the Next button to continue.

9. The last screen asks you to provide a name for your table. Type **MySAP** and click Finish. Microsoft Access then presents you with a confirmation window similar to that shown in Figure 22.13.

FIGURE 22.13
The Microsoft Access confirmation window declares that your data has finished importing.

10. Click OK in the final Import Spreadsheet Wizard confirmation window; you are returned to the Microsoft Access main window, and your new table is now listed under the Table tab.

11. To take a look at your table, select it and then click the Open button. Your SAP list now appears as a Microsoft Access table (see Figure 22.14); it includes an additional primary key field as well.

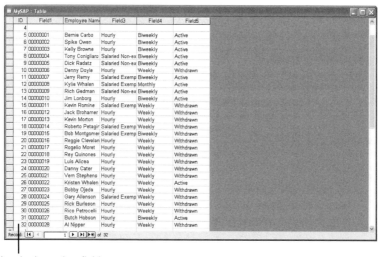

FIGURE 22.14
Your SAP data now appears in a Microsoft Access database table.

Note the additional primary key field

This process is certainly a few steps longer than exporting your SAP data into Microsoft Excel. However, Microsoft Access is a sound reporting tool used by a large number of SAP customers as their primary reporting tool—especially when other applications or tools like SAP Business Warehouse, Strategic Enterprise Management, Cognos, or Crystal Reports are unavailable. Its prevalence also speaks to the fact that Microsoft Access is popular across many companies regardless of size.

Another reason for its popularity is that Microsoft Access is simple to use. It leverages simple report wizards to guide you step-by-step in creating comprehensive reports. Now you will create one sample report using a Microsoft Access Report Wizard.

The Microsoft Access Report Wizard

Creating reports in Microsoft Access is easy using a tool called the Microsoft Access Report Wizard. The use of reports wizards simplifies the layout process of your fields by visually stepping you through a series of questions about the type of report that you want to create. The wizard walks you through the step-by–step creation of a report, while behind the scenes Access is formatting, grouping, and sorting your report based on selections you make.

Instead of having to create a report from scratch, Microsoft Access provides a number of standard report formats. Some of these, like tabular and columnar reports, mail-merge reports, and mailing label formats, lend themselves to meeting basic reporting requirements. Reports created using the Microsoft Access Report Wizard can also be customized to fit your needs. To use the Report Wizard, perform the following steps:

1. Close any open Access databases by using the menu path File, Close.

2. In the main Microsoft Access database window, click Reports.

3. From here, click the New button to launch the Microsoft Access Report Wizard (or choose the option to create a report in Design view).

4. Assuming you are running the Report Wizard, select the Report Wizard option in the top box and your table name in the second box. Click OK to proceed.

5. Next, you are presented with a field selection screen. From this screen, you can select which fields are output to your report. Select a field by highlighting it with your mouse, and then use the Next button to include it in the report. In the example, I selected the Employment Status field, as shown in Figure 22.15.

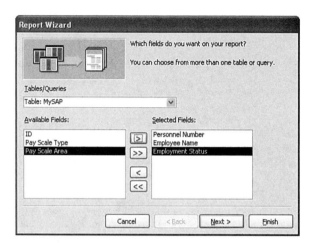

FIGURE 22.15
The Microsoft Access Report Wizard field selection window enables you to specify which fields you want to include in your report output.

6. After you click Next, the Report Wizard asks whether you want to add any grouping levels to your report. This is a helpful step when you are creating a report where you might want to group and subtotal portions of the output. For this example, you don't need grouping or subtotaling, so click the Next button to continue.

7. Now identify your sort order criteria. In the example, shown in Figure 22.16, I have sorted according to Employee Name.

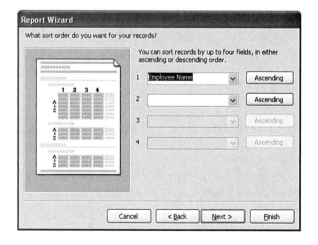

FIGURE 22.16
The Microsoft Access Report Wizard enables you to select multiple sorting criteria.

8. The Report Wizard enables you to specify formatting criteria. The orientation of the report (portrait or landscape) and the layout of the report (columnar, tabular, or justified) are designated on this screen. After making a selection, click Next.

9. You can choose from a selection of predefined formats for your report. After making a selection, click Next.

10. The last step asks you to type a name for your report. Do so, and click Finish to complete the creation of your report.

> Advanced Microsoft Access users can write a macro that automatically retrieves the latest SAP download file and imports it in to your existing Microsoft Access table—replacing the old data and thus automating the Microsoft Access import process. For more information on this function, search the Microsoft Access help for "automate importing."
>
> In the same way, advanced ABAP or Java programmers can write a program that automatically generates a file that can be used for the download portion of this process, thus automating the entire SAP-to-Access reporting process.

Microsoft Access is a great reporting tool that enables users with minimal Microsoft Access skills to create reports. Using Access, you can also include graphics in your reports, or you can create graphs and charts of your SAP data. If you take a few minutes to investigate the types of reports you can create using Microsoft Access, I'm sure you will discover the value of this reporting tool for SAP.

Quick References

The following sections provide simple step-by-step instructions for executing many of the reporting processes just discussed. Use the following sections as a quick reference to speed you through each respective reporting process. And remember, if you need more information, refer to each process's respective detailed sections provided earlier in this hour.

Quick Reference for Exporting Lists to Microsoft Excel

The following is a recap of the steps required to use the System List function to export SAP lists to Microsoft Excel.

1. Navigate to the SAP screen containing the list you want to output.

2. Follow the menu path System, List, Save, Local File.

3. Use the possible entries help button to change the location and filename of your new file.

4. Click the Transfer button.

5. Launch Microsoft Excel and open the file.

Quick Reference for Exporting SAP Query Reports to Excel

The following is a recap of the steps required to output SAP Query reports to Microsoft Excel.

1. Execute the SAP Query report that contains the data that you want to include in your report.

2. On the selection screen, select the Display As Table option, and execute the report.

3. Select the List, Download to File menu option.

4. Use the possible entries help button to change the location and filename of your new file.

5. Click the Transfer button.

6. Launch Microsoft Excel and open the file.

Quick Reference for Creating Form Letters with Microsoft Word

The following is a recap of the steps required to create SAP form letters using Microsoft Word.

1. Execute the SAP Query report that contains the data that you want to include in your report.

2. On the selection screen, select the Display As Table option, and execute the report.

3. Select the List, Word Processing menu option.

4. Click the Enter button on the Word Processing Settings dialog box.

5. Select your required options from the MS Word Settings dialog box, and then click the Enter button.

6. Type your document and insert merge fields using the Insert Merge Field button on the Microsoft Word mail merge toolbar.

7. Use the ABC view merged data button to review your document and the record selection buttons to navigate between records.

Quick Reference for Exporting Lists to Microsoft Access

The following is a recap of the steps required to use the System List function to export SAP lists into Microsoft Access. The initial steps of this process are the same for downloading files to Microsoft Excel.

1. Navigate to the SAP screen containing the list you want to output.

2. Follow the menu path System, List, Save, Local File.

3. Use the possible entries help button to change the location and filename of your new file.

4. Click the Transfer button.

5. Open your file in Microsoft Excel, and use the menu path File, Save As to save it as a Microsoft Excel worksheet. Close Excel.

6. Launch Microsoft Access and create a new database.

7. Use the menu path File, Get External Data, Import, and select your Microsoft Excel file to import the file in to Microsoft Access using the Import Spreadsheet Wizard.

Quick Reference for Exporting SAP Query Reports to Access

The following is an explanation of the steps required to output an SAP Query report to Microsoft Access. The initial steps of this process are the same for downloading files to Microsoft Excel.

1. Execute the SAP Query report that contains the data that you want to include in your report.

2. On the selection screen, select the Display As Table option, and execute the report.

3. Select the List, Download to File menu option.

4. Use the possible entries help button (down arrow) to change the location and filename of your new file.

5. Click the Transfer button.

6. Open your file in Microsoft Excel, and use the menu path File, Save As to save it as a Microsoft Excel worksheet. Close Excel.

7. Launch Microsoft Access and create a new database.

8. Use the menu path File, Get External Data, Import, and select your Microsoft Excel file to import the file in to Microsoft Access using the Import Spreadsheet Wizard.

Mendocino Review

Outside of the specific integration capabilities that OLE has historically made possible, SAP and Microsoft have worked together more recently to provide another level of integration. Called Mendocino, it's the first real joint product between the two giant software companies. Leveraging the openness of .NET-enabled Web Services and the capabilities of Enterprise Services Architecture (ESA), Mendocino enables Microsoft Office 2003 to extend and manage SAP-derived business process functions and the data traversing them.

Mendocino was announced in April 2005, made available in the final quarter of the year, and hailed as the "next big thing" for SAP/Microsoft integration. Its open interface enables independent software vendors (ISVs), other SAP customers, and systems integrators to extend workflows and improve functionality both in the "back office" and "front office" Microsoft product suites.

That is, Mendocino connects SAP with Outlook Exchange in the back-end, and with the usual Microsoft Office products like Excel and Word in the front-end. Additionally, Mendocino enables connectivity with other databases, servers, and clients. This is all accomplished through

▶ Extended Microsoft product application menus

▶ The use of an SAP-specific "smart pane"; SAP can pop up when it has something important to deliver or communicate

▶ Better business analytics made possible through Excel

▶ Better integration with Word via "smart" business documents

Improving Productivity with Mendocino

Mendocino improves end-user productivity by leveraging exposed business processes and Mendocino-improved desktop interfaces. What does this look like in the real world? As outlined here, the impact is widespread and compelling. Use Mendocino to

▶ Synchronize your SAP and Outlook calendars

▶ Synchronize SAP business processes with other processes managed through Microsoft products

▶ Conduct time-management activities and populate multiple data sources or impact extended business processes through a single interface (typically accomplished with SAP's Enterprise Portal or Microsoft's Outlook)

▶ View real-time data in SAP via Microsoft's products (as opposed to historical data often reflected by most reporting systems)

▶ Automate the creation and delivery of SAP reports via Microsoft Exchange and Outlook

▶ Bring together customer relationship management data with your meeting and conference call data, so that all relevant customer information, billing information, time-tracking data, and so on can be better leveraged for decision-making

▶ Deliver both "alerts" and "alert context" from SAP BW and then facilitate the execution of subsequent business processes—true management by exception

In the end, Mendocino helps SAP and Microsoft customers make the most of their respective investments. In doing so, it enables business processes to be extended and automated. This speeds up an organization's capability to intelligently respond to demands, and presumably serve customers, shareholders, and other stakeholders better than ever before.

Summary

Many tools on the market are designed to assist you in creating SAP reports. Yet with the integration naturally afforded by SAP for Microsoft's core suite of products, much of your reporting can be handled natively by SAP. This lesson gives you a look at how you can use Microsoft Excel, Word, and Access for such reporting purposes. Using the Microsoft Office family of products, you can therefore easily create the reports you need without expensive third-party tools, advanced technical knowledge, or the help of SAP technical professionals.

SAP's %pc functionality makes it easy to dump data from SAP into any number of other application formats. The processes discussed in this hour also highlighted how you can use Microsoft Excel to download SAP data into standard Excel spreadsheets. You discovered that Microsoft Word is ideal for creating merged SAP-fed form letters and mailing labels. Microsoft Access also helps you conduct reporting as well as manage data between multiple systems; use it as a comparison tool for data that is stored outside of SAP. Finally, the enhanced integration afforded by the joint SAP/Microsoft initiative known as Mendocino promises not only excellent workflow benefits, but greater integration between SAP and Microsoft Office's entire suite of productivity tools.

Q&A

Q *Instead of using the reporting tools provided by SAP, can custom reports be created from scratch in SAP?*

A Custom reports can be created from scratch in all SAP applications. These reports (or *programs*, as they are called in SAP) are written in the ABAP or Java by an experienced programmer. Some companies create many customized reports and others rely on customized reports only when absolutely necessary.

Q *If SAP data is output to a Microsoft Excel spreadsheet and then the spreadsheet is edited, is it possible to get that updated data back into SAP?*

A The easy answer is yes, but it is no easy task. It requires the skills of a programmer who can write a program that can upload the data in to SAP.

Workshop

The workshop is designed to help you anticipate possible questions, review what you've learned, and begin thinking ahead about putting your knowledge into practice. The answers to the quiz that follows can be found in Appendix A, "Quiz Answers."

Quiz

1. Name two methods you can use to create output files to be imported into Microsoft Excel.

2. Which type of integration interface is most often used to communicate with Microsoft Office?

3. Which Microsoft application do you use to create SAP-supplied form letters?

4. What does the term OLE mean?

5. Name some additional OLE-compatible applications.

Exercises

1. Create a file using the System List function and open the file in Microsoft Excel.

2. Create a new Microsoft Word form letter using an existing Microsoft Word document.

PART VI

SAP Support

Support Overview

Not too long ago, the extent of SAP's support consisted of a difficult-to-use Help system tied to each installation, tedious "online" documentation CDs, and an equally challenging-to-use and fairly slow Online Support System (OSS). These support mechanisms got the job done, but not without a bit of pain on the part of the users. These offline tools were completely replaced a number of years ago by a much more capable support umbrella consisting of SAP's Solution Manager and the SAP Service Marketplace website (along with other support resources covered in Hour 24, "Additional SAP Resources"). In addition, SAP refined its support organization with better tools and processes.

Highlights of this hour include

▶ Reviewing the SAP Solution Manager's support capabilities

▶ Investigating the SAP Service Marketplace

▶ Taking a closer look at field-specific F1 help

▶ An introduction to your SAP Support Team

SAP Solution Manager

Long time SAP veterans have a hard time forgetting the SAP Help system and online documentation CDs (the word "online" apparently didn't mean the same thing 10 years ago) used to provide post-Go-Live technical support for SAP. Much has changed since SAP AG provided Solution Manager a few years ago. SolMan, as it's often called, enables lifecycle management by providing the following resources, each discussed in more detail in the following sections:

▶ A portal back to SAP, tying together many behind-the scenes resources into something more easily accessible

▶ A set of tools covering implementation, SLA reporting, and much more

▶ Documentation, templates, best practices, implementation accelerators, and other such content designed to speed up implementations and smooth out learning curves

Portal

Solution Manager provides seamless access to the SAP Service Marketplace (discussed later in this hour), enabling great control and capabilities from a single interface. With SolMan, access to SAP Notes, the capability to conduct remote EarlyWatch sessions, and insight into SAP's solution areas, an administrator can easily stay on top of things.

An SAP EarlyWatch session is the label given to the process whereby SAP AG logs in to your SAP system, pokes around unobtrusively, collects performance and other data, and then provides you with a report of your system's overall configuration. EarlyWatch highlights problem areas, potential problem areas, and areas that are configured well, thus helping you proactively maintain sound performance and solid availability.

Tools

Beyond access to SAP's EarlyWatch service, SolMan provides a number of native tools. Business Process Monitoring (BPM) helps you track the performance of business processes across one or more SAP systems. SolMan gives you insight into source systems, interfaces to other systems, and visibility into background jobs tied to a business process. In this way, administrators can quantify and measure true end-to-end performance, and then compare it to a set of performance thresholds. When a threshold is exceeded, alerts can be escalated. This enables proactive management by exception, freeing your IT resources and business analysts to focus their time fixing problems that truly matter.

SolMan can monitor business processes because of a feature called Solution Monitoring. Solution Monitoring drills down into individual SAP systems, looking for potential issues and minor problems before they become major problems. Through another tool, Service Level Reporting, administrators can compare the performance of individual system components to baseline and target business goals (which are jointly set between IT and the business units served by the system). Through these tools and targets, it becomes an easy matter for an IT administrator to monitor and proactively support SAP. By verifying that everything is working well and addressing potential issues quickly, SolMan saves time and money.

Content

Important to implementation teams as well as post-Go-Live support teams, Solution Manager also provides a great many tools and templates under the guise of "content." Some of this content helps project managers and implementation specialists plan for, design, and install SAP systems. *Business content* helps business analysts create SAP business solutions atop these freshly installed SAP systems. Samples include business scenarios and best-practices templates—tools that make it easier to get SAP up and running.

To facilitate a smooth implementation, SAP Solution Manager includes *Road Maps* (essentially customized methodologies for implementing specific business solutions). SAP Solution Manager also includes *Implementation Accelerators,* which are enabled through the creation of a custom knowledge repository complete with templates, check lists, test scripts, and more.

SAP Service Marketplace

Although SolMan is certainly one of SAP's premier support vehicles today, SAP's Service Marketplace is king. It's where you can find nearly all the support you ever need to plan for, implement, and support an SAP solution. Around for a number of years now, it consolidates what used to be spread out across many different websites, CDs, SAP-proprietary support mechanisms (such as the old OSS site), and more. Access this website by opening your browser and typing `http://www.service.sap.com` or simply `http://service.sap.com`. Major resources available from this website—service.sap.com—include

- ▶ SAP Support Portal
- ▶ Education, Consulting, Solutions Areas, and User Groups
- ▶ SAP Business One Customer Portal
- ▶ SAP Developer Network
- ▶ SAP Partner Portal
- ▶ SAP Channel Partner Portal
- ▶ SAP Help Portal
- ▶ SAP Community

For a quick snapshot illustrating the breadth of support options available, see Figure 23.1.

The SAP Support Portal

For many users, the SAP Support Portal is arguably the most useful site within the SAP Service Marketplace. It provides access to

- ▶ SAP Notes
- ▶ Messages
- ▶ The Software Download site
- ▶ SAP Support Center Addresses
- ▶ SAP Service Channel—your "Inbox"

FIGURE 23.1
The SAP Support Marketplace provides great one-stop-shopping when it comes to customer, developer, partner, and general help, as well as other support mechanisms.

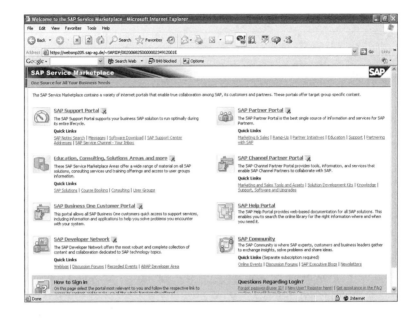

SAP Notes

Access to SAP Notes is one of the keys to troubleshooting application and technical problems with your SAP system. SAP Notes enables you to search by application area (SAP product or component, like CRM, Public Sector), by technology (for example, Oracle-based SAP systems running on IBM hardware), by language (English or German), and more. With SAP Notes, you can also quickly review HotNews (customized based on your preferences), along with SAP TopNotes, a great tool for reviewing SAP component-specific and even module-specific popular SAP Notes, other findings, and miscellaneous published documents.

You can also post (send) notes to SAP, to be reviewed, answered, and ultimately shared with others. This two-way communication is what makes SAP Notes such a great collaboration and troubleshooting tool. You need a special SAP user ID to access SAP Notes, though. Work with your SAP Account Manager, Competency Center, or implementation partner to acquire this access.

Messages

From the Messages link, you can run the SAP Message Wizard, a new way of creating Customer Messages. Simply select one of the systems associated with your SAP user ID, conduct a solution search, find a solution, and if necessary create a message. With the SAP Notes search integrated into this process, escalating issues has never been easier.

Software Download

The Software Download link takes you to the SAP Software Distribution Center, where you can either download media via the Web or request that software be shipped to you on CD or DVD. Based on the unique licenses paid for by your company (or customer, as the case may be), you have access to the latest and greatest NetWeaver and mySAP Business Suite releases, bug fixes, Support Packages, SAP Notes, and much more. This is also a great way to stay on top of the latest technical tools used in the course of installing and maintaining SAP—you can download the newest versions of tools like SAPCAR, SAPRouter, the SAP Exchange Connector, the Java Log Viewer, and more.

SAP Support Center Addresses

Use this link to quickly access SAP's country-specific Support websites for upwards of 50 countries or regions. This is an invaluable tool for SAP support organizations tasked with managing SAP systems spanning the globe. Each link provides a wealth of contact information, ranging from local telephone and fax support numbers to mailing addresses and more.

SAP Service Channel—Your Inbox

Access your SAP "inbox" to receive feedback from SAP Notes you have posted, customer messages, or other communiqués. Assign delegates or substitutes while you're away, so that hot items don't stack up unattended. You can also track orders for software and services you have purchased from SAP.

Education, Consulting, Solutions Areas, and User Groups

Use the Education, Consulting, Solutions Areas, and More link from the SAP Service Marketplace to gain access to training and education sites, including a site used for managing training. Read about the various training and certification programs. Review the most current Online Training Catalog to find a particular course, review where it is being offered, look into hotel and other accommodations, and book a class or certification test—all online. There's also a wealth of information relative to consulting services, various SAP solutions areas, user group forums, and much more. Note that as of this writing, SAP has more than 9,000 consultants, whereas another 180,000 SAP-experienced and certified consultants exist worldwide as well.

One of my favorite links is the User Community; from here, you can participate in web events, read about current events in any number of SAP-sponsored newsletters, and participate in real-time discussion forums. Other favorites include the documentation and training sites, discussed in more detail next.

SAP Documentation

SAP AG maintains documentation for many products, and indeed a host of different releases of these products, each geared toward an equally complex number of computing platforms. It will come as no surprise that product documentation continues to be an area fraught with challenges. Truth be told, great strides have been made since 2002, though, when independent surveys conducted by SearchSAP.com uncovered obvious deficiencies in satisfaction. The documentation team at SAP buckled down at that time to focus on delivering consistent and updated documentation as quickly as possible. Today, SAP's Service Marketplace provides easy access to what amounts to often-updated and typically very useful documentation. Have patience when it comes to new products, though—until a product has matured a bit, SAP provides something of a framework rather than fully fleshed-out documentation.

You will still find that some of the SAP support materials, like the training materials you are given at SAP-sponsored training courses, do not reflect perfect English. Why? Because much of this documentation is first written in German and then translated to English. Unsurprisingly, clarity is sometimes lost in the translation. In addition, in many places, the translation process is not yet complete; some screens, websites, and other materials, for example, might appear with certain words and definitions in German. This is rarely anything more than a nuisance, though.

Training Materials

When you attend an SAP training course, in most instances, you receive a notebook binder containing your training materials. The standard documentation provided is in the format of a Microsoft PowerPoint presentation. This means that each page of the notebook contains a large screen print followed by a few bullet points of information, and much white space for note taking.

The bullet points usually only scratch the surface of a concept, however. Although the concept might be discussed and instructed at length in the class, the training materials therefore serve as a poor post-classroom reference for the topic at hand. And you might find that, as with other forms of documentation, some pages have been translated poorly or not at all. In these cases, be sure to remember the resources available to you elsewhere in the SAP Service Marketplace. In particular, look for newly revised documentation.

SAP Business One Customer Portal

Through this special portal, SAP's SMB (small and medium business) customers who have deployed SAP Business One have access to specific SAP Notes, problem management resources, and other specialized support processes and applications. The Business One Customer Portal provides nearly everything found in the larger SAP Service Marketplace portal, scaled toward supporting SAP's SMB audience—the capabilities to order software, obtain SAP installation and upgrade CDs, download patches, and request license keys are good examples. You can also access SMB-relevant TopNotes and HotNews from here.

SAP Developer Network

Another outstanding resource available through the SAP Service Marketplace is the SAP Developer Network. Use it to participate in weblogs (blogs), timely discussion forums, or replay recorded events at your convenience, for instance. This site is especially useful after major SAP conferences, when SAP posts a host of materials ranging from keynote addresses to technical presentations for its developer community. And because the Developer Area is carefully constructed around supporting NetWeaver, it's easy to find resources geared toward Enterprise Portal, Exchange Infrastructure, Business Information Warehouse, xApps, Mobile Infrastructure, and everything else NetWeaver.

For hardcore ABAP developers, there's nothing more valuable than the ABAP Developer Area, another entire site dedicated to developing within the NetWeaver framework or platform. Download developer's guides, ABAP FAQs and articles, access ABAP eLearning resources, and participate in ABAP-specific discussion forums. Stay abreast of recent developments via a regular newsletter, and access online ABAP Language and Workbench *Help*—much of it SAP component- or technology-specific. For example, use the ABAP Language Help site to access APO liveCache-centric ABAP tips, SAP Knowledge Warehouse information, materials focused on Basis and CCMS, the NetWeaver Security Guide, and a wealth of other valuable resources.

SAP Partner and Channel Partner Portals

For SAP partners and channel partners, these two sites within the SAP Service Marketplace umbrella are invaluable. Note that only registered partners can access these sites, which are used for collaboration, joint problem escalation and resolution, support for joint partner initiatives and marketing events, and so on. Specialized education, support and marketing tools, and access to all the software and support resources at SAP's disposal (as opposed to a subset of these that are available to a specific customer) are enabled through these portals as well.

SAP Help Portal

Long ago, SAP only provided help via CDs that shipped with their products. Today, all this "near-line" help is also available online 24 hours a day, for all products and components, covering all major technology platforms and supported options. Powerful search facilities make the SAP Library, as it is called, useful to all members on your implementation or post-Go-Live support teams. An offline version is available as well (that is, you can still order this excellent resource on CD-ROM). And because the content is managed through SAP's Knowledge Warehouse environment, it can be quickly introduced and adopted within the larger context of other materials you or your IT team host via SAP KW.

As you might expect, all product documentation is available via this venue— whether you're running SAP NetWeaver '05 or mySAP ERP, or the Industry Solution for any number of verticals, the SAP Help Portal gives you one-stop-shopping like no other SAP documentation resource. Best practices, a terminology database, and documentation for the SAP Tutor (used to create interactive training courses called "learning units") are also available here.

Accessing Extended Help

Although the SAP Help Portal and SolMan-enabled help/support tools are all wonderful in their own right, such real-time access might not always be possible. Sometimes, you might find yourself on a particular SAP screen, wondering what a particular field is used for. In these cases, rather than launching a browser session and logging in to the SAP Service Marketplace, you can instead select the menu path Help, Extended Help from the screen that you have questions about. Your Online Documentation application launches with topic-specific help related to your current SAP screen.

Retrieving Field-Specific Help

SAP provides you with help information embedded into most of the SAP applications available today. For instance, you can retrieve field-specific help by performing the following steps:

1. Use transaction code /nME21 to navigate to the Create Purchase Order: Initial screen (for example).

2. Position your cursor in the Vendor field and press the F1 key (see Figure 23.2).

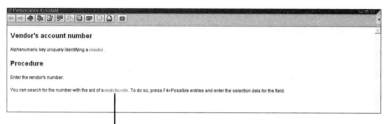

FIGURE 23.2
You can access field-specific help by positioning your cursor in an SAP field and pressing the F1 key.

Field Specific Help contains hypertext, which can be used to navigate additional Help topics.

The Performance Assistant

After you press F1 to retrieve field-specific information, you are presented with the Performance Assistant, which displays context-sensitive help. Oftentimes, you will find that this help is sufficient. When you need more details or additional clarification, though, the Performance Assistant provides a number of buttons:

▶ The Application Help button provides application-specific insight. Your System Administrator must set up this feature, however.

▶ The Technical Information button (see Figure 23.3) provides SAP-specific details regarding the Screen Data (comprised of the current report name, program name, and screen number), GUI Data (comprised of the GUI's program name and status), Field Data (comprised of the table and field names, and data element), and the Field Description for Batch Input (comprised of the screen field).

▶ The Edit Documentation button allows users with this special access the capability to update and maintain F1-specific documentation.

▶ The Glossary button provides a glossary of terms. Like Application Help, though, your System Administrator must set it up.

▶ The SAP Help Portal button opens a browser window and connects you to http://help.sap.com (assuming you have an Internet connection).

The Performance Assistant also features a handy Print button along with a button used to close the Performance Assistant window.

Abbreviated Technical Information

An abbreviated Technical Information button is available when you highlight a button (instead of a field, as discussed previously) and press F1. Highlight a button by clicking it once and then moving the mouse off the button. You will notice that the button is then surrounded by dashed lines instead of a solid line. When you press F1, you see an abbreviated button-specific Technical Information window like that shown in Figure 23.4.

FIGURE 23.3
Additional tech-
nical help is
provided via
the Technical
Information
button found
in the SAP
Performance
Assistant.

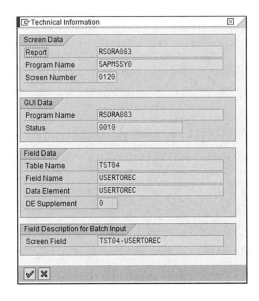

By highlighting a button and pressing F1, you can determine the button's relevant program and function calls. On the rare occasion when you're without a mouse, this can be handy. I actually use this feature to *avoid* mouse-clicks (which can occasionally be problematic) when scripting automated transactions. In the command field, simply type the function call (WKLD in the figure) and press Enter. It's just like pressing the button, but requires no tabbing or mouse clicking.

FIGURE 23.4
SAP GUI button-
specific program
and function
data are dis-
played by high-
lighting a
button and
pressing F1.

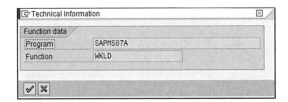

Field-Specific Help Settings

You can customize the way your field-specific help functions by modifying your Personal Settings. Follow the menu path Help, Settings, which presents the Personal Settings for User dialog box, as shown in Figure 23.5.

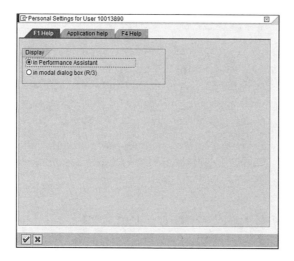

FIGURE 23.5
You can modify
the display of
your F1 settings
through the use
of the Personal
Settings
dialog box.

The Personal Settings dialog box defaults to your F1 settings. However, you can also update your Application and F4 Help settings by clicking their respective tabs, making any desired changes, and pressing the green check mark to save them. Use the F4 Help tab (see Figure 23.6) to make changes to your user-specific settings. Probably the most common use of this screen is to update the value associated with max number of hits to be displayed. I often change the default from 500 to 100, for example, to reduce the amount of time spent waiting for search results to be displayed.

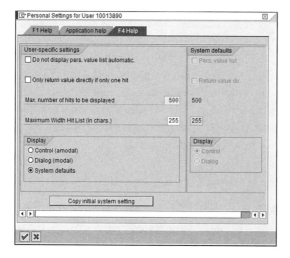

FIGURE 23.6
From the F4
Help tab of the
Personal
Settings dialog
box, update
user-specific
settings such
as the maxi-
mum number of
hits displayed
as the result of
a search.

The SAP Support Team

When you reach the Go-Live milestone, your SAP implementation turns a new corner. Now, issues and challenges must be resolved in a production environment where downtime is likely hard to come by, and end users are reluctant to give up anything beyond what they've agreed to in their Service Level Agreements with IT. In these cases, the SAP Support Team, or simply SAP Support, shines.

SAP provides you with contact information necessary to work with your customer-specific SAP Support Team. Keep in mind the resources available via the SAP Support Portal as well—they were covered previously.

Supporting Unplanned Downtime

SAP has always been very good about providing support during mission-critical "down" situations. They are famous for sticking with a problem until it's resolved, rather than transferring helpless customer victims from one phone support person to another. In the U.S., this support typically comes from resources located in Newtown Square, although SAP provides follow-the-sun support enabled by resources in Europe and India as well.

The key is to know when to use your support team. When searching through another batch of SAP Notes or drafting another customer message seems a waste of time, and when your circle of support and user group resources (covered in more detail in Hour 24) have been exhausted, don't hesitate to turn to your SAP Support Team.

Summary

In the past hour, you have learned where and how to obtain support for your SAP solutions. SAP Solution Manager and the SAP Service Marketplace are two primary vehicles for obtaining real-time support around the clock. SAP Help is also built into your SAP system. Finally, turn to your SAP Support Team when a live person is necessary to quickly work through or escalate a mission-critical issue. These resources are supplemented by a host of additional support resources, too, covered in Hour 24.

Q&A

Q *What is the website's URL for accessing SAP's Service Marketplace?*

A In your browser, type `http://www.service.sap.com`, or simply `http://service.sap.com`.

Q *What are the three primary components of SAP Solution Manager?*

A A portal to SAP Service Marketplace, a set of tools, and a collection of content.

Q *What has essentially replaced SAP's "online documentation CD?"*

A SAP offers a number of portal-based documentation resources that include access to all SAP's product- and component-specific documentation, help-based resources, and more. The SAP Library is another such resource, available both online and in CD format.

Workshop

The workshop is designed to help you anticipate possible questions, review what you've learned, and begin thinking ahead to putting your knowledge into practice. The answers to the quiz that follows can be found in Appendix A, "Quiz Answers."

Quiz

1. What is the common abbreviation for SAP Solution Manager?

2. List three primary tools that you can access within Solution Manager.

3. What is the primary online support vehicle for SAP developers?

4. How can you obtain field-specific help?

5. List two ways to access SAP Notes from the SAP Support Portal.

Exercises

1. Log in to the SAP Service Marketplace and find installation documentation relevant to your current SAP technology stack.

2. Navigate to transaction code /nCRC0 and retrieve context-sensitive help for the Resources screen.

3. From the SAP Developer Network, participate in a blog or other online discussion.

HOUR 24

Additional SAP Resources

Although SAP is one of the largest software vendors in the world, and still the market leader in Enterprise Applications software (despite Oracle's best attempts!), there is not an overabundance of freely available support and similar resources. True, there are a couple hundred books available, but at any point in time perhaps only 20 to 30 of these are current enough to be useful. In the same way, there are a number of magazines dedicated to SAP, a number of websites outside of SAP's own web-based resources, and certainly hordes of consulting companies teeming with billable resources. But if you simply have a few questions and little money to spend, where should you go?

This hour discusses additional SAP resources available to users, developers, and other SAP professionals. This material complements the material covered in Hour 23, "Support Overview," and seeks to answer the question posed previously.

Highlights of this hour include

- ▶ A closer look at some professional resources, such as SAP-focused books, magazines, user groups, and other professionally delivered materials

- ▶ A review of helpful SAP websites

- ▶ An introduction to select SAP career resources

- ▶ A review of additional SAP resources, including SAP-sponsored and other SAP-focused conferences and events

Professional Resources

Professional resources for SAP span the gamut from inexpensive books to magazine subscriptions, membership in professional user-based organizations, and more. Part of the reason for this diversity is SAP's size—beyond its installed base and the hundreds of thousands of users who depend on SAP day in and day out, there's a supporting cast of another hundred thousand consultants, contractors, developers, engineers, and other support personnel. Some of the more prominent and useful professional resources are outlined in the following sections.

Americas' SAP Users' Group (ASUG)

In almost every facet of business, it is helpful to network with people who are using similar products in the pursuit of similar goals. SAP is no exception. An organization, Americas' SAP Users' Group—known as ASUG—is an independent, not-for-profit organization comprised of SAP customer companies and eligible third-party vendors, consulting houses, hardware vendors, and others. Visit ASUG's website at http://www.asug.com (see Figure 24.1).

FIGURE 24.1
ASUG is an independent, not-for-profit organization of SAP customer companies and eligible third parties.

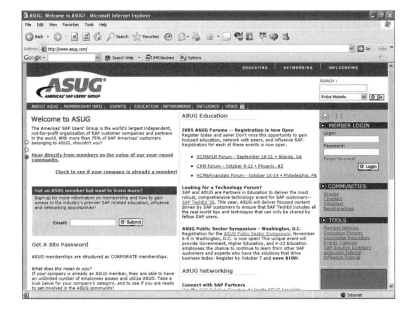

ASUG's goals of educating members, facilitating networking among colleagues and SAP representatives, and influencing SAP's global product and service direction forms the foundation of all that ASUG does. ASUG provides a forum for members to communicate mutual concerns to SAP, influence software development, exchange ideas and best practices, and establish future priorities. ASUG is dedicated to the advancement, understanding, and productive use of SAP products.

Brief History of ASUG

Founded in 1990, ASUG began immediately following the SAPPHIRE conference that year in Orlando, Florida. One year later, ASUG was officially incorporated. Starting with a group of 15 participants, by the end of 1996 the organization had grown to more than 450 member companies, representing both R/2 and R/3 installations in North, Central, and South America. In the same year, ASUG expanded its customer-only membership to include third parties (vendors and consultants) under a new Associate Membership category. By the close of 1998, the organization was 950 corporate memberships strong, with more than 12,000 participants. And by the middle of 2004, ASUG boasted an installation base of nearly 1,200 companies and more than 34,000 members. With more than 80% today, ASUG continues to grow as it strives to reach its goal of representation by 100% of SAP America's customers.

There are two types of membership—Installation Member and Associate Member. The former reflects membership at a corporate level of those companies that have installed and run SAP. A nominal annual fee of $1,400 gives all employees of the company benefits from ASUG. Each company designates a Champion (the single point of contact for the company), along with a Primary Contact, Executive Contact, and up to six Secondary Contacts.

Associate Members include licensed vendors (that is, entities that are licensed Logo, Platform, Alliance, or Implementation Partners) along with certified Complementary Software Program (CSP) participants. Noncertified partners such as small consulting firms can qualify for Associate Member privileges too.

With ASUG membership comes access to the members-only site within the parent ASUG website. This provides access to a Discussion Forum, the Member Network, various ASUG-sponsored webcasts, and past presentations and other materials. ASUG members also enjoy discounted rates to attend the annual ASUG conference, access to local and regional chapter meetings, webinars, teleconferences, group meetings, symposiums, and more. Joining ASUG enables a member company to learn from the shared experiences of other users, forging solutions to common user challenges and influencing and shaping SAP's product development over the next few years. And with Installation Membership, the special opportunity to influence SAP AG makes for probably the most compelling reason to "join the club!"

For more information about ASUG, use the following contact information:

> Americas' SAP Users' Group
>
> 401 North Michigan Avenue
>
> Chicago, IL 60611-4267
>
> Phone: 312.321.5142
>
> FAX: 312.245.1081
>
> Email: hq@ASUG.com
>
> www.asug.com

SAP Professional Journal

A bimonthly publication, the *SAP Professional Journal* targets a wide cross-section of SAP professionals, from developers to Systems Administrators to infrastructure/basis support personnel and more. But the journal also targets the business professionals who rely on SAP to keep their respective companies running. Within the pages of the *SAP Professional Journal,* you'll find technology tutorials, reviews of new products and options, coding and other technical tips, case studies, integration and systems management advice, migration and upgrade guidance, and a wealth of installation and support best practices. And these are not cursory articles or short abstracts—we're talking detailed materials here, the kind that are at once useful.

Perhaps even better than the printed journal is access to their online version, though. Take a look at www.sappro.com for a list of articles in the latest issue (plus abstracts). Even better, use this resource as a search engine, helping you to find some of the best technical materials and SAP best practices available anywhere. With more than 5,000 pages worth of published articles and other documents, the investment of $495 for personal access or $4,995 for a handy site access (up to 100 users, including five printed copies of the journal) represents the kind of investment that pays big dividends for the entire SAP support department.

SAPinsider

SAPinsider is published by the same organization that publishes the *SAP Professional Journal*—Wellesley Information Services (WIS). Its format is decidedly different, though, in that it's a quarterly publication, it's free to qualified subscribers (typically anyone supporting or using SAP), and it's sponsored directly by SAP AG. In fact, *SAPinsider* is a joint venture between WIS and SAP. To this last point, the Editorial Board of Directors responsible for publishing valuable real-world *SAPinsider* content reflects a cross-section of some of SAP's most well-known executive and technical names. This helps ensure leading-edge insight. Important lessons learned are imparted every quarter, making *SAPinsider* an excellent addition to any SAP professional's reading.

In addition to solid technical advice, *SAPinsider* provides product walk-throughs and reviews, up-to-date news from SAP developers, and a number of useful regular columns—NetWeaver, Under Development, Recommended Reading (book reviews, slanted naturally toward SAP Press), and a New and Noteworthy section used by partners and SAP product organizations alike to share important findings. This variety of resources and information can help you stay well rounded and abreast of the most current developments in the SAP community. It's no wonder that more than 125,000 professionals who develop, implement, support, and use SAP applications depend on *SAPinsider*. For information, visit www.sapinsideronline.com.

SAPNetWeaver Magazine

The newest addition to the small circle of SAP-focused magazines on the market today is *SAPNetWeaver Magazine*. Founded in 2005, it is the self-described independent authority on SAP NetWeaver. The purpose of this magazine is to share insight and findings that reflect the real world of SAP NetWeaver implementations. Thus, you will find that this is one of those magazines that seeks to align the business and IT sides of SAP, marrying them such that its articles appeal to a broad readership. It succeeds in doing just that.

Although the magazine is young, it's proven itself an excellent read thus far. And why not—it fills an important void. Managers will find the analysts' coverage, thoughts from industry experts, and real-world anecdotes and high-level case studies just what they need to build a business case for moving in a particular direction. Technologists and architects will find the best practices, detailed case studies, an independent insight proffered by SAP experts indispensable as well, enabling them to make better and bolder decisions while mitigating the risk of deploying products without the benefit of long histories (a nicer way of saying "new products are necessarily immature products"). *SAPNetWeaver Magazine* is offered quarterly. Go to www.sapnetweavermagazine.com to learn more about why this might be the magazine you've been waiting for.

Books

There are a few hundred books available on the market today for SAP. Using online bookstores such as Barnesandnoble.com (www.bn.com) and www.amazon.com, you can easily search for and uncover the latest SAP-related books. It's worth your time looking at www.SAP-press.com as well; unsurprisingly, they offer a wealth of SAP books covering topics as diverse as SAP Solution Manager, Performance Optimization, various books on ABAP and Java programming, Workflow, SAP Service and Support, and nearly every SAP product sold by SAP.

Additional sites include www.SAP-Resources.com/saprbooks1.htm, useful simply because it's both up-to-date and fairly comprehensive. This site mentions nearly 100 of the best-selling SAP books on the market. And because each book is hyper-linked to Amazon, it's a simple matter to quickly read over reviews, examine pricing and shipping options, look for used-book deals, and ultimately place an order for a copy.

Technical Newsletters

WIS Publications, the same entity who publishes the *SAP Professional Journal,* offers a number of technical newsletters as well. Each newsletter is laser-focused on a particular topic. Some of these include

▶ *SAP Financials Expert*—Geared toward finance and IT teams who use or support FI, CO, or mySAP ERP Financials, it covers quite a bit of reporting options, ranging from R/3 and BW Reporting, to SEM, Financial Accounting (FA), Profitability Analysis (PA), G/L, Treasury, A/P, A/R, Controlling, and more. See www.ficoexpertonline.com for details.

▶ *BW Expert*—If you are tasked with deploying, upgrading, optimizing, or supporting SAP BW (or in a broader sense, business intelligence), this newsletter focused on deploying and tuning BW for use as the central hub in a sea of transactional systems is what you are looking for. Look to www.bwexpertonline.com for more information.

▶ *SCM Expert*—If your SAP team is tasked with optimizing your company's supply chain, this is your newsletter. All the usual supply chain functions are covered, including procurement, warehousing, manufacturing schedules, sales, and distribution. But more than SAP APO is targeted; *SCM Expert* targets core R/3 and ECC modules as well, including SD, PP, MM, QM, and PS. Refer to www.scmexpertonline.com for details.

▶ *HR Expert*—Although SAP HR is relatively mature in this day and age, HR projects are critical simply because of the people and paychecks that are at stake. To the rescue comes HR Expert, touting documented ROI gains from deploying SAP HR technology, guidance from industry experts, insight into new HR functionality, and more. Use it to avoid common configuration, integration, and customization mistakes and to reduce your dependence on expensive HR and Employee Self Services (ESS) consultants. See www.hrexpertonline.com.

▶ *CRM Expert*—If your team is responsible for unlocking critical CRM functionality such as marketing, sales, service, and analytics, including the various CRM user interfaces (three different ones exist), *CRM Expert* is just the ticket for you. Check out www.crmexpertonline.com as well.

Internet Resources

Many SAP Internet resources are available for you to communicate, learn, and share your own ideas and findings about your SAP system with SAP professionals, vendors, and the entire virtual user community. Always on and always available, the Internet is an ideal source for obtaining troubleshooting information in a pinch, too. I suggest searching the Net every now and then for new SAP resources—you'll be amazed at the wealth of new material made available practically every day. In the course of my own career with SAP, my colleagues and I have found a host of Internet-based resources quite useful. The best of these are covered next.

SAP Fans

SAP Fans, located on the Internet at www.sapfans.com, continues to be an excellent source of unbiased SAP information (they are not affiliated with SAP AG). SAP Fans is designed as a forum to exchange ideas with other SAP customers working with SAP R/3, R/2, and other SAP systems. This website includes user-based, technical, and other "discussion" forums that provide you with the opportunity to post questions, comments, and experiences about your SAP system, and retrieve responses from other SAP professionals. These forums are grouped into a number of areas. Arguably the most useful is the Technical area, which includes

Logistics	Financials
Human Resources	Basis
SAP Security	SAPscript/Smart Forms
ABAP	SAP CRM
Business Workflow	Business Warehouse
SEM	APO and SCM
Implementation Issues	Industry Solutions
SAP Portals/Internet	Interfaces
Third-Party Products	"Other"

There's also a Non-Technical forum area, intended to host general discussions, share job postings and resumes, and address educational services, list training courses, and address certification questions. Finally, a Knowledge Corner moderated in real-time lets you pose functional, technical, or ABAP-related questions. Using these discussion forums, you can easily post a question or problem that you are having with your SAP system (see Figure 24.2).

Other SAP Fans users will see your posting and (hopefully!) respond with possible solutions (see Figure 24.3).

The network of contacts you gain as you discuss and share similar experiences can prove invaluable. As of this writing, SAP Fans boasts more than 32,000 registered users and more than half a million posted articles. And because it's an ideal source for SAP news, events, products, books, and employment opportunities, I suggest you bookmark SAP Fans as one of your favorites. Yes, some of the material is outdated. But much of it is extremely current, making it a very useful (not to mention very free!) resource.

FIGURE 24.2
In the SAP Fans discussion forum, you can post comments or questions or respond to other users' comments or questions.

FIGURE 24.3
The SAP Fans discussion forum can prove an ideal source for answers to your SAP questions.

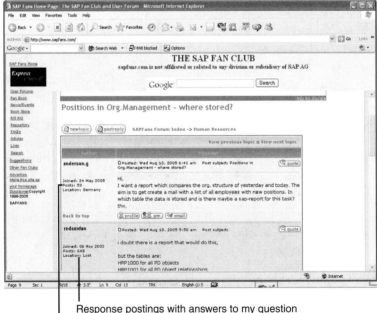

Response postings with answers to my question

My original posting

The Wayback Machine

Although there are plenty of recently constructed and oft-updated SAP-related websites at your disposal, you might find yourself looking for something that is no longer available on the web. Most sites change significantly every few months or years. And some very useful sites have completely faded away with the times, like the *SAP Technical Journal* (www.saptechjournal.com) and ERPcentral (www.erpcentral.com), the latter of which was a nice portal site featuring information on the ERP leaders in 2003 and earlier: SAP, Oracle, PeopleSoft, JD Edwards, Baan, and more. ERPcentral was a good source for installation and support best practices, for example.

But with ERPcentral "gone," how do you access the content on its site? For example, if you're still running an older version of R/3 and have misplaced your CDs and guides, but remember similar information once available at ERPcentral, what can you do? The folks at SAP might be able to send you updated media, and your SAP Competency Center might have filed away some of its legacy documentation, too. But trying to dig up data using this hit-and-miss approach can become a very big problem when time is of the essence.

The answer might be as simple as navigating to the Wayback Machine at www.waybackmachine.org (note the "org" extension). As you can see in Figure 24.4, the site provides a search box where you can enter the URL of any site that has existed in the last 20-odd years. Simply enter the site name (like `http://www.erpcentral.com`) and press the Take Me Back button.

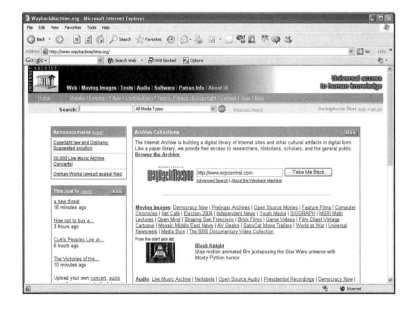

FIGURE 24.4
With the Wayback Machine, it's a breeze to pull up materials from websites that have been changed or decommissioned.

A list of search results spanning a great number of years appears. Click any of the hyperlinked dates to navigate to the version of the site as it looked on that particular day. Keep in mind that restricted sites, password-protected sites, and some materials on other sites are unavailable. But you'll be amazed at the wealth of newfound "old" data suddenly at your disposal. Old sites can be helpful when you're looking for a particularly difficult-to-find document, too—I've found myself going through SAP's primary website on many occasions, for instance.

SAP FAQ

The SAP FAQ originated in 1994 as a web-based adjunct to the `de.alt.sap-r3` Usenet discussion forum from Germany's University of Oldenberg, a pioneering SAP academic installation site. As a longstanding, not-for-profit, technology-specific resource, the SAP FAQ has earned and maintained a position of global credibility and respect. Its objective is to serve as a comprehensive point of information about SAP for those who work with SAP, companies that are implementing SAP, students, and those who are looking into SAP as a potential ERP solution or career option.

TechTarget and SearchSAP.com

What used to be termed the SAP FAQ's "by-subscription" discussion forum, ask-the-experts forum, and other similar resources are now accessed through TechTarget, the parent to SearchSAP.com. In fact, when you type **www.sapfaq.com**, you are rerouted to http://searchsap.techtarget.com/ITKnowledgeExchange/, a wonderful portal into a wealth of materials, moderated discussions, salary surveys, events and conferences, great tips, useful newsletters, and so much more. It's a great way to exchange ideas while staying on top of new trends and products. An awesome SAP product directory covers much more than the usual ERP, CRM, and Supply Chain topics. You can access hard-to-find information pertaining to disaster recovery and capacity planning, for example. Or if you're interested in trying to understand what kind of products are available in the hot areas of Business Process Management (BPM) or Reporting, there is much to be reviewed as well. From general, core FI and HR module–related discussions, to industry-specific dialogue, subscribers can select a customized combination of discussions that fit very specifically into their areas of interest and expertise. And given the no-cost approach to subscription, SearchSAP.com and TechTarget in general are no-brainers for SAP professionals on a budget. For more information or to subscribe, visit http://searchsap.techtarget.com.

Cambridge Publications' Searchable Archive

From the team who helped SAP AG create and assemble the templates for the ASAP and ValueSAP implementation methodologies comes a wealth of both archived and more recent data. Although much of its SAP content is indeed dated, the SAP-R3-L list is still useful relative to discussing SAP from both technical and nontechnical perspectives. MIT hosts and administers the list; the university's Searchable Archive provides the forum to search through all postings to retrieve information about most any SAP R/3 topic. You can access the Searchable Archive at http://www. documentation.com/archives/saplist/saplist.html, and for any questions about the SAPR3-L list, you can write to the list owners at the email address, SAP-R3-L-request@MITVMA.MIT.EDU.

What I particularly appreciate about this list and website is that recruitment, product, and service advertisements are not permitted. This list is all "SAP business" and is therefore one of the more focused tools available in gaining help and contacts with which to share SAP concerns and experiences. To subscribe to the SAP-R3-L list, send the command SUBSCRIBE SAP-R3-L *Your-Real-Name* to LISTSERV@MITVMA.MIT.EDU. Note that *Your-Real-Name* should be in the format first name, middle initial, last name. Be sure to include the spaces you normally use when typing your name, taking care to ensure no quotation marks or special delimiters or separators are included.

The SAP ITtoolbox and SAP Assist

With more than 2.2 million registered users, and a history of serving those users with integrity, a subscription to the ITtoolbox portal is a must-have for nearly everyone. ITtoolbox takes care to not inundate you with weekly trash; instead, you choose cafeteria-style your interests, and ITtoolbox works to provide you with updated interest-specific content as it becomes available. Interested in SAP careers, training, or certification? Want to review knowledge bases focused on PeopleSoft, SCM, or Hardware? ITtoolbox has it all. Register at their main site at www.ITtoolbox.com.

For its SAP community members, the *SAP Knowledgebase* link at the bottom of the main site takes you directly to what used to be known as the "SAP Assist website"—a site now simply known as the SAP ITtoolbox site. Although its label changed a few years ago, www.sapassist.com still takes you to the SAP-specific ITtoolbox website, an online service providing wonderful tools and information geared toward assisting SAP practitioners in making informed decisions and completing their daily activities. Like its sister sites, the SAP ITtoolbox combines a functionally organized database of information with the benefits of global communication capabilities to quickly bring useful information to your fingertips. I find this site one of my favorites, even after six years of personal use. Just check out the weekly SAP decision makers and SAP-doers newsletters (delivered through email), and I trust that the SAP ITtoolbox will soon become one of your favorites as well.

SAP Conferences

In addition to the ASUG conference and regular ASUG-sponsored events, a growing number of other SAP conferences is available to SAP professionals, users, and others. Some of these, such as SAP TechEd, are geared toward technologists and developers, whereas others, such as SAPphire, are geared toward executives and other decision makers. There's also a wealth of product-specific conferences and events hosted throughout the year by the same folks that publish the *SAP Professional Journal* and *SAPinsider*—WIS Publications. Some of my favorite annual conferences hosted in North America are discussed next.

SAPphire

If you are seeking a high-level or executive-level perspective on where SAP is heading, consider attending the annual SAPphire conference. One is held every year in the United States, Europe, and most recently Asia. A certain amount of technical sessions are offered, but SAPphire is better known for touting a who's who of keynotes, customer case studies and success stories, and a great number of business-oriented presentation sessions. For example, SAPphire '05 boasted 10 conference tracks ranging from core Financial Services and Discrete/Process Industries (SAP's bread and butter in many ways) to SAP NetWeaver/ESA, SAP xApps and Business Process Innovation, and others—reflecting 22 SAP solutions and 24 industry verticals. Review www.sapsapphire. com for information about the most recent or upcoming SAPphire.

SAP TechEd

Since I first attended SAP TechEd in 1998, it's been my absolute and most favorite all-time technical conference. I've had the opportunity to speak at two of them since then, have attended all but two, and can tell you from experience that it's worth both your money and your time. There is no better way to get the inside SAP scoop on everything out there and everything coming around the corner. And like I've said before, because SAP TechEd is not interested in hosting marketing sessions, you actually learn things that are immediately useful in your day-to-day life, whether optimizing your current system or planning for your next functional upgrade. Finally, only SAP TechEd consistently provides you the opportunity to easily, quickly, and cheaply take certification exams—this alone can save your travel and expense budget thousands, because you can combine multiple training and certification trips into one four- or five-day jaunt to great destinations like San Diego, Boston, New Orleans, Las Vegas, and Orlando. Celebrate afterwards with a family vacation!

Managing SAP Projects

If you're on a team tasked with planning and deploying SAP, consider attending one of the newer SAP conferences out there, WIS's Managing SAP Projects. By offering real-world advice focused on resolving issues and duplicating successes, Managing SAP Projects gives you the chance to drill down into what makes or breaks a successful implementation or upgrade, to walk through customer case studies, or to hear about high-level strategies and leadership tactics used by SAP project leaders and their teams. Such practical guidance learned in the trenches is worth the fee of $1,695.

Because of the decidedly project management focus of this annual conference, certified Project Management Professionals (via the Project Management Institute, or PMI) will be glad to know that they can also earn PDU credits by attending many of the more than 90 sessions. This is helpful in maintaining PMP certification. And because this is very much a vendor-neutral conference—SAP AG does not sponsor it, although many of the speakers hail from various SAP organizations—those interested in perhaps a less biased view of SAP will find the sessions refreshingly straightforward. Check out www.SAPprojects2005.com for more information on the 2005 conference, and links to other conference opportunities.

Other WIS-Sponsored Seminars and Conferences

Wellesley Information Services offers a host of other content-specific or product-specific conference venues. In 2005 alone, WIS brought a slew of conferences, ranging from mySAP ERP for Managers and Managing SAP Projects to technology-focused SCM, PLM, HR, BW, CRM, and other conferences. And the new SAP Admin conference has received high marks from many SAP professionals. Like all of WIS's conferences, their SAP-neutral stance makes an excellent platform for knocking back a whole lot of great real-world information in just a few days. See www.wispubs.com/eventCalendar_SAP.cfm for a list of upcoming SAP-focused conferences near you.

Employment and Career Opportunities

Even today, one of the first things you will notice when you begin an SAP project is that you're suddenly in demand from others. Your email inbox and voice mail box will be bombarded with messages from recruiters offering to out-do your present salary, reduce your travel, increase your opportunities for advancement, and so on. It's not a bad deal, actually, but can catch you off guard; you need to be prepared for it.

SAP knowledge is a hot commodity today; a wealth of positions is available and growing for people with the right skills. This includes functional as well as technical skills, development as well as configuration expertise. Possessing in-depth knowledge on how to configure and set up a module in ECC is just as valuable as being able to write ABAP or Java code for SAP, or navigate an SAP system through a complex functional upgrade or OS/DB migration. And people with program management and project management skills gleaned through an SAP project are in great demand as well. Unsurprisingly, a great number of websites are devoted to making their employment opportunities available to you. A sample of these websites is provided next.

SAP-Resources.com

Touting itself as the "independent home of SAP-only jobs since 1998," SAP-Resources still provides sound value seven years later. It provides a web-based recruitment service focused solely on the SAP marketplace. SAP-Resources enables you to approach the task of finding an SAP career opportunity in a couple of ways through the following services:

▶ The Jobs Database, which is constantly being added to, includes details of some of the hottest SAP positions currently available. Just enter some relevant keywords to perform a search.

▶ The Skills Profile Service is aimed at professionals who know that some of the best opportunities are never advertised and want to make their skill details available to the widest audience possible. It's simple to create and activate your skills profile and to be contacted by recruiters handling the hottest SAP opportunities. All levels of experience are always in demand. Check out the full details at the Professionals Information page.

▶ Lastly, the Jobs-by-Email service provides subscribers with a daily email message listing the latest jobs posted to SAP-Resources (see Figure 24.5). For more information and to review employment opportunities, visit www.SAP-Resources.com.

One of the coolest things about the site is the Top Recruiters box off the main page. Look here to find who's placing the most people (based on job posting popularity). And click the hyperlinked Company Names to review the actual postings in real-time.

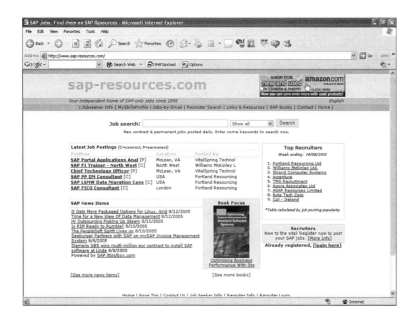

FIGURE 24.5
All services offered on SAP-Resources.com are free.

Softwarejobs.com

Another great venue for posting and reviewing SAP employment opportunities is www.softwarejobs.com. Its online career resources are free and useful, including consultation and resume writing help, links to free industry-related magazines and similar materials, access to career events and continuing education, and even access to a free personality test, a free career test (hosted by www.LiveCareer.com), and a cadre of career-boosting-related articles.

The site also offers free email (with a CareerMail.net extension), inexpensive background checks (to make the decision to hire you over 500 other candidates weigh in your favor), and a full-blown Resource Center portal site to provide access to all this and more. Finally, softwarejobs.com's Job Seeker Tools section makes it easy to build a portfolio, manage and post your resume, conduct advanced job searches, and distribute your resume through a number of venues.

ITtoolbox for Careers

As discussed previously, the ITtoolbox website provides outstanding career and job assistance. From the home page you can launch the Career Center, giving you rapid access to recently posted jobs, the capability to sign up for "job alerts," the capability to introduce yourself to the IT industry's top recruiters, and access to the career-specific ITtoolbox knowledge bases.

Need to hire a couple of contractors for one of your own projects? ITtoolbox also features a section for employers. Use it to post a job opening, review the site's online Resume Database (access costs you $495; use your credit card and you'll be knee-deep in the middle of thousands of resumes in no time), and review recent employers. Be sure to bookmark this site as one of your favorites—one day, you'll use it.

Summary

This hour looked at some of the additional resources available to you, many of which are free, and all which are intended to help you get the most out of your SAP system. As time goes on, I suspect these resources will only continue to grow—especially the Internet-based resources, diversity in SAP conferences, and career resources.

Through your personal exposure to SAP ECC, NetWeaver, and so on, coupled with the resources highlighted here and the skills you have learned, you will find yourself quickly moving from "sapling" status to a true "sapper" (or "sapman," or whatever—insert your favorite title here!). Again, welcome to the world of SAP, and I hope that you have enjoyed the past 24 hours—it's been my pleasure. I look forward to seeing or hearing from you soon!

Q&A

Q *What points should you keep in mind when shopping for SAP books?*

A One of the most important points to keep in mind when looking for SAP books is the SAP release or version number covered by the book. Almost anything written earlier than 1999 covers SAP R/3 exclusively, for example. And anything written before 2003 doesn't even mention NetWeaver or SAP ECC.

Q *How can you stay abreast of job opportunities as well as obtain career advice and other counsel?*

A Frequently visit websites such as www.softwarejobs.com, www.SAP-Resources.com, and www.ITtoolbox.com.

Q *How can you keep up to date with the latest SAP information available on the Internet?*

A It is a good idea to use an Internet search engine such as www.yahoo.com, www.google.com, or www.hotbot.com to search for new SAP sites on a periodic basis to keep up to date with the latest SAP information available. And be sure to visit SAP's primary website frequently as well!

Workshop

The workshop is designed to help you anticipate possible questions, review what you've learned, and begin thinking ahead to putting your knowledge into practice. The answers to the quiz that follows can be found in Appendix A, "Quiz Answers."

Quiz

1. How can you quickly find the top 100 or so books on SAP?

2. Who sponsors most of the least-biased SAP conferences?

3. Which SAP conference is primarily intended for executive and other decision-maker audiences?

4. How can you view what a retired website looked like in 1999?

Exercises

1. Check out www.SAP-Resources.com.

2. Subscribe to the SAP-R3-L list by sending the command SUBSCRIBE SAP-R3-L *Your-Real-Name* to LISTSERV@MITVMA.MIT.EDU (keeping in mind that *Your-Real-Name* should be in the format first name, middle initial, last name).

3. Visit www.sapinsideronline.com and obtain a free subscription to *SAPinsider*.

Appendixes

APPENDIX A

Quiz Answers

Answers to Quiz for Hour 1

1. SAP stands for Systems, Applications, and Products in Data Processing.

2. SAP provides bolt-on solutions for nearly 30 industries, including SAP Aerospace & Defense, SAP Automotive, SAP Banking, SAP Chemicals, SAP Consumer Products, SAP Engineering & Construction, SAP Healthcare, SAP High Tech, SAP Insurance, SAP Media, SAP Oil & Gas, SAP Pharmaceuticals, SAP Public Sector, SAP Retail, SAP Service Provider, SAP Telecommunications, and SAP Utilities. See www.sap.com/industries/index.epx for a complete and up-to-date list.

3. The presentation server, application server, and database server constitute SAP's system design; all three are required to be installed, although all can be installed on separate physical computers (servers) or even the same computer. The presentation server runs the SAP GUI or other SAP user interface, and is the system that users enter data into or use to manage and monitor the system. The application server handles the SAP administrative functions, including background processing and spool requests for the printer; it contains the business logic (programs) for SAP. The database server houses all the data associated with the SAP system.

4. The successor to SAP's wildly successful R/3 product is ECC, or ERP Central Component.

5. Although there are many benefits to SAP's integrated design, the most important is that it facilitates communication between modules and components that make up SAP's business environment, and therefore affords visibility and enables smarter decision-making.

6. A cross-application business process spans multiple SAP components (applications). A business process that completes all its work within just ECC is not a cross-application business process.

7. ESA provides the roadmap or blueprint for designing an adaptable enterprise computing solution; it's the architecture rather than the enabler or toolset (NetWeaver provides the platform and tools to construct a solution that embraces ESA).

8. An SAP logical unit of work contains all the steps of a transaction, often con-cluding with the update to the SAP database.

Answers to Quiz for Hour 2

1. By default, users can have a maximum of six sessions open at one time in SAP, although this number can be increased or reduced by your System Administrator during post-installation configuration.

2. The transaction code for the Users Overview screen is SM04.

3. If you are navigating using the command field in SAP from any screen other than the initial screen, you must enter an /N (N for New session) or an /O (O for Open New session) before the transaction.

4. The System and Help options are consistent across the menu bar of all SAP screens.

5. Using multiple sessions in SAP enables you to begin and complete multiple tasks at once without losing your place in a current task; in this way, true multitasking is made possible.

6. You need a user name, password, and client number. Optionally, you can also include a language identifier.

7. The menu path to create a new session from the menu bar without using a transaction code in the command field is System, Create Session.

Answers to Quiz for Hour 3

1. A database is a container used to store, retrieve, process, and present data.

2. A database is composed of tables, columns (called fields), and rows (called records or data).

3. An RDBMS or Relational Database Management System consists of multiple tables connected through relationships.

4. A primary key in a database table is composed of one or more fields that make a record in that table unique.

5. A foreign key is a field (or fields) used to link a primary key field in another table.

6. If a value is entered in a field that does not match an entry in that field's Check table, you will receive a Check Table violation.

7. A database index is used to decrease the time it takes to retrieve records from a database table.

Answers to Quiz for Hour 4

1. The button to the right of the help icon is the Customizing of Local Layout button. You can use it to make many different kinds of changes to the SAP GUI's display.

2. Before making any changes in the Customizing window, be sure to document the current settings in case you need to restore to the defaults.

3. Selecting the Insert button on your keyboard changes the SAP system setting from OVR to INS mode and vice versa.

4. The JavaGUI, or SAP GUI for Java, supports Unix, Linux, Mac OS, and in older cases OS/2 and other operating system alternatives.

5. On the Options tab from the Options selection in the Customizing drop-down menu, select the Dialog Box at Error Message check box. Then select Apply and OK.

Answers to Quiz for Hour 5

1. The transaction code for the main SAP screen is S000.

2. The Microsoft Windows Paint application can be used to paste and then save or print SAP screen prints in formats like BMP, JPEG, GIF, TIFF, and others. Microsoft Word and PowerPoint are also useful tools in this regard.

3. You would select the Delete After Print check box on the Print Screen List window in order for your spool request not to be saved by the SAP system.

4. The F10 function key activates the menu bar so that you can navigate through the menu paths using only your keyboard.

5. Using the menu path System, Status, you can determine the shortcut transaction code for the current screen.

6. You can access the history list of all transaction codes processed since you logged in by selecting the down arrow on the right side of the SAP GUI command field.

7. The Retention Period determines how many days a spool request (print job) is to remain in the spool system before it is deleted.

Answers to Quiz for Hour 6

1. You can use the Enter key on your keyboard or the green check mark on your Windows toolbar to check the entries made on an SAP screen.

2. The Hold Data feature enables you to overwrite the default value that you have set for an input field.

3. To expand an SAP tree structure, use the (+) sign located to the left of the desired line.

4. A dialog box appears to a user to provide messages, feedback, or specific information about a current task.

5. The length of an input field determines how many characters you can enter in that field.

6. The Possible Entries Help button (down arrow on the right side of an input field) can be used to display valid entries for that input field.

7. Required input fields display a box with a check mark (older systems displayed a question mark) in the SAP system. These must be filled in to continue.

Answers to Quiz for Hour 7

1. There are three levels of SAP training: Level 1 focuses on awareness, Level 2 concentrates on readiness, and Level 3 focuses on proficiency.

2. Level 1 training classes are designed as an introduction and do not require any prerequisite courses.

3. A Functional Analyst focuses on your SAP business process. Functional Analysts are not technical people but work in the functional end of the business: Human Resources Managers, Shipping Clerks, and so on. Technical Analysts are IT professionals who are bringing a technical savvy to the Project Team because of their computer and technical experience.

4. Your selected SAP Project Team is one of the most important factors in a successful SAP implementation.

5. Although the Project Manager leads the project, the highest level in the project management structure is the Executive Steering Committee, led by a Chair or Project Sponsor.

Answers to Quiz for Hour 8

1. Knowledge transfer refers to the transference of SAP know-how from one individual to another.

2. The five consecutive phases of the AcceleratedSAP (ASAP) roadmap are Project Preparation, Business Blueprint, Realization, Final Preparation, and Go-Live.

3. There are three levels of SAP training courses: Levels 1, 2, and 3.

4. In addition to ASAP, GlobalSAP, ValueSAP, and SAP Solution Manager all offer alternative methodologies and tools for SAP implementation.

5. The SAP Project Implementation Guide contains only the customizing steps necessary for the application components that your company is implementing.

6. The Reference, Enterprise, and Project IMGs are the three project views available for the IMG.

7. You use the transaction code /nSPRO to launch the initial screen of the IMG.

Answers to Quiz for Hour 9

1. Buy-in includes that given by executives and that granted by end users.

2. An execution window is the time allotted to complete a particular task. Exceeding the execution window implies a penalty of sorts.

3. The most prevalent end-user lesson learned is that an unwillingness to change current business practices and processes leads to a less-than-optimized or successful SAP implementation.

4. Technical Change Control implies managing changes to the SAP technology stack, not the application-layer business logic associated with end users and functional change management.

5. Load testing (workload, stress, volume, and so on) makes it possible to validate that a particular technology stack is indeed capable of hosting a particular workload while meeting the SLAs for which IT has signed up.

6. Long-term consulting arrangements can cost considerably more than hiring, and such arrangements do not foster knowledge transfer to company-internal personnel. This tends to prolong the consulting arrangement. And such an approach to solving problems can foster organizations that become addicted to spending more money than probably necessary to resolve business issues, thereby further adding to costs.

Answers to Quiz for Hour 10

1. SAP NetWeaver is an umbrella term used to describe the collection of SAP products and technologies that combine to create a platform for building, extending, and integrating enterprise applications.

2. The common technology platform for most SAP NetWeaver components and products is SAP's Web Application Server (WebAS).

3. Unicode speaks to the method of encoding the characters in each language supported by SAP, such that all languages are supported by a single system.

4. Web Services represent the standards-oriented communication method used to facilitate communication between disparate technology platforms. In this way, SAP's Enterprise Architecture Services vision can be realized.

Answers to Quiz for Hour 11

1. The Funds Management component is designed to support your company in creating budgets.

2. The Controlling submodule provides the functions necessary for effective and accurate internal cost accounting management.

3. The General Ledger Accounting subcomponent serves as a complete record of all your company's business transactions.

4. The SAP term profit center refers to a management-oriented organizational unit used for internal controlling purposes.

5. The main benefit from the Human Resources, Recruitment component is its automation.

6. An infotype is a carrier of system-controlling characteristics, such as attributes or time constraints, and so on.

7. The two methods that you can use for R/3 Employee Self Service are web-based technology and interactive voice response functionality.

8. The components available in the Materials Management module include Inventory Management, Warehouse Management, Purchasing, Invoice Verification, Materials Planning, and Purchasing Information System.

9. The focus of the Production Planning and Control module is to contribute solutions for production planning, execution, and control.

10. You can access data on products, marketing strategies, sales calls, pricing, and sales leads at any time to facilitate sales and marketing activity in the Sales and Distribution module.

11. Sales and Operations Planning creates realistic and consistent planning figures to forecast future sales.

Answers to Quiz for Hour 12

1. The three SAP components that make up the Information Integration trio within the SAP NetWeaver stack are SAP BI, SAP KW, and SAP MDM.

2. Instead of using Microsoft Office for XML editing in SAP KW, you can obtain Epic Editor or Authentic.

3. The required components of MDM include the SAP MDM Server, the MDM Console, the MDM Command Line Interface, and typically the MDM Client and Catalog Manager. Many other components are optional, depending upon the specific MDM scenario.

4. The SAP BW Precalculation Service is required for SAP BW Reporting using the Business Explorer Analyzer.

5. You use Crystal Enterprise SAP Edition Version 10 and Crystal Reports when you need additional formatting capabilities in your reporting.

6. To translate SAP documents in SAP Knowledge Warehouse, you use the TRA-DOS translation tools.

7. SAP KW supports searching for documents through the use of a web browser; you can conduct full-text searching, attribute-based searching, a combination of these, or you can search for similar content objects.

Answers to Quiz for Hour 13

1. NetWeaver's Rapid Installer is used to quickly install SAP Enterprise Portal. It is also used to set up connectivity between the portal and a mySAP ERP system, Business Warehouse, SAP CRM, and any system you might deploy to help you manage and monitor the portal via SAP CCMS.

2. SAP Enterprise Portal is used to host SAP Knowledge Management.

3. SAP XI uses the following to connect systems: SAP IDocs, SAP RFC, SAP BC, file copies, XML over JMS, XML over plain HTTP, XML over Java proxy-based messaging, XML over JDBC Data Access, web services via SOAP, RNIF, a Mail Adapter, and a Marketplace Adapter.

4. Arguably the biggest factor in deploying SAP XI is the potential for complexity; optional components, various connection protocols, and the number of systems being tied together make for a naturally complex environment.

5. Data replication for SAP Mobile Infrastructure entails rationalizing what needs to be moved to the client in the form of a data package, defining the contents of each data package, packaging the data, moving the data, resolving any data version issues that crop up, and monitoring the overall process. Fortunately, MI handles this entire process.

6. Any Java-compliant device can potentially be used as a client for SAP MI. This includes cell phones, PDAs, pagers, and more.

7. The core value of SAP xApps lies in the fact that they are easy to create. They are designed to facilitate business innovation while addressing a company's need to rapidly address updated business and regulatory requirements.

Answers to Quiz for Hour 14

1. The most popular interface form used for Internet applications is EDI. EDI is the electronic exchange of structured data between environments that use different hardware, software, and communication services.

2. Object linking and embedding (OLE) is used to integrate PC and similar applications with SAP. OLE is the technology for transferring and sharing information among applications such as SAP and Microsoft Office.

3. The three types of data transmitted through ALE are control and customizing data, master data, and transaction data.

4. The two primary types of update processes are synchronous and asynchronous processes, also called V1 and V2 work processes.

5. Middleware is the layer of software that functions as a conversion or translation layer between two different layers.

6. A Common Program Interface Communication (CPI-C) facilitates the communication (talking back and forth) and the processing of applications and programs within the SAP system.

7. Session start-up, session control, communication, and session termination are the four areas of rules for CPI-C.

Answers to Quiz for Hour 15

1. Any of the following examples can be found on your user master record: user name, assigned client, user password, company address, user type, start menu, logon language, personal printer configuration, time zone, activity group authorizations, expiration date, and default parameter settings.

2. The SAP_ALL authorization profile gives users access to everything in your SAP system.

3. The SAP Profile Generator assists in the implementation of your company's security and it is based on the concept of authorization objects, authorizations, and authorization profiles.

4. The acronym CCMS stands for SAP's Computing Center Management System, used for monitoring and managing SAP.

5. You can access the SAP Servers System Monitoring screen by following the menu path Tools, Administration, Monitor, System Monitoring, Servers or by using the transaction code /nSM51.

6. An instance is an administrative unit used to group together SAP system components that provide one or more services to SAP end users.

7. The user authorizations are stored in the master record of each user.

8. Useful SAP CCMS monitoring transactions include SM66, SM51, AL08, SMLG, SSAA, ST03N, ST06, ST07, and ST22.

Answers to Quiz for Hour 16

1. Transaction ST03N (or ST03) enables you to view workload statistics collected over time, as does STAD, ST03G, and to some extent ST07.

2. To view active users grouped by application server, execute transaction /nAL08.

3. To view active users grouped by SAP functional areas, execute transaction /nST07.

4. ST03G provides visibility into global matters, like extended business processes, unavailable to ST03N.

5. Use transaction /nSMLG to validate how well your particular logon load-balancing scheme is working—press F5 from the main screen to view response time statistics.

6. Both SM50 and SM66 are useful in displaying work processes; the former enables you to drill down into a specific application server and view the status of both active and inactive work processes, whereas the latter provides cross-application-server visibility of all active work processes.

Answers to Quiz for Hour 17

1. Transaction code /nSE16 can be used to access the General Table Display function of the SAP ABAP Dictionary.

2. A structure is a group of internal fields that logically belong together.

3. The three components for defining data in the ABAP Dictionary are tables, domains, and data elements.

4. Selection screens are used to specify criteria for the output that will be displayed.

5. Pooled tables contain a one-to-many relationship.

6. One major distinction between cluster tables and pooled tables is that pooled tables hold a large number of tables and table clusters hold only a handful of tables.

7. Transparent tables contain a one-to-one relationship with tables in the database.

8. ABAP Dictionary objects are broken into basic objects, other objects, and fields.

9. Environment objects are composed of development coordination, authorizations, and automatic tests.

10. The Find button (which looks like a pair of binoculars) is used to search for objects in the Repository Information System.

11. The Repository Information System is a tool designed to assist you in retrieving information on the objects in your ABAP/4 Dictionary.

12. In the Repository browser, you can search by object attributes, research relationships between tables, do data review, and query the SAP system for modified objects.

13. Modeling objects, ABAP Dictionary objects, Programming objects, and Environment objects comprise the four types of SAP objects in the Repository Information System.

Answers to Quiz for Hour 18

1. The primary mode of the SAP Screen Painter is called the Graphical Screen Painter.

2. SAP refers to screens as dynpros, or dynamic programs.

3. Screen elements consist of the items on your screen—elements with which the user interacts, such as check boxes and radio buttons.

4. The programming code behind your screen that makes it work is called the *flow logic*.

5. The Field List screen is where you maintain the ABAP Dictionary fields or program fields for your screen.

6. The four components of a GUI status in the SAP Menu Painter include the menu bar, standard toolbar, application toolbar, and function key setting.

7. By using the Menu Painter and selecting the Title List subobject, you can view all the title bars for every screen in your program.

Answers to Quiz for Hour 19

1. The Ad Hoc Query reporting mechanism is used to pose ad hoc queries to the database.

2. ABAP List Processing requires the user to write code in the ABAP language in order to generate reports.

3. To take a look at the attributes of a particular report in the General Report Selection Tree, select the report and then follow the menu path Edit, Node Attributes.

4. The menu path used to search for reports in the General Report Selection is Edit, Find, Node.

5. A *variant* is a group of selection criteria values (used to create a report) that has been saved, and can then be used as a "shortcut" in the future—instead of entering all the data fields again, you simply enter the variant name.

6. A variant is "protected" when the variant can be changed only by the person who created it or last updated it.

7. The primary advantage of background processing is that it enables multitasking. A report started in the background running on your SAP ECC system, for example, arguably has no direct influence on your interactive real-time work—you can do both at the same time, with no or very little impact on your overall response time or report throughput/processing time.

Answers to Quiz for Hour 20

1. The transaction code to access the Create Users screen is /nSQ03.

2. The transaction code to access the Create InfoSets screen is /nSQ02.

3. The transaction code to access the Create SAP Queries screen is /nSQ01.

4. Queries designed in the global area are used throughout the entire system and are client-independent.

5. The three components of SAP queries are Query Groups, InfoSets, and administrative decisions.

6. A Query Area includes SAP query elements, queries, InfoSets, and Query Groups.

7. The two Query Areas in R/3 are standard and global.

8. After creating or modifying an InfoSet, you must save and generate it.

9. The transaction code to access QuickViewer is /nSQVI.

10. The InfoSet (Ad Hoc) Query tool is now available in all modules, although it is still referred to as the Ad Hoc Query when executed through the Human Capital Management module.

Answers to Quiz for Hour 21

1. SAP SCM can maximize profitability through improved responsiveness via real-time insight into your supply chain, via greater inventory turns, and via increased collaboration with supply chain parties and subsequent analytics.

2. The three components of SCM include Advanced Planner & Optimizer (SAP APO), SAP Inventory Collaboration Hub (SAP ICH), and SAP Event Management (SAP EM).

3. SAP CRM maximizes your profitability in that it helps you retain your existing customer base while also maximizing profit per transaction.

4. PLM's use of HTML, XML, and the Wireless Application Protocol (WAP) enables LAN- and WAN-based clients, as well as users on handheld and mobile devices, to access your PLM data.

5. Four business benefits of SRM include making sourcing strategy improvements, compressing procurement cycle times, reducing process costs, and lowering overall unit prices.

6. The technology used to connect and integrate your SRM-enabled suppliers with your procurement team is XML-based document exchange.

Answers to Quiz for Hour 22

1. The System List function method and the export method from the SAP Query tool are the two methods you can use to create output files to be used in Microsoft Excel.

2. Object linking and embedding is used to integrate Office applications with SAP.

3. You can use Microsoft Word to create form letters using your SAP data.

4. OLE means object linking and embedding. OLE is the technology for transferring and sharing information among applications.

5. Some additional OLE-compatible applications include Microsoft Office, Corel Office, Star Office, Lotus Smart Suite, Microsoft Outlook, and a host of web and application development tools.

Answers to Quiz for Hour 23

1. The common abbreviation for SAP Solution Manager is SolMan (you might see SSM used occasionally as well).

2. Three primary tools accessible via SolMan include Business Process Monitoring, Solution Monitoring, and Service Level Reporting.

3. The primary online support vehicle for SAP developers is the SAP Developer Network, accessible via the SAP Service Marketplace.

4. You can access field-specific help by navigating to the field in your SAP GUI and pressing the F1 key.

5. Access SAP Notes from the SAP Support Portal's SAP Notes Search link, or from the Messages link.

Answers to Quiz for Hour 24

1. You can find the top 100 or so books covering SAP by searching through Amazon, Barnes and Noble, and a host of other such online sites. Sort by date to find current titles, or by best-selling status to find titles that other people are actually buying. Look to www.SAP-Resources.com as well for a link to the most popular SAP books.

2. The primary sponsor of most of the least-biased SAP conferences and events is WIS Publications. These are the same folks who publish the *SAP Professional Journal* and have a joint venture with SAP to publish the *SAPinsider*.

3. The conference geared toward executives and decision makers is the annual conference SAPphire, held every year in three regions around the world.

4. To view a website as it appeared many years ago prior to being retired or changed, use the Wayback Machine (www.waybackmachine.org). Note the org extension.

Index

J - K

JavaGUI (SAP GUI for Java)
 installation requirements, 46
 language support, 46
 latest versions, downloading, 46
 platform suitability, 46

KANBAN Production Control processing, 155
keyboards, menu path navigation, 63
KM Content (SAP BW), 163-164

L

Last Page button (SAP GUI standard toolbar), 31
Layout Editor, screens, designing (Screen Painter), 251-252
layout elements (Screen Painter), 248
leasing services industry, SAP CRM processes, 306
legal change packages, 102
levels in report trees, viewing (General Report Selection screen), 265-266

lists
 SAP
  exporting to Microsoft Access, 330
  exporting to Microsoft Excel, 328-329
  versus reports, 270-271
load tests, importance of, 127
lock downs of production systems, failure to execute, 127
logical databases, 275
logical unit of work (LUW), 16
Logistics Information Systems (LIS) module (mySAP ERP Operations), 156
logoffs, executing, 23
logons
 load balancing management, SMLG transaction code (CCMS), 218
 SAP Logon Pad
  configuring, 24-25
  low-speed connections, 24-25
long-term consultants, reliance on, 129-130

M

Maintain Queries screen, SAP queries, creating, 284-287
maintenance
 ECC versus R/3, 143
 R/3 versus ECC, 143

Manager Self Service (mySAP ERP Human Capital Management), 15, 153
Manufacturing Performance Improvement xApp, 185
manufacturing vertical industry, SAP CRM processes, 306
master data, Application Link Enabling (ALE), 196
Master Data Management (MDM), 137
master records, user authorizations for, 208-209
Materials Management module (mySAP ERP Operations), 155
MDM CLIX (Command Line Interface), 170
MDM Import Manager, 170
MDM Syndicator, 170
media industry vertical services industry, SAP CRM processes, 306
members of Project Team
 executive steering committee responsibilities, 99-100
 Functional Analyst responsibilities, 101-102
 key characteristics of, 98
 Project Management Office responsibilities, 100-101
 Project Manager responsibilities, 99
 Project Sponsor responsibilities, 98-99

QuickViewer, 273
accessing, 295
function of, 294
output options, 295-296
toolbar options, 296
versus
Ad Hoc Query, 294
InfoSet Query, 294
SAP Query, 294
views, creating, 294-296

R

R/3, 141
business modules,
144-145
Asset Accounting, 145
Basic Components,
145
Business Workplace,
145
Controlling, 145
Customer Service, 145
Enterprise Controlling,
145
Financial Accounting,
145
Materials Management,
145
Personnel
Administration and
Payroll Accounting,
145
Personnel
Development, 145

Plant Maintenance,
145
Production Planning,
145
Project System, 145
Quality Management,
145
Sales and Distribution,
145
SAP Quick-Sizer web-
site, 145
Treasury, 145
Warehouse
Management, 145
versus ECC, 141-142
business processes,
143-144
installation process,
142-143
platforms, 142
support and mainte-
nance, 143
radio buttons, 89
Rapid Installer, SAP
Enterprise Portal (EP), 176
IT challenges, 176-177
legacy challenges, 177
RDBMS (Relational Database
Management System), 37
check table violation,
39-40
foreign key, 39
primary key, 37-38
readiness phase, Level 2
Project Team training, 104

Real Estate Management
module (mySAP ERP
Corporate Services), 157
Realization (ASAP Phase 3),
110
configuration testing,
110-111
knowledge transfer, 111
recording system logs for
monitoring, 204
records, 79
viewing via ABAP
Dictionary selection
screens, 237-238
Reference IMG view, 114
Relational Database
Management System
(RDBMS), 37
check table violation,
39-40
foreign key, 39
primary key, 37-38
Release Notes screen,
Implementation Guide
(IMG), 120
Remote Function Calls
(RFCs), WebAS/Basis layer,
193
replicating screen data, 85-86
report trees (SAP Information
System), 265
attributes, viewing, 267
levels, viewing, 265-266
searching, 267-268